# Radical Prince

For Jane

and in memory of
Kathleen Raine
(1908–2003)

# Radical Prince

## The Practical Vision of the Prince of Wales

David Lorimer

Floris Books

First published in 2003 by Floris Books
This revised paperback edition published in 2004
© 2003 David Lorimer

David Lorimer has asserted his right under the
Copyright, Designs and Patents Act 1988
to be identified as the Author of this Work.

British Library CIP Data available

ISBN 0-86315-463-8

Printed in Great Britain
by Bell & Bain Ltd, Glasgow

# Contents

Where is the wisdom we have lost in knowledge?
Where is the knowledge we have lost in information?
The cycles of heaven in twenty centuries
Bring us further from GOD and nearer to the Dust.

T.S. Eliot, Chorus I from *The Rock*

# Preface

*Radical Prince* owes its origins to an autumn drive down the A9 from Inverness to Perth, when it struck me that no one had presented the full range and context of Prince Charles's ideas and work. The reader will find that I share many of the Prince's views and concerns, but I try to place them in a wider contemporary context and respond to criticisms levelled by those who understand the world differently. My approach is therefore broadly sympathetic. Even if readers do not find themselves sharing the Prince's views, I hope that they will at least be impressed by the scope of his practical work. I have kept the Prince and his office at Clarence House informed about the progress of the book, but at no point have they given any editorial direction. The concept, the context, the analysis and the conclusions are entirely my responsibility.

The Prince takes a spiritual view of reality, which I happen to share, while many of his critics understand the world as an entirely material system devoid of purpose and meaning, which they claim is the only position supported by modern science. However, modern science itself rests on philosophical assumptions that are open to question. I argue that a spiritual understanding of reality offers a more complete and adequate worldview, and one that is consistent with scientific findings.

It is a great pleasure to be able to thank friends and colleagues — many from the Scientific and Medical Network — who have helped in various ways or who have commented on the book. Emilios Bouratinos has patiently read the whole manuscript and generously given me the benefit of his very considerable historical, linguistic and philosophical insight. Dr Peter Fenwick, Dr Larry Dossey and Dr James Witchalls commented on the medical chapter, Rod Parker and Professor Jules Pretty on the agricultural chapter and Dr Kathleen Raine, who died as this book went to print, on the architecture chapter. And at Floris Books my editor Christopher Moore has given a perceptive editorial steer. I have also received enormous encouragement from friends to whom I have spoken about the book. Finally, I owe the largest debt to my wife Jane for her constant support and to my children Charlotte and George for putting up with a father working through weekends and having less time to spend with them.

The original hardback edition of *Radical Prince* was published in the autumn of 2003, and contains much background technical material as well as extensive notes and references that have been omitted from this abridged paperback edition. Readers who would like a more comprehensive treatment are therefore referred to the original hardback.

In July 2004 the Prince of Wales published his first Annual Review, a comprehensive account of his activities. The Review is an impressive document that runs to 48 pages with photos. It is divided into five sections: Introduction, Supporting the Queen, Charitable Entrepreneur, Promoting and Protecting, and Income, Expenditure and Staff. The Prince raises around £100 million a year for his 17 core charities alone, which makes him the country's largest multi-cause charitable enterprise, all the elements of which are covered in this book. In addition to his official and charity work (517 engagements and 150 formal briefings), the Prince deals with a huge volume of paperwork and writes over 2,000 letters personally, with a further 10,000 written on his behalf by his office in response to some 33,000 sent in by members of the public. The Review can be ordered directly from The Office of the Prince of Wales, Clarence House, London SW1A 1BA. An online version can be viewed at www.princeofwales.gov.uk under the heading 'About the Prince'.

# Introduction: A Time to Heal

Consider the following headlines:

**Experts Pour Scorn on Prince's NHS Crusade**
**The Rural Prince — Useful Thoughts on the Countryside**
**Scientists Condemn Prince's 'Woolly' Lecture on GM Food**
**Prince and Sophisticated Populist**

Why have the Prince of Wales's views evoked such strong and contradictory reactions? One answer is that he has not been properly understood. Another, perhaps more significant, is that these contradictions represent a profound division at the centre of our society concerning our understanding of the very basis of reality and therefore the significance of human life. This book has been inspired not only by a desire to set out the Prince of Wales's philosophy in a coherent and comprehensive way but also to understand the source of that division and the imbalance it represents. Does the Prince's philosophy go some way towards restoring the balance? Are the contradictory reactions to his views evidence of the very polarity they seek to heal?

As will become apparent below, the Prince has a wide range of interests but the public catches only glimpses of his concerns on the occasion of major speeches and the ensuing press reaction. One month it is medicine, a few months later agriculture, and the following year business in the community. The very nature of major speeches is occasional and hence coverage of the Prince's views is not only episodic, but public understanding of how his interests link up is inevitably fragmented. This book aims, first, to show how the Prince's views on ecology, agriculture, religion, architecture, medicine, business and education reflect wider currents of thought and are the expression of his personal philosophy; and secondly to illustrate how this philosophy is translated into action through a multitude of practical projects. The Prince is no armchair philosopher, but a man of action with a passion for helping bring about improvements in his various fields of interest.

The last fifty years have seen extraordinary scientific and technical achievements but these have been underpinned by a bleak philosophy that sees the universe and human life as devoid of meaning and purpose beyond the material world. Marxism may have been largely abandoned, but materialism is rampant. However, a sense of technological triumph (at least in the West) has been matched by a profound spiritual malaise as people have lost their traditional bearings at the same time as having to live at a frenetic pace. As a jet pilot reportedly said, 'I'm lost but I'm making record time!' The Prince is acutely aware of these tensions and has repeatedly castigated the shortcomings of a modernistic and mechanistic approach while calling for a restoration of the place of the soul and an inner spiritual life.

The Prince's approach is radical in three respects. First, he insists that we need to rediscover our roots in a living tradition in order to retain a sense of meaning and direction. In this sense he can be called a radical traditionalist. Second, the Prince identifies the root cause of many of our current problems in the one-sided philosophy of modernism, which we discuss below. If the root lies in the philosophy and values, then it shows up in our attitudes to the environment, agriculture and medicine, among other areas. This means that a change of thinking or philosophy is required before corresponding policies will be implemented. The third sense in which the Prince is radical is in his belief that the kind of action required is that which addresses the level of causes rather than tinkering with symptoms, and that one of the best ways of demonstrating this is through example.

Modernism, the Prince argues, has carried out a demolition job by literally pulling up our traditional roots. This has affected 'the very ground of our being which had been nurtured for so long in the soil of what I can only describe as perennial wisdom. And I think the destruction was utterly comprehensive and deadly in its effect and it has particularly affected the four areas in which I have battled away about for the last 25 years or so — that is, agriculture, architecture, medicine and education.'

The Prince elaborates:

> As far as agriculture is concerned, I remember when I was
> a teenager, miles of hedges were uprooted, ancient
> meadows and woodlands ploughed up and removed in a
> matter of days. You try putting them back, it takes
> hundreds of years — I'm trying.
>
> The land was forcibly drained and laced with chemicals
> of all descriptions — look at the problems now. Familiar
> landmarks, as far as architecture is concerned, ancient
> town centres that escaped Hitler's bombs, entire streets
> housing cohesive communities, great complexes of finely
> designed eighteenth and nineteenth century cotton mills
> for instance, were all swept away and comprehensively
> re-developed.
>
> In medicine, as in architecture, the doctrine of man as a
> machine has held sway. God was declared dead — I
> remember it happening. The soul was declared moribund
> and redundant. Ancient well-tried therapies and
> diagnostic techniques were simply abandoned and
> thrown away. The balance of the rational and the intuitive
> was destroyed.
>
> In education, I believe, the same doctrinal brutality
> reigned supreme resulting in a complete wasteland of
> moral relativism and the deliberate disruption of an
> approach that had always ensured the transmission from
> one generation to another of a shared body of knowledge,
> of a cultural, historical and moral heritage. And what has
> been the result of all this brutal vandalism for the sake of,
> I believe, a gigantic social experiment?
>
> I believe that it has created a profound malaise, a deep
> dis-ease, a dis-integration and a dis-functioning of the
> natural harmony in human existence all because
> modernist ideology demands that all history and all
> tradition be pulled up by the roots so that we can all start
> again with what they like to call a *tabula rasa*, a clean slate.

Many of us share the Prince's sense of unease about the excesses
of modernism and support efforts to redress the balance, as we

shall see, in the environment, agriculture, medicine, architecture, philosophy, education, business and the community.

## Wisdom and Information

*Where is the Life we have lost in living?*
*Where is the wisdom we have lost in knowledge?*
*Where is the knowledge we have lost in information?/*

The introductory quotation from T.S. Eliot is arguably more relevant today than when he wrote it over seventy years ago. Eliot did not have to live in our 24/7 world where we struggle to keep information overload at bay. Perhaps you are reading these lines with a drink in a comfortable chair but the chances are that you may be in a crowded train where a mobile phone could go off any second — at which point people generally give a graphic description of where they are and why they will be late! Your neighbour may be working on a laptop or reading a book on time management about how to prioritize her life and fit even more activities into it ('the endless cycle of idea and action'). So where is the time for quiet reflection, for that knowledge of stillness rather than motion, knowledge of silence rather than speech that Eliot speaks of?

This predicament brings us to a core theme in the thinking of the Prince of Wales: the need for balance and harmony between head and heart, reason and intuition, outer and inner, action and contemplation. Eliot also reflects on the eternal cyclical nature of spring and autumn, birth and death, light and darkness. Most of us are less immediately aware of these cycles than our ancestors, but they frame our lives nevertheless — especially if we are lucky enough to live in the country — and enable us to feel connected to the perennial cycles of nature.

As the Prince put it in his Reflection on the 2000 Reith Lectures:

I believe that we need to restore the balance between the heartfelt reason of instinctive wisdom and the rational insights of scientific analysis. Neither, I believe, is much use on its own. So it is only by employing both the intuitive and the rational halves of our own nature — our hearts and our minds — that we will live up to the sacred trust that has been placed in us by our Creator — or our 'Sustainer,' as ancient wisdom referred to the Creator.

Implicit in the Prince's analysis here is that modern Western culture is currently in a state of imbalance. There is too much emphasis on reason and scientific analysis at the expense of intuition and wisdom. At worst, reason cuts itself off from its roots in a deeper part of the human mind. It is important to stress the Prince's insistence that he is 'not suggesting that information gained through scientific investigation is anything other than essential.' His scientific critics frequently ignore such carefully worded qualifications and launch into impulsive attacks on his speeches as a 'return to superstition and ignorance,' roundly accusing him of being anti-science. Although the Prince himself argues for the importance of intuition and wisdom, he is clearly advocating a *both-and* approach that values intuition and reason together, rather than privileging one mode of knowing over the other. This *both-and* approach is reflected right across the range of his concerns. The Prince calls for a combination of the best of the old or traditional with the best of the new and innovative. He deplores the cult of the new when it means a wholesale repudiation of traditional wisdom and often refers to the danger of throwing the baby of tradition out with the bathwater of superstition.

In a more recent speech the Prince goes further than harmonization of opposites by insisting that his deeper motivation is healing:

> Now all my life I've been driven by a desire to heal the festering wounds produced by what I believe is an aberration, and will be proved to be, in the soul of humanity. In other words, to heal the landscape, to heal the soil, to work in harmony with nature once again. To build in a way that actually respects the sacredness of the land and reconnects man with the organic roots of his being, with the ancient principles of traditional urbanism that reflect our human scale with the healing timelessness

of a living tradition, not a dead thing. It's not a dead language, it can be a living tradition, contemporary in each generation. Not a genetically modified disruption to the invisible patterns of our existence.

To treat the whole individual, not merely one part of us, to restore the soul to its rightful place, to integrate, this is the most important thing, the best of modern medicine with the best of ancient therapeutic wisdom. To reorientate the damaged psyche in terms of stress, trauma and the problems associated with frenetic lifestyles.

In educational terms to reconnect our young people to their literary, historical and moral roots. To provide the disciplined framework that paradoxically provides the genuine opportunities for creativity.

The Prince of Wales is not alone in advancing a diagnosis of imbalance in modern life. It is not simply work-life balance that is at stake here but, more profoundly, the balance between contemplation and action, between being and doing. The philosopher René Guénon refers to much of our action as 'agitation as unprofitable as it is trivial.' He goes on (writing as long ago as 1942!):

This, indeed, is the most conspicuous feature of modern times; a craving for ceaseless agitation, for continuous change, for ever-increasing speed like that with which events follow one upon another. On all sides we see dispersion into multiplicity, and in a multiplicity no longer unified by consciousness of any higher principle; in daily life, as in scientific thinking, analysis is driven to extremes, resulting in an endless subdivision, a veritable disintegration of human activity in every sphere in which that activity can be exercised; and hence the inaptitude for synthesis and the incapacity for any sort of concentration that is so striking a feature in the eyes of Orientals.

Since Guénon's time, the situation has deteriorated. Attention spans have been further reduced and tens of thousands of children have so-called attention deficit disorder while being exposed to never-ending sources of stimulation and distraction. It is significant that we refer to 'information overload' rather than 'knowledge overload,' while 'wisdom overload' would seem a contradiction in terms. We tend to conflate the urgent with the important, spending our time in inverse proportion to the respective importance of information, knowledge and wisdom. We struggle to absorb ever-increasing piles (or screens) of information, leaving us little time for recreational study and practically none for contemplation or reflective reading. We give ourselves mental indigestion but do not nourish our deeper roots. We are then in danger of joining Dr Elisabeth Kubler-Ross's patient who, when told he had six weeks to live just as he was looking forward to retirement, said: 'I made a good living but I never really lived.' To recall Eliot, 'Where is the Life we have lost in living?'

The consequence of this breakneck pace and the dominance of instant information is that our knowledge is not tempered or balanced by wisdom. Wisdom comes from life experience, although there is no guarantee that life experience will bring wisdom. Wisdom is a timeless but elusive quality rooted in depth of character and insight into life. It is traditionally associated with the great sages of religion and philosophy, and, to a lesser degree, with kings and judges. Sages spend long periods in silent meditation and contemplation, thereby gaining what Eliot calls the knowledge of stillness and silence, which in turn informs the sage's actions. This may be a counsel of perfection for harassed professionals and parents, but we all feel better when our lives are in a better state of balance.

## The Fundamental Divide

I referred above to a profound divide at the centre of our society, which I believe stems from fundamentally differing interpretations of the nature of reality. Can our existence be accounted for, as some vocal scientists would have us believe, entirely in material terms, or is there an underlying spiritual reality? Is the universe a chance occurrence — 'one of these things that happen from time to time' — or does life have some kind of intrinsic purpose? Is conscious awareness simply a by-product of brain function or does our deepest experience suggest that it may in some sense transcend physical space and time? Is the death of the brain the extinction of the person or a gateway to a new form of existence?

The wider cultural context of the Prince's speeches — and the reactions to them — can be found in the relationship between science and religion and the related questions of the authority, scope and validity of different kinds of knowledge. Public understanding of the relationship between science and religion is regrettably much cruder than the current state of scholarship. Spurred on by the adversarial structure of many TV and radio programmes, people are encouraged to think in terms of a grand battle between science and religion, which science is obviously winning. It is argued that science has disproved most of the doctrines previously upheld as infallible by the Church. It is assumed that modern evolutionary theory has entirely displaced God. It is supposed that neuroscience has negated the existence of the soul. Anyone disagreeing with these views, their proponents maintain, must be either scientifically illiterate or steeped in outdated superstition.

While it is true that scientific advance has immeasurably enhanced our knowledge of the physical universe, it is not true to say that it has by the same token comprehensively eliminated the possible existence of a spiritual dimension. Scientists who give this impression fail to make the crucial distinction between scientific findings and the philosophical assumptions underpinning the whole scientific enterprise. They suppose that the fact that something cannot be measured means that it does not exist. However, science need not be logically wedded to currently fashionable materialistic assumptions about the nature of reality. It can be expanded to include inner experience. Indeed, the zoologist Sir Alister Hardy did precisely this over thirty years ago when analysing religious experiences, which he wrote up in his book *The Spiritual Nature of Man*. And William Blake makes the point: 'the desires and perceptions of man, untaught by anything but organs of sense, must be limited to organs of sense.' So going beyond these sense organs can widen the horizon of reality, as the Prince himself maintains.

Our modern situation is more serious if one agrees with Bede Griffiths that the essential thing is to maintain contact with the

Transcendent so that human life does not become closed on itself: 'but the modern world has removed every such point of contact ... wherever modern civilization spreads, all holiness, all sense of the sacred, all awareness of a transcendent Reality disappears.' It is one of the Prince of Wales's passions, shared by all serious spiritual seekers and aspirants, to find ways of recovering the sense of the sacred in our time and to explore its implications for the way we live and treat each other and the earth.

From this perspective, the Prince's philosophy is a deeply felt response to our cultural crisis and is the articulation of a spiritual worldview, the implications of which are worked through into medicine, architecture, education, ecology, agriculture and gardening. This book will argue that widespread adoption of the kind of integrated philosophy advanced by the Prince is essential if we are to restore the necessary inner and outer balance to our lives.

## *Leadership by Example*

The Prince of Wales's current and future constitutional position imposes on him a role of leadership, about which he has reflected long and hard. The question is not whether to lead but how to do so. His starting point is service (the motto of the Prince of Wales is *Ich Dien* — I Serve) and a real concern for people, their welfare and potential. He could have chosen a quieter life by simply not speaking out on the range of issues that he has addressed, but, as he writes, 'there's something somewhere telling me that I can't do that and that I wouldn't be true to myself if I did stay quiet instead of taking the risk and accepting the challenge ... Anyway I hope that what I said helps to stir up the debate and raise *some* people's awareness.'

In another letter, written in 1993 to Tom Shebbeare, he comments: 'In order to put the Great (back into Britain) I have always felt that it is vital to bring people together, and I began to realize that *one* advantage of my position has over everyone else's is that I can act as a catalyst to help produce a better and more balanced response to various problems. I have no "political" agenda — only a desire to see people achieve their potential.' Reflecting on the overwhelming response to his original speech to the British Medical Association he remarked that 'people often remain silent about what they really think ... They are terrified of saying something in case "everyone" should think they are mad.'

The Prince of Wales sees the monarchy as a living tradition, woven into the fabric of our national life. It serves as a link with what is valuable and worth preserving from the past and as a symbol of continuity from past through the present into the future. The Prince has always reminded us of the value of preserving the best of the past, but he is equally concerned for the future welfare not only of the country but also of the planet as a whole. It stems naturally from his role that he should take the long and therefore sustainable view. The plants of the present grow in the soil of the past, and the Prince above all is aware of the importance of the quality of soil for healthy growth.

In this context it is important to grasp the Prince's understanding of tradition, which is much richer than his critics realize:

> I am not interested in returning to the past, and that applies — I might as well tell you — whether I am talking about farming, architecture, education or complementary medicine! What I do believe, passionately, is that we should learn from the past, accept that there are such things as timeless principles, operate on a human scale, look firmly to the long-term, respect local conditions and traditions, and be profoundly sceptical of people who suggest that everything new is automatically better — invariably it turns out to be a short-lived fashionable approach anyway.

It is no mean tribute to the Prince of Wales's integrity and moral courage that he has not flinched from taking public stands and stirring up hornets' nests in the interests of enlarging debate and finding constructive ways forward in the fields outlined above. Wilful ridicule or gross misrepresentation of his efforts in the press has been partly compensated by the avalanche of letters from the public — the vast majority of which are supportive — that follow any major speech. This public response demonstrates that the

Prince is much more in touch with ordinary people and is using his role in a constructive way to voice their concerns and interests. The Prince can also take quiet satisfaction in seeing public opinion catching up with what he was saying more than a decade previously, especially in relation to the natural and built environment, organic agriculture and gardening and integrated medicine.

However, the Prince of Wales does more than just talk about his ideas. He puts them into practice right across the board. Albert Schweitzer once said that there were three ways of changing the world: the first is through example; the second is through example; and the third — well, you've guessed it, through example. The integrity and consistency between the Prince's philosophy and actions — his practical idealism — is truly impressive and inspiring. He has made his estate at Highgrove into a famous organic garden and has also converted the Duchy of Cornwall home farm to organic production; he founded Duchy Originals to market the produce and the company turned over £35 million in its latest financial year and has given a total of nearly £3.5 million of its profits to the Prince's Charitable Foundation; he has worked tirelessly through the Prince's Trust to give young people better opportunities to fulfil their potential; he has supported the regeneration of local communities through his Business in the Community schemes and is now applying the same principles to rural life; through the Prince's Foundation he has been responsible by means of the Phoenix Trust and Regeneration through Heritage for the preservation or restoration of many historic buildings; he set up his own Institute of Architecture (now a part of the Prince's Foundation), has inspired the building of Poundbury in Dorset and is Patron of the Temenos Academy to encourage arts and the imagination; at the Prince's Foundation he has also set up a drawing studio and a degree course in Visual Islamic and Traditional Arts; he has established the Prince of Wales's Foundation for Integrated Health to encourage research in complementary medicine and forge a coherent future for healthcare as a whole. The list goes on.

I said at the beginning of this introduction that a core theme of the Prince's approach was the need for balance and harmony between head and heart, reason and intuition, outer and inner, action and contemplation. One could add past and present, tradition and radicalism, individual and community. As the Prince himself explains:

> Ever since I was quite young I have felt most strongly the need to contribute in whatever way I can towards a renewed search for balance and harmony in our existence and in the way we use and enjoy the world around us. I have done so in the heartfelt belief that tradition is not a dead or irrelevant thing, but a crucial and living means by which we can experience a sense of belonging and meaning in a rapidly changing world. I have attempted to express this deep-rooted belief in a Sacred dimension in a practical way when it comes to those aspects of life in which I have taken most interest over the years — for instance, in architecture, the environment, agriculture, medicine and education. It is a belief which tries to understand the profound links in the chain of our existence in such a way that we do not lose sight of the wider nature of our being.

With this approach, the Prince has forged a unique role as the heir to the throne by formulating a personal philosophy that gives him the courage and conviction to encourage debate, bring people together in partnership and translate his ideals into practical projects that can inspire others to do the same. His ideas are rooted in the living traditions derived from the past at the same time as representing the rising culture of the new century, a worldview centred on spiritual principles that are also holistic and ecological. Reflecting what Onora O'Neill calls 'a culture of suspicion,' the Prince's critics tend to dwell negatively on his personal and organizational problems in ways that undermine and obscure the real contribution that he has made to our national life and in recognition of which the Queen awarded him the Order of Merit in her Jubilee Year. However, his integrated vision, his passion for practical solutions and his real concern for people mark him out as a leader for the new century. I hope that this book will make a small contribution towards explaining his philosophy and the work that stems from it.

David Lorimer, Fife, March 2003.

# 1. Sustaining the Web of Life

*The major problems in the world are the result of the difference between the way nature works and the way man thinks.*

Gregory Bateson

*We cannot put an end to nature; we can only pose a threat to ourselves.*

Lynn Margulis

## *The Web of Life*

The late 1960s were significant years for the Earth: the first man walked on the moon in 1969 and we began to receive images, now so familiar, of the Earth from the Moon. Especially poignant was one called 'Earthrise' showing the Earth rising over a barren lunar landscape. Two years earlier, Professor James Lovelock was formulating what later became known, thanks to his friend the novelist Sir William Golding, as the Gaia hypothesis, the theory that the Earth is maintained as a benign habitat for life by the actions of living organisms themselves. The post-war generation, including the Prince of Wales, came of age during this same period. The Prince celebrated his 21st birthday in 1969, and presided for the first time over a meeting of the Prince's Council, the body responsible for overseeing the Duchy of Cornwall, an estate destined for the heir to the throne since its creation in 1337 by Edward III for his son Edward the Black Prince. As we shall see, the Duchy of Cornwall plays an important role as an expression of the Prince of Wales's philosophy from the 1980s onwards.

The Prince made one of his first major public speeches in 1970 on the environment, and many of the themes that he highlighted have not only proved prescient but have also resurfaced in his ecological work in the intervening years. The occasion was the Countryside Conference held in Cardiff in February of that year.

He was then already drawing attention to problems posed by overpopulation, various forms of pollution and waste disposal. But in one respect he has happily been proved wrong when he quoted Dr Frank Fraser Darling as saying that 'people will get tired of the word ecology before they know what it means.'

The Prince's approach to the environment and ecological matters reflects some broad trends within the scientific disciplines of biology and ecology. Since the discovery of the DNA helix in the 1950s, biology has been dominated by work at the molecular level, leading directly to today's preoccupation with biotechnology and genetic engineering. This approach is underpinned by a reductionist and mechanistic philosophy and methodology that focuses on the smallest elements such as cells and genes rather than on the organism as a whole. This focus, when combined with data from evolution, neuroscience and cognitive psychology, has led to a bleak materialistic view of the human being which many people, including the Prince of Wales, find so impoverished.

However, there is an alternative tradition stemming mainly from developmental rather than molecular biology. Here the emphasis lies on growth rather than structure, on organisms rather than genes, on wholes rather than parts. The basic metaphor of this tradition is not the atom or building block, but rather the *web of life*, an image that strongly evokes our mutual interconnectedness and interdependence. We are not separate from nature but form an integral dynamic part within larger Earth systems. Nor is the organism wholly shaped and determined by the environment, but creatively engages with it. The dominance of competition — 'nature red in tooth and claw' — in the neo-Darwinist understanding has obscured the role played by co-operation in Nature. The picture of the web of life is a complex, dynamic, self-organizing and interacting whole in which human beings are deeply embedded.

Biologists Brian Goodwin, Elisabet Sahtouris and Mae-Wan Ho have suggested that the essential issue here is a fundamental divergence in ways of thinking about life and the world. This has far-reaching implications not only for ecology, biology and agriculture but also for our overall worldview. Metaphors exert a powerful hold over the imagination, so the replacement of a dominant cultural metaphor is no small matter. Sahtouris points out that:

One of the distinguishing characteristics of a holistic biology is in the metaphors used. The reductionistic neo-Darwinist literature is replete with such metaphors as 'information' in the DNA, genetic 'program,' 'competitive' interactions among species, 'survival of the fittest,' 'selfish genes' and survival 'strategies.' In the neo-Darwinist view of evolution, species either work, and hence survive, or they don't; they have no intrinsic value or holistic qualities, and the metaphors reveal this. In a holistic biology, by contrast, we find such metaphors as continuum, co-operation, altruism, creativity, agency, and intentionality.

More generally, science has been dominated by the metaphor of the machine since the seventeenth century. Galileo's famous experiments established the science of mechanics and led on to Newton's laws of motion. Descartes regarded animals as automata and was fascinated, like Voltaire after him, with mechanical contrivances that mimicked organic functions. In the eighteenth century Vaucasson invented a mechanical musician and even a shitting duck, about which Voltaire famously remarked that without it 'what would there be to remind us of the glories of France?' And in 1749, Julien de la Mettrie's *L'Homme Machine* appeared, a book that might be regarded as the forerunner of modern Artificial Intelligence and cybernetics. Newton's physics, with its mechanical clock-work framework, became the dominant metaphor for the aspiring natural sciences. His God becomes the Divine Clockmaker responsible for starting up the whole process, who interferes with miracles from time to time when the process goes awry. The idea of such arbitrary interventions was anathema to Enlightenment philosophers like David Hume and was repudiated by later thinkers like the astronomer Laplace, who famously explained to Napoleon that he had no need for the hypothesis of God in his system. The machine worked very well on its own.

The last twenty years have also witnessed a revival of interest in the mediaeval understanding of nature as an organism as the notion of nature as a machine has begun to lose its grip on the imagination. During the seventeenth century a seismic shift of thinking took place, which resulted in nature no longer being considered sacred. This had far-reaching consequences, but there is currently some prospect of a resacralization of our understanding of nature. The essence of the shift is expressed by the environmental historian Carolyn Merchant, when she says in her seminal book *The Death of Nature* that 'between the sixteenth and seventeenth centuries the image of an organic cosmos with a living female earth at its centre gave way to a mechanistic world view in which nature was reconstructed as dead and passive, to be dominated and controlled by humans.' There is a corresponding transfer from organic to mechanistic metaphors, a move away from a perception of human embeddedness and belonging in the natural world to seeing human beings as detached observers of nature and economic manipulators of resources. This separation from nature in turn leads to widespread feelings of alienation — we no longer seem to belong to the universe but are strangers in it.

The views of the Islamic philosopher Seyyed Hossein Nasr go even further by making an intimate connection between this inner attitude and the destruction of the environment:

> The destruction of nature is ultimately the destruction of our own inner being and finally our external life as well. Of course, from the point of view of cause and effect, it is the reverse; it is the pollution of our inner being that has caused the pollution of the natural environment. It is our inner darkness that has now extended outward into the world of nature. The chaos of the outward reflects like a mirror what has happened within ourselves.

Nasr does not doubt that we have a major crisis on our hands and that no kind of quick economic or technological fix will rescue us. Nor will a readjustment of our ideas of sustainable development be sufficient. What is required — a view shared by most other spiritual writers in the field — is 'a very radical transformation in our consciousness, and this means not discovering a completely new state of consciousness, but returning to the state of consciousness which traditional humanity always had. It means to rediscover the traditional way of looking at the world of nature as sacred presence.'

So there we have it: alienation or belonging, separation or connectedness, control and domination or harmony and co-operation. Does all this mean going backwards to a bucolic idyll? Not at all, since the new philosophy of biology and ecology, complemented by a resacralization of our understanding of life and nature, can provide us with a new and necessary conceptual framework. As Fritjof Capra observes:

> There are solutions to the major problems of our time;
> some of them even simple. But they require a radical shift
> in our perceptions, our thinking, our values. And,
> indeed, we are now at the beginning of such a
> fundamental change of worldview in science and society,
> a change of paradigms as radical as the Copernican
> Revolution.

Here Capra puts his finger here on a central thesis of this book: that we are gradually undergoing a radical shift in worldview away from a purely materialistic and mechanistic understanding of life towards one based on holistic, ecological and spiritual principles. The Prince of Wales is fully aware of this shift and indeed articulates the essential elements of a new view. The key ideas of *holism* can be characterized in terms of 'connectedness, relationships, context', while *reductionism* asserts that organisms can be understood as machines (like car engines) that are simply the sum of their parts. The Prince is a committed holist who understands the inherent limitations of a reductionist viewpoint and combats it vigorously when it implies an impoverished view of human beings. In practice, the holistic and reductionist approaches should be complementary, since we need an understanding of both wholes and parts. It is absurd to see them as mutually exclusive or to claim that the organism can be understood as a mere survival machine for 'selfish' genes. Indeed, organisms are *by their very definition not machines*.

Capra concludes that:

instead of being a machine, nature at large turns out to be more like human nature — unpredictable, sensitive to the surrounding world, influenced by small fluctuations. Accordingly, the appropriate way of approaching nature to learn about her complexity and beauty is not through domination and control but through respect, co-operation, and dialogue.

This is a radical statement that challenges not only the current consensus in biology but also in economics (and even politics), where an ideology of domination and control is endemic. So this new understanding of biology leads directly into what Capra calls the basic principles of ecology, which recur frequently in the Prince of Wales's speeches: 'interdependence, recycling, partnership, flexibility, diversity, and, as a consequence, sustainability.

## The Reith Lecture 2000 — A New Vision of Sustainability

*After decades of ignoring the implications of what we are doing to the Earth, we now know that our current way of life is wholly unsustainable. In evolutionary terms, unsustainability ultimately equals extinction. Sustainability is, therefore, not an option; it is a non-negotiable imperative.*

Sir Jonathon Porritt

The most comprehensive statement of the Prince of Wales's views on the environment — and indeed of his overall approach — was delivered in his Reflection on the Reith Lectures of 2000. Although the ostensible theme was sustainable development as a matter of enlightened self-interest, the Prince chose to emphasize the centrality of the spiritual dimension of existence. He does not feel that enlightened self-interest goes nearly far enough, commenting that 'we will need to dig rather deeper to find the inspiration, sense of urgency and moral purpose required to confront the hard choices which face us on the long road to sustainable development.' He continued:

The idea that there is a sacred trust between mankind and our Creator, under which we accept a duty of stewardship for the earth, has been an important feature of most religious and spiritual thought throughout the ages. Even those whose beliefs have not included the existence of a Creator have, nevertheless, adopted a similar position on moral and ethical grounds ... I believe that if we are to achieve genuinely sustainable development we will first have to rediscover, or re-acknowledge, a sense of the sacred in our dealings with the natural world, and with each other. If literally nothing is held sacred any more — because it is considered synonymous with superstition, or in some other way 'irrational' — what is there to prevent us treating our entire world as some 'great laboratory of life,' with potentially disastrous long-term consequences?

Here the Prince plunges into one of the most central issues at the interface between science, society and the sacred, namely the question of the limits of science and its application in new technologies. He reflects the views of Seyyed Hossein Nasr when Nasr remarks that 'that although science is legitimate in itself, the role and function of science and its application have become illegitimate and even dangerous because of the lack of a higher form of knowledge into which science could be integrated and the destruction of the sacred and spiritual value of nature.'

The Prince goes on to explain his reasons: 'Fundamentally, an understanding of the sacred helps us to acknowledge that there are bounds of balance, order and harmony in the natural world which set limits to our ambitions and define the parameters of sustainable development.' Without any limits, everything is permitted, especially when driven by competitive commercial pressures. The limits of science have to be decided by society, but society itself has become secularized and has arguably lost its moral bearings in favour of studiously pragmatic compromises. At one level, limits are easier to define:

In some cases, Nature's limits are well understood at the rational, scientific level. As a simple example, we know that trying to graze too many sheep on a hillside will, sooner or later, be counter-productive, for the sheep, the hillside, or both. More widely, we understand that the over-use of insecticides or antibiotics leads to problems of resistance. And we are beginning to comprehend the full, awful consequences of pumping too much carbon dioxide into the earth's atmosphere. Yet the actions being taken to halt the damage known to be caused by exceeding Nature's limits in these and other ways are insufficient to ensure a sustainable outcome.

As we all know, there is a lack of political will to translate scientific findings on climate change into practical policy — the issues seem too long-term for the normal short political horizon. As Sir Martin Holgate put it: 'Cure does not follow automatically from diagnosis, any more than people practise what they preach.'
The Prince then highlights this shortcoming:

> In other areas, such as the artificial and uncontained transfer of genes between species of plants and animals, the lack of hard scientific evidence of harmful consequences is regarded, in many quarters, as sufficient reason to allow such developments to proceed. The idea of taking a precautionary approach, in this and many other potentially damaging situations, receives overwhelming public support, but still faces a degree of official opposition, as if admitting the possibility of doubt was a sign of weakness or even of a wish to halt 'progress.' On the contrary, I believe it to be a sign of strength and of wisdom. It seems that when we do have scientific evidence that we are damaging our environment we aren't doing enough to put things right, and when we don't have that evidence we are prone to do nothing at all, regardless of the risks.

His concluding observation here is aimed at two separate groups: on environmental matters there is a scientific consensus that is not acted upon by politicians — for instance with respect to global warming. While in the second case a different argument is used: many scientists are persuaded, as in the case of biotechnology and especially GM crops, that their risk assessment methodology is watertight, a judgement that is hotly contested by independent holistic biologists (see www.indsp.org). The Prince rightly identifies the ideology of mechanistic reductionism as a significant overall factor:

> Part of the problem is the prevailing approach that seeks to reduce the natural world, including ourselves, to the level of nothing more than a mechanical process. For whilst the natural theologians of the eighteenth and nineteenth centuries, like Thomas Morgan, referred to 'the perfect unity, order, wisdom and design' of the natural world, scientists, like Bertrand Russell, rejected this idea as rubbish. 'I think the Universe,' he wrote, 'is all spots and jumps without unity and without continuity, without coherence or orderliness.' Sir Julian Huxley wrote in 'Creation: a modern synthesis' that 'modern science must rule out special creation or divine guidance.' But why? As Professor Alan Linton of Bristol University has written — 'evolution is a man-made "theory" to explain the origin and continuance of life on this planet without reference to a Creator.' It is because of our inability or refusal to accept the existence of a guiding Hand that Nature has come to be regarded as a system that can be engineered for our own convenience, or as a nuisance to be evaded and manipulated, and in which anything that happens can be 'fixed' by technology and human ingenuity. Fritz Schumacher recognized the inherent dangers in this approach when he said that 'there are two sciences — the science of manipulation and the science of understanding.'
>
> In this technology-driven age it is all too easy for us to forget that mankind is a part of Nature, and not apart from it, and that this is why we should seek to work with the grain of Nature in everything we do.

A living philosophy of nature is surely the only viable option in the long run:

> This, to my mind, lies at the heart of what we call sustainable development. We need, therefore, to

rediscover a reverence for the natural world, irrespective of its usefulness to ourselves — to become more aware, in Philip Sherrard's words, of the 'relationship of interdependence, interpenetration and reciprocity between God, Man and Creation.' Above all, we should show greater respect for the genius of Nature's designs — rigorously tested and refined over millions of years. This means being careful to use science to understand how Nature works — not to change what Nature is, as we do when genetic manipulation seeks to transform the process of biological evolution into something altogether different.

Here, two contrasting attitudes to Nature are again apparent. Much modern science — and indeed medicine, focuses on the defects of Nature that require correcting. In some cases, such as gene therapy, this is a laudable view, but it is dangerous, and in the long run lethal, for humanity to be in a state of war against Nature — engaged in an arms race with bacteria and pests that can mutate much more rapidly than us. As Woody Allen put it: 'I have seen the enemy — and it is us.' The second attitude — what Schumacher is quoted above as calling 'the science of understanding' — tries to work with rather than against the grain.

As an example of working with the grain of Nature, I happen to believe that if a fraction of the money currently being invested in developing genetically manipulated crops were applied to understanding and improving traditional systems of agriculture, which have stood the all-important test of time, the results would be remarkable. There is already plenty of evidence of just what can be achieved through applying more knowledge and fewer chemicals to diverse cropping systems. These are genuinely sustainable methods. And they are far removed from the approaches based on monoculture which lend themselves to large-scale commercial exploitation, and which Vandana Shiva condemned so persuasively and so convincingly in her lecture.

We will discuss agriculture later in a separate chapter. In the face of the unknown, the Prince calls for humility:

> Our most eminent scientists accept that there is still a vast amount that we don't know about our world and the life forms that inhabit it. As Sir Martin Rees, the Astronomer Royal, points out, it is complexity that makes things hard to understand, not size. In a comment which only an astronomer could make, he describes a butterfly as a more daunting intellectual challenge than the Cosmos! Others, like Rachel Carson, have eloquently reminded us that we don't know how to make a single blade of grass. And St Matthew, in his wisdom, emphasized that not even Solomon in all his glory was arrayed as the lilies of the field ...
>
> Faced with such unknowns it is hard not to feel a sense of humility, wonder and awe about our place in the natural order. And to feel this at all stems from that inner, heartfelt reason which, sometimes despite ourselves, is telling us that we are intimately bound up in the mysteries of life and that we don't have all the answers.

Here the Prince makes an appeal for the use of intuition to supplement reason, a faculty creatively used by the greatest twentieth century physicists like Albert Einstein, Niels Bohr and Paul Dirac:

> So do you not feel that, buried deep within each and every one of us, there is an instinctive, heartfelt awareness that provides — if we will allow it to — the most reliable guide as to whether or not our actions are really in the long-term interests of our planet and all the life it supports? This awareness, this wisdom of the heart, may be no more than a faint memory of a distant harmony, rustling like a breeze through the leaves, yet sufficient to remind us that the earth is unique and that we have a duty to care for it. Wisdom, empathy and compassion have no place in the empirical world, yet traditional wisdoms would ask 'without them are we truly human?' And it would be a good question. It was Socrates who,

when asked for his definition of wisdom, gave as his conclusion, 'knowing that you don't know.'

The Prince elaborates this by making it clear that he is advocating a balanced approach:

> In suggesting that we will need to listen rather more to the common-sense emanating from our hearts if we are to achieve sustainable development, I am not suggesting that information gained through scientific investigation is anything other than essential. Far from it. But I believe that we need to restore the balance between the heartfelt reason of instinctive wisdom and the rational insights of scientific analysis. Neither, I believe, is much use on its own.

The Prince stresses that he is advocating a *both-and* approach to knowledge. He feels that our culture has become skewed towards an exclusively rational approach at the expense of that deeper wisdom that is a vital part of our nature. Many of his critics responded to this passage as if he was decrying scientific analysis, which he is emphatically not doing. What he is saying is that feelings have an important role to play, especially in motivating us towards the action required to achieve sustainable development. He adds:

> As Gro Harlem Brundtland has reminded us, sustainable development is not just about the natural world, but about people too. This applies whether we are looking at the vast numbers who lack sufficient food or access to clean water, but also those living in poverty and without work. While there is no doubt that globalization has brought advantages, it brings dangers too. Without the humility and humanity expressed by Sir John Browne [now Lord Browne of Madingley, Chief Executive of BP-Amoco] in his notion of the 'connected economy' — an economy which acknowledges the social and environmental context within which it operates — there is the risk that the poorest and the weakest will not only see very little benefit but, worse, they may find that their livelihoods and cultures have been lost.

So, if we are serious about sustainable development then we must also remember that the lessons of history are particularly relevant when we start to look further ahead.

This process also involves a new kind of education:

Of course, our descendants will have scientific and technological expertise beyond our imagining, but will they have the insight or the self-control to use this wisely, having learnt both from our successes and our failures? They won't, I believe, unless there are increased efforts to develop an approach to education which balances the rational with the intuitive. Without this, truly sustainable development is doomed. It will merely become a hollow-sounding mantra that is repeated ad nauseam in order to make us all feel better. Surely, therefore, we need to look towards the creation of greater balance in the way we educate people so that the practical and intuitive wisdom of the past can be blended with the appropriate technology and knowledge of the present to produce the type of practitioner who is acutely aware of both the visible and invisible worlds that inform the entire Cosmos.

Here the Prince reflects widespread concern about the uneven effects of globalization, a theme to which he returned in 2001. He described the whole concept as 'deeply flawed and utterly unsustainable' unless 'we can find ways of achieving a much wider acceptance that responsible corporate behaviour includes the need to address these issues comprehensively, in partnerships with Governments and civil society.'

Returning to the Reith extract above, the Prince also stresses the importance of tradition, of not throwing out wisdom along with superstition, which brings him on to education. The point he makes here is that a spiritual understanding of life, a development of our intuitive faculties, is an important element in education. After all, creativity — whether artistic or scientific — depends on intuitive insights; rational or mathematical analysis comes afterwards in working out the details.

The Prince, however, goes further than the simple development of intuition by stating that there are both 'visible and invisible worlds that inform the entire Cosmos,' returning to the original Greek meaning of the word as the 'ordered totality of being'. Here he parts company with Enlightenment rationalists — whether in the science or arts (or even theology) departments of universities — by positing the existence of an invisible, that is spiritual, dimension to life. All religions are founded on this basis, all the great mystics assert the existence of subtle realms perceptible by subtle senses, and indeed experiences from transpersonal psychology and near-death experiences — largely ignored by mainstream science — point in the same direction. The contention that the world is entirely physical, that there is no spiritual dimension to existence, is not so much a scientific finding as a philosophical assumption maintained by studiously ignoring all evidence to the contrary.

> The future will need people who understand that sustainable development is not merely about a series of technical fixes, about re-designing humanity or re-engineering Nature in an extension of globalized industrialization — but about a re-connection with Nature and a profound understanding of the concepts of care that underpin long-term stewardship. Only by re-discovering the essential unity and order of the living and spiritual world — as in the case of organic agriculture or integrated medicine or in the way we build — and by bridging the destructive chasm between cynical secularism and the timelessness of traditional religion, will we avoid the disintegration of our overall environment.

The Prince ends with a plea for a new philosophy of Nature, an understanding of the unity and order of both spiritual and natural worlds, commonly called the Way, the Tao, Dharma, the Path, depending on one's tradition. We are part of Nature, not set apart from it. And, as former US Vice-President Al Gore points out in *Earth in the Balance*, a failure to recognize this can have drastic consequences:

Believing ourselves to be separate from the earth means having no idea how we fit into the natural cycle of life and no understanding of the natural processes of change that affect us and that we in turn are affecting. It means that we attempt to chart the course of our civilization by reference to ourselves alone. No wonder we are lost and confused. No wonder so many people feel their lives are wasted. Our species used to flourish within the intricate and interdependent web of life, but we have chosen to leave the garden. Unless we find a way to dramatically change our civilization and our way of thinking about the relationship between humankind and the earth, our children will inherit a wasteland.

The Prince also makes connections with his other interests to be explored later in this book — agriculture, medicine and architecture or the built environment. He passionately espouses our role as stewards of creation and puts this idea at the centre of his case for sustainable development.

Public reaction to this speech was mixed. The environmentalist Jonathon Porritt began his *Guardian* article: 'So what does the word "sacred" do for you? Does it induce a nice warm glow, or bring on an instant fit of apoplectic rage?' He went on to observe that it was the rage that seized the great and the good of the UK's scientific establishment when the Prince chose to organize his contribution around the simple notion of rediscovering a 'sense of the sacred.' The press naturally called on those most likely to criticize the Prince so as to generate good old controversial copy. Steve Jones, professor of genetics at University College London is quoted as saying that the Prince was a 'classic woolly thinker ... he is mixing up theology and science.' He went on to say that he had no time for those 'who prefer ignorance to knowledge.' Richard Dawkins applauded the Prince's concern with the long-term stewardship of the planet but regretted that his enlightened view was tied to 'a wholly unnecessary hostility towards scientific rationalism.' Martin Bobrow, professor of medical genetics at Cambridge said: 'I think it is extremely unhelpful to convey a general attitude of being antagonistic to a scientific process. Science is about inventing things and understanding what we do know and what we don't know.'

As Jonathon Porritt observed, the Prince's fundamental concern is with the dehumanizing imagery and language conveyed by genetic science. He quotes from Jeremy Rifkin's *The Biotech Century*: 'living things are no longer perceived as birds and bees, foxes and hens, but as bundles of genetic information. There is no longer any question of sacredness or specialness. How could there be, when there are no longer any recognisable boundaries to respect? How can any living thing be deemed sacred when it is just a pattern of information?' The underlying position behind the responses quoted above is that theology or metaphysics has no bearing whatever on science; and that science itself is value-neutral and has no inherent philosophical presuppositions of its own. Neither of these propositions is true. Furthermore, there is a conflation of science with the ideology of 'scientism,', which is science plus materialism. It is quite possible to support the scientific processes of openness, scepticism and rigour while at the same time being critical of dogmatic scientism. Much of what passes for 'anti-science' is more precisely 'anti-scientism.'

## The World Commission on Environment and Development (WCED)

> *Time is not on the side of indecision. Important choices must be made now, because we are at the threshold of a new era. It needs leadership that is proactive, not simply reactive, that is inspired, not simply functional, that looks to the longer term and future generations for whom the present is held in trust. It needs leaders made strong by vision, sustained by ethics, and revealed by political courage that looks beyond the next election.*
> Our Global Neighbourhood

The Prince of Wales has supported the work of the WCED since its groundbreaking report in 1987, which has set the agenda for much environmental and green economic policy and thinking since that time. He gave a major speech to the Brundtland Commission in 1992 and another one to the Local Agenda 21 conference in 1995.

His 1992 speech begins on a light-hearted note when he

admits that the whole area is strewn with elephant traps and the best he can do is 'to explain, as frankly as possible, why you care enough about the issues to risk being accused of exaggerating the problems, of being excessively gloomy, or of getting your facts wrong.' He notes the progress made since 1987 but his diagnosis of the situation remains the same:

> I happen to believe we live in dangerous times, and I think it worth listening carefully to all those intelligent observers of the natural environment who are increasingly speaking with one, agitated voice [this is even more true in 2004]. The difficulty, of course, is that to the vast majority of lay observers everything seems to function perfectly happily in our immediate environment. On the whole, we cannot smell, feel, hear or sense anything particularly wrong with the world about us. We have only the scientists' word to go by — and, people will say, they have got it wrong in the past, haven't they? And anyway, when all is said and done, Nature's capacity to heal itself is infinite and we must not be panicked into hasty action. Unlike the obvious threat of a nuclear holocaust, the environmental threats we face are far from clear.

He quotes the report by the Royal Society and the US Academy of Sciences in support of the gravity of our ecological situation, the first issued jointly by the two leading scientific societies of the English-speaking world:

> The future of our planet is in the balance. Sustainable development can be achieved, but only if irreversible degradation of the environment can be halted in time.' They set out with great cogency their reasons for thinking this way. Again I quote: 'Unrestrained resource consumption for energy production and other uses, especially if the developing world strives to achieve living standards based on the same levels of consumption as the developed world, could lead to catastrophic outcomes for the global environment.' What could be clearer or more authoritative than that? None of these bodies is known for

its tendency to exaggerate, rather the reverse. This makes it all the more amazing that so many people still prefer to turn their backs on the signs of planetary stress that are by now indisputable. The issues raised are never going to be comfortable subjects for polite conversation.

Two of the key issues are the interacting ones of resource consumption and population growth:

> I think we have to ask ourselves, firstly, whether we can continue to ignore the prospect of a virtual doubling of the world's population — somewhere approaching 10 billion [this estimate has since been reduced] — by 2050? Secondly, can we look forward to any kind of real security as the global gap between rich and poor continues to widen? If we compare the *per capita* wealth of Europe with China, or India, the ratio in 1890 was two to one. By 1940, that ratio was 40:1, today it is 70:1. With these statistics in mind, is it really any wonder that the 'South' are approaching the Rio conference event with open economic demands? For them, it is essentially a conference about development and justice.
>
> I do not want to add to the controversy over cause and effect with respect to the Third World's problems. Suffice it to say that I don't, in all logic, see how any society can hope to improve its lot when population growth regularly exceeds economic growth. The factors which will reduce population growth are, by now, easily identified: a standard of healthcare that makes family planning viable, increased female literacy, reduced infant mortality, and access to clean water. Achieving them, of course, is more difficult — but perhaps two simple truths need to be writ large over the portals of every international gathering about the environment: we will not slow the birth rate much until we find ways of addressing poverty. And we will not protect the environment until we address the issues of population growth and poverty in the same breath.

Much of what the Prince says here could equally well have applied to Johannesburg ten years on. He went on to criticize the Commission for recommending economic growth as a panacea to Third World problems, commenting that this may well be incompatible with their aim of sustainability. Moreover, 'Gross National Product is merely a reasonably good indicator of the overall level of a nation's economic activity. It is a thoroughly misleading indicator of national well-being, let alone sustainability. We clearly need some measure of "green GNP", which calculates the nation's output after deducting the depreciation on nature's capital.' Much work has in fact been done on new quality of life indicators in the last ten years, but these have yet to make any impact on mainstream politics. The Prince's own approach is based on a dual concept of stewardship:

> For me, stewardship operates at two levels; firstly, at the level of good housekeeping: living thriftily, saving energy, repairing, re-using and recycling, not wanting by not wasting, accepting personal responsibility and so on.
>
> Secondly, it also operates at a level which recognizes that we are as much a part of the living world as it is part of us. Good stewardship celebrates the beauty and diversity of the natural world. We should not, I believe, just be 'managing the Earth's resources more efficiently' (relying on a traditional utilitarian ethic), but seeking to live in balance with the rest of creation, even if we cannot discern any direct and immediate material benefit to ourselves in that process.

This requires a further shift in our thinking where, as the ecologist Lester Brown explains in his book *Eco-Economy*, economics becomes a part of ecology instead of the other way round. The Prince takes the same view:

> We must, in fact, get back to Nature — not in any romanticized, drop-out, 'under the greenwood tree' sort of way, but through the application of both science and philosophy. From very different perspectives, both disciplines teach us that the reality of the natural world within which we live is not linear, but essentially circular. There is no such thing as 'waste' or even 'pollution' in the

natural interaction of different species within their own eco-systems. This is still understood — indeed, lived out in practice — by those whom we so patronizingly describe as 'primitive.' As we thrash around with various theoretical definitions of the sustainability of today's economic orthodoxy — and some alternative (as yet undefined) models of progress — it remains a sobering experience to encounter sustainability in action amongst tribal people, without any great fanfares or the assistance of voluminous reports.

Again (and I say this only to ward off those who might be inclined to misrepresent my respect for the traditional wisdom and stewardship of tribal people), I am not advocating any kind of mass return to a 'hunter-gatherer' society. But the real challenge, as I see it, is to find the right blend of dynamic Western systems in all their purposeful linearity, with the closed loop circularity of the natural world. In effect, to combine modern science with traditional wisdom.

This passage is another example of the Prince's integrated *both-and* philosophy while many of his critics remain embedded in an *either-or* framework and assume that he is hostile to science simply because of his criticism of scientific materialism. The Prince is sensitive to thinking through solutions appropriate to local conditions:

Tragically, too many so-called solutions to environmental problems miss their mark because they fail to recognize the nature of the societies which have to put them into effect. Unless there is a really critical analysis of the roles of the different components of these societies — women as well as men, and young as well as old — there is every risk that the proposals will be unworkable, the development assistance projects will be on the wrong scale, and the communities will be left with inappropriate, imposed technology that they cannot operate.

In southern India, where I was in February, the simple act of giving people tenure over the land they work day in and day out, and secure access to water, has not only transformed the quality of their lives, but is also giving them an incentive to rehabilitate their environment. This simple formula of meeting basic needs, empowering communities and safe-guarding the environment — Primary Environmental Care — not only works; it is where the solution to everything else starts. Environment, much like charity, really does begin at home. Things may be starting to improve but the world is already littered with corroding bulldozers and mechanized farm implements, paid for by development aid yet unworkable under the circumstances of life in rural communities. Starting with people, analysing their needs, taking account of their culture and traditional practices, making certain that the roles of all sectors of the community are understood and, above all, asking people to frame their own, local, environmental goals are all pre-requisites to satisfactory solutions.

Remarking that 'your Commission also pointed out the crucial importance of democracy and individual participation in achieving a more sustainable world,' the Prince notes the momentous changes that took place in Eastern Europe in 1989. He is also encouraged by the British Government taking the lead in 'making a much more explicit linkage between aid flows and the establishment and maintenance of democracy, as well as compliance with international conventions on human rights.' He adds that 'unless the human spirit is first unshackled, environmental protection and development will remain just a dream for many.' The thrust here is as Gro Harlem Brundtland herself stated: environment, plus development, plus democracy.

The Earth Summit came and went, as has the 2002 meeting ten years on in Johannesburg. By 1995 the Local Agenda 21 process was well under way and a conference was held in London in March to take stock, with speakers including the Secretary of State for the Environment and Jonathon Porritt. The Prince reminded the audience that Local Agenda 21 is the new agenda of sustainable development which seeks to integrate environmental, economic and social factors with a strong community consensus. He attributed its success to the fact that it embodies many things that people — individual people — believe deep down in themselves. It is a planned, democratic process involving the whole community. It is about improving the quality of life for everyone — but within the constraints set by the natural environment. It sees local government as the steward of the local environment (with responsibilities not only for land use planning, management of open areas and environmental protection but also for local economic development and social issues). It integrates commitment to the local environment with local economic development and local social care.

The Prince gives two reasons why he puts such an emphasis on the local dimension:

> Firstly, because in an increasingly cosmopolitan world, with much talk of such things as the global village, the information super highway and the Internet, it is worth remembering that in this country two-thirds of the population still live within five miles of their place of birth. And, secondly, because applying policies — whether they are devised in Rio, Whitehall, Brussels or Geneva — at a local level is perhaps the ultimate test of whether or not they can actually be made to work.

It also means taking a long-term view of the resources available in the locality and generally taking environmental constraints seriously:

'In the past, the major constraints on our actions were technological, financial or intellectual. Now and in the future, if we are to behave responsibly towards future generations — leaving them the maximum number of options — I believe the constraints will increasingly be environmental. '

## Environmental Security and the Precautionary Principle

*The insistence on complete certainty about the full details of global warming — the most serious threat that we have ever faced — is actually an effort to avoid facing the awful,*

*uncomfortable truth: that we must act boldly, decisively,*
*comprehensively and quickly, even before we know every last*
*detail about the crisis. Those who continue to argue that the*
*appropriate response is merely additional research are simply*
*seeking to camouflage timidity or protect their vested interest*
*in the status quo.*

Al Gore

The Prince of Wales's WCED lecture appeared in a volume called *Threats without Enemies*, edited by Professor Gwyn Prins, Director of the Global Security Programme in the University of Cambridge. This collection is subtitled 'Facing Environmental Insecurity' and contains thoughtful essays from a number of key political, military and scientific figures. For many years the Cold War gave the West a context for security with its stand-off of nuclear arsenals relying on a policy of deterrence embodied in mutually assured destruction (MAD). All this changed from 1989 onwards and left something of a vacuum in US foreign policy, which had to be formulated without reference to a specific enemy. September 11, 2001 brought a new and powerful focus on global terrorism as the main security threat, and has redefined US foreign and defence policy and consequent military expenditure. This means that environmental matters are once again very much on the back burner — indeed it is only public concern that can bring them back into focus again under the 'business as usual' scenario.

However, in a broader sense, the problems of environmental insecurity have not only not gone away (despite comfort taken by governments from Bjorn Lomborg's book, *The Sceptical Environmentalist*), but they are likely to intensify. As Professor Prins says:

Environmental insecurity is a range of things in the here and now. It is the pattern of increasingly violent storms in the recent past. It is the disappearing rainforests. It is the hole in the ozone layer. It is the promise of more, and maybe worse, of the same: runaway global warming; losses of biodiversity beyond the point of retrieval; an unsustainably large and resource-hungry human population.

Environmental security is therefore *not* something in the here and now. It is a goal. It means capping the trends which are enhancing climate change. It means defining and practising sustainable development. Critically, it means modifying conventional, contemporary political theory and practice to make this possible.

This is a tall order, as Prins himself explains. However, there are specific flashpoints in terms of resource conflicts— water for example and transnational pollution — to address. Typically, these are dealt with in a confrontational mode that fails to address the underlying issue of the difference between human linear logic and Nature's circular or cyclical logic, as the Prince explains above.

The Prince returned to this theme of global security in a lecture at Cambridge University to mark the publication of Gwyn Prins' book. The stated aims of Prins' Global Security Institute are Stewardship, Sustainability and Survival, all themes close to the Prince's heart:

> What I suppose I am getting at here is that security starts at home and, when we're lucky, it stretches in an unbroken chain from individual concerns all the way through to the kind of concerns the Earth Summit addressed. It is wholly natural that things closer to home are likely to matter more to people than things in far-off countries or far off on the horizon.
>
> It may be that one of the most useful contributions that the emerging discipline of global security can make is to widen our very understanding of security by taking on broader, non-military interpretations (social, economic and political security), and by emphasizing the different levels at which security ceases to be an abstraction and becomes a very hard-edged reality for people in their own daily lives, in their communities, and in their workplaces.

A personal sense of security begins in the home and at work, which 'means so much more to people than the relatively straightforward business of being paid for selling one's labour.

Security, dignity, purpose, fulfilment, conviviality, status, service to others, reassurance, solidarity, variety; in an industrial society, some or all of these psychological benefits are delivered primarily through the jobs that people have or the work they do, paid or unpaid.' Hence unemployment can radically undermine this security, so the Prince asks:

> How then are we to organize matters to give everyone
> some status, some self-respect and the sense of personal
> security that comes from having a job? At present we live
> in a society where some people are fully employed and
> some are wholly unemployed. In the long run, should we
> perhaps try to get away from thinking in those terms?
> Ought we not to be examining ways of ensuring that all
> people (but particularly all young people) have a chance
> to serve others and the community, thereby improving
> their own prospects through the work they do?

This is precisely the aim and work of the Prince's Trust, which will be described in a later chapter. All of this work takes place within the community, which represents another level of security and stability. Returning to the overall theme, the Prince reminds his listeners that poverty and pollution are also security threats:

> Stewardship, sustainability and survival; these are as much
> national security goals as they are global security goals.
> Sustainable development is not a doctrine which can be
> embraced in isolation; only when national goals for
> sustainable development can be achieved in cooperation
> with other nations will we be able to anticipate a future that
> is not littered with increasingly bitter disputes over those
> natural resources which define and limit sustainability.

The Prince highlighted a number of specific security threats, beginning with water shortages. He rightly says that demand will continue to grow at a time of increased shortages. Some rivers like the Ganges, Nile, Jordan and Colorado flow through more than one country, making it possible for the upstream country to syphon off more than its fair share. In the light of the complexity and multiplicity of strategic threats involving the environment and development, the Prince makes a case for adopting the precautionary principle, a bulwark of post-war defence policy: 'In military affairs, policy has long been based on the dictum that we should be prepared for the worst case. Why should it be so different when the security is that of the planet and our long-term future?' He is not optimistic, though, that our existing institutions are adequate to the task. Nor is it an easy task, as metaphorical boiled frogs eventually find out when the water is already too hot for them to escape:

> A particular difficulty is that many of these non-military threats are insidious, they creep up on us slowly and are difficult to recognize. Our reactions, even under favourable circumstances, are likely to be late. Often they will also be inadequate. We may well pass the danger point before we wake up. Here perhaps we should take a lesson from military strategists, who pay great attention to indicators and warnings, meaning indicators and warnings of a potential trouble-maker's intentions. I see great merit in co-ordinated international attention being paid to indicators and warnings of environmental problems, resource disputes and local difficulties which could flare up.

A comprehensive recent volume on the precautionary principle speaks of 'late lessons from early warnings, cataloguing a series of situations like fisheries, asbestos, chemical contamination of the Great Lakes and BSE where early warnings were ignored — to our later cost.' This means being able to respond not only to scientific uncertainty but to ignorance and formulate appropriate policy options; this is easier said than done, especially with pressure from lobbies with a vested interest in certain outcomes. So the Prince sees that the specific challenge is to:

> bridge the gap between today's crisis management and tomorrow's pending ecological disasters. When more and more people in the developing world are unable to obtain

enough energy to meet their basic needs, it is easy to understand why the still hypothetical horrors of long-term climate change cut mighty little ice. But governments and non-governmental organizations alike can drag those long-term eventualities back to current realities — through specific programmes to eliminate energy shortages, through the introduction of new market instruments and incentives to promote energy efficiency, through active measures (as is happening here in Cambridge), to promote cycling and walking, and to improve public transport. The list is endless! The short-term benefits to the local economy and to people's immediate quality of life are enormous. The long-term ecological benefits are not insignificant either!

A new slogan might be coined in this context: 'Not just "think globally — act locally". But also "protect tomorrow — act today".' Perhaps, the Prince fears, we will need a catastrophe to bring us collectively to our senses but 'do we not have an obligation to minimize the likelihood of such a grim eventuality by addressing the threats in terms and through policies which make sense to people today?' He continues on a more positive note that 'we are all slowly learning to re-interpret short-term self-interest (which is likely to remain the most intoxicating political brew for some time to come!) within a longer-term framework of stewardship and the reciprocal rights and obligations of citizenship on a finite planet.' He concludes that:

> There is no 'quick fix' for the problems we face, and technology alone will certainly not suffice. We somehow have to find the wisdom, courage, restraint and humility to confront the fundamental realities of living on a finite planet. Developing a clearer vision of how we can do this will require new levels of openness and creativity, utilizing all the intellectual and philosophical resources at our disposal. The discipline of global security, with its clear-sighted focus on stewardship, sustainability and survival, interpreted in a spirit of practical idealism, has a major contribution to make to this process.

The Prince ranges across a wide canvas of environmental issues in his more general environmental speeches but he has addressed more specific themes on a number of occasions, and it is to these that we now turn.

## Rainforests and Timber

> *Nature depends on cycles to maintain life. In nature, there are no linear flow-throughs, no situations where raw materials go in one end and garbage comes out the other. In nature, one organism's waste is another's sustenance. Nutrients are continuously cycled. This system works. Our challenge is to emulate it in the design of the economy.*
>
> Lester Brown

The Prince's major speech on this issue was given in 1990 at Kew Gardens for Friends of the Earth. Since that time he has not only maintained an active interest in this issue, but has implemented a sustainable forestry policy in the Duchy of Cornwall woodlands. He himself says at the outset that there is probably little new to be said about tropical forests but it is nevertheless a critical issue of which we should all be aware. And it is one for which the industrial world must shoulder much of the responsibility since they have instigated most of the logging projects, having used up their own forests centuries ago. We need to remind ourselves that tropical forests are in fact the natural assets of other countries.

Showing our anxiety about their problems must be done in a way which shows respect for their sovereignty, and an understanding of their needs. We must also examine our own consciences. We talk about the need to avoid irreversible damage to fragile habitats, and the requirement to guard shrinking non-renewable resources. But what about the wrong sort of afforestation in the Flow country of Scotland, and large-scale, highly mechanized, peat extraction? If any exploitation is to be carried out at all then surely it should be one in a more traditional way, rather than utilizing such utterly inappropriate methods. It seems

to me important that any discussion about the tropical
forests should start by looking at the people who depend
directly on them for their livelihood. This includes both
indigenous people and relatively recent settlers, but the
main focus of concern must be on the remaining tribal
people for whom the tropical forest has been their home for
many generations. Their story has been told many times,
and it is one of which we must all be profoundly ashamed.

Deforestation, the Prince maintains, affects people at a number
of different levels. First, the forest-dwellers themselves; then the
other inhabitants of the country by means of local climate
change; and finally the rest of us through the wider impact of
climate alteration. The next aspect is species extinction, with
tropical deforestation as the leading cause — amounting to
losses of as many as ten million in the next half century. This has
a considerable potential impact in the medical and agricultural
fields. As an example, the Prince cites that:

> genes from wild rice helped to combat a new disease
> which was threatening to wipe out much of Asia's rice
> crop. As it happened, that crop-saving plant was found in
> the Silent Valley forest in India, which itself was only
> saved by the intervention of the kind of environmental
> activists whose activities are so often derided by those
> who do not share their single-minded commitment ...
> [He concludes:] ... It really does seem extraordinary that
> we should be destroying our genetic inheritance at
> precisely the time when we most need it, and at a time
> when advances in science and technology are providing
> incredibly precise and sophisticated tools to open up some
> of nature's secrets — to the benefit of medicine, nutrition
> and industry. What possible justification can there be for
> systematically stripping future generations of their options
> — in a way that defies even conventional economic logic?

Turning to the causes of deforestation, the Prince identifies a
number of factors: the poverty of people who live around the
tropical forests in developing countries; pressure of human

numbers; commercial logging and cattle ranching; and, principally, the clearance of land for agricultural purposes. This is
usually achieved through 'slash and burn,' a method that in
itself exacerbates greenhouse warming, adding an estimated 1.4
billion tons of carbon dioxide a year. And despite the fact that
two new international organizations — the International
Tropical Timber Organization (ITTO) and the Tropical Forestry
Action Plan (TFAP) — have been established in the past eight
years to address forestry problems, the Prince observes that
'deforestation has actually increased massively during the time
that these institutions have been at work.' Hence his suggestion
for 'an international agreement or convention on the world's
tropical forests.'

He proposes that the goals of a separate Rainforest
Convention would be as follows:

~ to establish a rationale for sustainable use;
~ to maintain ecological and physical processes essential to
   the maintenance of local, regional and global climates;
~ to maintain maximum biological diversity;
~ to establish the fundamental rights of forest dwellers; to set
   targets for re-afforestation;
~ to establish mechanisms of compensation for countries that
   suffer financial loss by controlling destruction of their
   forests; and
~ to establish funding mechanisms to meet the cost of such
   compensation.

The Prince recognizes that this is a 'massive challenge,' but
believes that 'we cannot simply go on talking about the need to
protect the world's tropical forests, and not create the kind of
institutions and mechanisms which will actually make that possible.' He is, however, not optimistic about the prospects for
stemming the flow of so-called 'shifted cultivators' from the
forests, especially given the pressures of debt servicing that
involve a transfer of resources from South to North on a massive
scale. Once again, sustainable forest management has to proceed on the basis of using interest sustainably rather than eating
through the irreplaceable capital resource.

His visit to Indonesia had given the Prince some first-hand experience, but he was dismayed to find that forest management education was still focused on obtaining the maximum economic return in the shortest time period. The British Government did in fact launch a forestry scheme through the Overseas Development Agency in 1988 and, at the time of this speech in 1990, was supporting 115 projects, with another 50 in preparation, at a total cost of £145 million. Given the finding that even the most selective and sensitive types of timber extraction are unsustainable, the Prince suggests that 'with the tropical forests at such risk, it would seem to me to be eminently sensible to work towards the restriction of timber extraction to secondary forest — to those forests which have already been logged over. We could then look towards future timber needs being met from hardwood plantations established on the vast area of already degraded land.' He recognizes the strength of economic considerations, but observes that even conventional economics bears out the superiority of sustainable use over outright destruction. However, he acknowledges that the demand for hardwood is international and hence earns valuable foreign exchange, which is not the case with alternative non-timber products.

The way forward, the Prince suggests, is to find out what Nature will allow and to work within these limitations. He cites a disastrous venture by Henry Ford — Fordlandia in Brazil — as a cautionary tale:

> Here the single-minded energy of American industry, aided by a welter of concessions from the Brazilian government, was unable to establish a viable rubber plantation, because of an oversight concerning some very basic laws of Nature. In 1927, Ford took control of what was described as 'a fertile rolling plateau, forested with tall and lovely trees.' By 1929 he had cleared nearly one and a half thousand acres but the project failed because the seedlings would not thrive. The main problem was that *Hevea brasiliensis*, whose latex provides the raw material for rubber, was attacked by a leaf rust fungus. This is not a serious problem when the trees are grown

singly in the jungle, but spreads with devastating effect when they are planted as a monoculture.

This underlines an important lesson, which has been taken up in the years since this speech — a lesson that also helps to maintain vital biodiversity:

> The importance of working with indigenous tribal peoples, and respecting them for their all-embracing knowledge and experience of the forest. Generations of observation and bodily trial and error have honed their judgement in a process as rigorous as any laboratory testing. As a result, local people often have keener insights into the intricately balanced harmony of the forests, and how simultaneously to exploit and sustain that harmony, than do the peripatetic experts. Yet local communities have too often been ignored. We must systematically, I would suggest, bring them into efforts to safeguard the forest, right from the start of the planning process.

After some concrete examples of agreements to hand land back to indigenous peoples, the Prince concludes with a number of policy recommendations: 'avoid purchasing tropical hardwood products unless we are satisfied that they come from "sustainably managed forests",' although there are labelling problems here. He himself had begun (and has continued) to plant hardwoods for furniture making in about seventy years time. He suggests that the use of tropical hardwoods in the built environment be minimized — at least until the introduction of a proper sustainability labelling scheme. Most importantly, 'we have to find a way of doing something about the burden of international debt. I really don't see how developing countries can be expected to achieve sustainable development and at the same time meet huge debt repayments.'

He reminds us that the tribal notion of 'management' and indeed stewardship is very different from our own while warning against patronizing or romanticizing them. He reiterates his theme of the need for a less arrogant, Man-centred philosophy and the development of a reverence for the natural world, urging us, as some tribes do, to consider the effects of our actions on the seventh generation.

The Prince returned to timber and forestry issues in a speech to the World Wildlife Fund (WWF) Timber seminar in 1994, remarking that the picture in the tropics had changed only slightly in the intervening period. And in some places like Nigeria the situation had deteriorated so sharply that this country was now a net importer of timber when it had once been a leading exporter. However, the environmental movement had been successful in raising public awareness of tropical deforestation and is sceptical about assurances from producers. Nevertheless, some specific targets had been set, for instance the WWF target that by 1995 all 'wood and wood products from all forests to be based on sustainable sources by the end of 1995.' The Prince reported that twenty-four companies had taken up the challenge, but that there was still no credible international certification scheme as he had recommended in his 1990 speech. So he recommended a voluntary scheme whereby value is added to timber that can be certified as coming from a sustainable source.

The Soil Association has since made considerable progress on the certification front, and the Prince himself said that he had asked the Soil Association to inspect, and hopefully certify, the Duchy of Cornwall's woodlands near Liskeard so that 'Royal Household's timber suppliers have been asked to supply only timber which comes from independently certified sustainable sources after the 1995 deadline.' The way ahead has to include partnerships between government and industry, increased consumer pressure for sustainability labelling and, most importantly, personal commitment and action on the part of individuals.

## Water and the Seas

*It is a curious situation that the sea, from which life first arose, should now be threatened by the activities of one form of that life. But the sea, though changed in a sinister way, will continue to exist; the threat is rather to life itself.*

Rachel Carson

The Prince of Wales applies the key themes of sustainability and stewardship to both drinking water and life in the oceans. In a speech to the Institute of Water and Environmental Management in 1990, he called for long-term solutions to the problems of over-extraction and pollution, the balance of supply and demand within industry and consumers generally, and charging schemes that 'reflect not only the cost of providing a scarce resource, but the damage that is being done to the environment.' He reminds us that water management includes sewage disposal as well. The core of his message translates into an obligation for each generation:

> I believe that the aim of our stewardship should be to pass on to future generations water resources that will allow them no less a range of uses and benefits that we currently enjoy. We cannot foretell their precise requirements. They may have much greater needs than us, or new technology may enable them to exist with less high quality water than we need today. But I do believe that certain aspects of human nature do not change and that they, like us, will see plentiful supplies of clean water as making an important contribution to their quality of life. They will want healthy bathing beaches, clean rivers and lakes to fish in, sail on, and walk by, with a wide variety of unspoiled aquatic wildlife habitats — in addition to ample water from the tap. A clear goal for our generation to set itself is to work out how we can hand on at least the same quantity, quality and variety of water resources as we currently enjoy. And to do whatever we can actually to improve things. If each succeeding generation can set itself the same goal we will really be on course for the sustainable use of water.

The Prince believes that 'this sort of approach, in which all users have to balance their requirements for water against the costs of meeting them, is sustainability in action. And if we are serious about our role as stewards then the sooner we get used to thinking this way, the better.' Among the chronic problems that we need to address are the cleaning up of groundwater, the effects of acid rain, coastal bathing waters and agricultural pollution resulting from intensive farming practices, of which the Duchy of Cornwall has direct experience, having been involved in over forty pollution prevention schemes in the previous ten years.

The Prince has been actively concerned with the quality of the marine environment for many years. At the North Sea conference in November 1987 he launched a powerful plea to cut the dumping of toxic waste into the sea, 'which we have treated like a rubbish dump.' Here again he advocates a precautionary line against those who 'argue that we do not have enough proof of danger to justify stricter controls on dumping or to warrant the extra expenditure involved. They say that we must wait for science to provide that proof. If science has taught us anything, however, it is that the environment is full of uncertainty. It makes no sense to test it to destruction. While we wait for the doctor's diagnosis, the patient may easily die!' Only joint action is sufficient, and, since the sea is part of our global commons, we all have an interest in preserving it for the future.

A further and critical issue is the unsustainability of our current fishing practices and the related threat that new methods pose to marine species including the albatross. The basic issue is this: 'Can we find the necessary combination of scientific and traditional knowledge, technical skill, management ability, consumer pressure and political will to get the world's fisheries, however gradually, back to sustainability?' As regards the overall situation, first highlighted by Rachel Carson in 1950, the Prince is under no illusions:

> There is a more general point here too, which is that our stewardship of the world's oceans has been truly appalling. We have polluted them, used them as dumps for every sort of waste, and exploited most of their fish stocks beyond the point at which they can maintain their numbers. Sadly, at sea, 'out of sight' really is all too often 'out of mind.'
>
> Our 'solution' to diminishing fish stocks has been laughable to say the least. First, more and bigger fishing boats, spending longer at sea and using ever more powerful equipment. Second, fishing 'down the food chain,' seeking ever smaller species — to the point where some people

have even discussed fishing for plankton (no, that's not a joke). Third, fish farming, which in many cases has only exacerbated the problems, by taking food away from wild stocks and causing yet more and newer forms of pollution.

On another occasion he remarked that he thought that 'more could be done to limit the use of over-powerful technology in fishing, swinging the balance back towards smaller-scale fisheries and the coastal communities they support.' A prominent Scandinavian politician once dismissed this view as 'wanting to put the clock back' and thoroughly inefficient, to which the Prince responded: 'if the alternative is overfishing, with collapsing fish stocks, a devastated marine ecosystem and local unemployment, a little more "inefficiency" might be worth considering, providing it does not compromise safety at sea.' The Prince suggests that the principle of Environmentally Sensitive Areas might equally be applied to the sea with the concept of Highly Protected Marine Areas that is now on the table.

As an indication of species connectedness, the Prince mentions the illegal fishery of the Patagonian toothfish or Antarctic seabass, which is a staple food for the albatross. Not only is the albatross itself threatened, but the very existence of the Patagonian toothfish is in question. Pirate vessels operating under flags of convenience account for up to a quarter of the world's fish catch, according to a recent UN report. Thousands of tons of this particular fish are smuggled into ports every year. The Patagonian toothfish lives up to fifty years and takes ten years to reach breeding capacity; it is currently being caught at a rate that will lead to its extinction if fishing continues at present levels. If one asks why this fish is being pursued in this way, the answer is:

> simply that all of the more accessible fisheries have largely been ruined. Sixty per cent of the world's fisheries are now assessed as either fully exploited or over-exploited. The renowned Grand Banks cod fishery off the coast of Newfoundland was closed in 1992 to allow stocks to recover, and forty thousand people lost their livelihoods. Eight years later there is still no real sign of recovery.

Scientists now suggest that the Irish Sea and North Sea cod fisheries may be on the brink of a similar collapse.

Since this speech, unpopular but necessarily severe restrictions have been imposed by the EU and an agreement on sustainable fish stocks was reached in Johannesburg, but with a thirteen year timeline in which illegal overfishing is sure to continue unabated. Moreover, as the Prince has observed, we are now targeting sand-eels in the North Sea, which are at the bottom of the food chain. And although the total allowable catch in 2004 is 826,000 tons, the fleet could only net 300,000 tons in 2003 simply because there were not enough sand-eels! This lack of sand-eels has a knock-on effect on the population of sea birds, particularly on kittiwakes in places like Shetland. There is, however, some hope of consumer pressure being exerted with the establishment of the Marine Stewardship Council's labelling scheme for sustainably produced seafood. The Prince has been a strong supporter of the work of the MSC and has made several speeches on their behalf in the last year. There are now 200 MSC-certified products for sale in 14 countries.

The Prince's company Duchy Originals has followed the MSC lead with its Cornish mackerel pate made from fish caught with handlines. Their latest product is a kipper and lemon pâté using Thames Herring, a fish unique to our coastal waters which comes from the MSC's first British certified fishery. The fish are caught in season using driftnets — a highly sustainable method which protects the young fish stock — and are kippered by a local smokery.

The Prince has taken a special interest in the plight of the albatross, as well as in the wellbeing of other sea birds whose numbers have been affected by modern fishing methods. Of the 24 known species, 21 are now considered endangered, up from only three in 1996. The reason for this is connected with longline fishing practices: 'each ship sets anything up to eighty miles of line equipped with thousands of baited hooks, in search of high value fish such as tuna and swordfish. The problem occurs as the baits enter the water. Any accompanying albatross sees a free meal, swoops down and, if the hook takes hold, is dragged inexorably to its death.' A grim scenario, especially when repeated: 'it is clear that some tens of thousands of these birds are drowned by fishing gear every year' (the latest estimate is 100,000). This is why the charity BirdLife International is lobbying for more environmentally friendly fishing practices to protect seabirds: 'It points out that, since the biggest albatrosses may take ten years or more to reach breeding age, and then produce only one chick every other year, the impact of these losses on overall numbers is severe and unsustainable.'

For instance, the Prince continued, 'British scientists are in no doubt that longlining is to blame for the relentless decline (by nearly a third) in the numbers of Wandering Albatrosses on Bird Island, South Georgia, since the 1960s. Hooks, broken lines and other longline debris even turn up in the food that the parent birds regurgitate to their unsuspecting chicks.' However, there are some simple but effective measures such as 'setting lines under water, or only at night, trailing a bird-scaring line, prohibiting offal discharge while fishing and observing a closed season at the most vulnerable times.' It is encouraging that an international agreement was signed in 2004 to protect albatrosses and petrels.

Nevertheless, the most recent statistics are still chilling. The estimated number of seabirds perishing annually through longline fishing has risen to 300,000. It is clear that similar challenges to sustainability exist in the oceans as on land, and that the same principles can, as the Prince argues, be applied to both. In both cases there is a conflict between short-term economic exploitation and longer term stewardship that can arguably be overcome by policies of enlightened self-interest. But is this enough? Will we have to wait for a catastrophe before we radically change course? Might a spiritual renaissance help mitigate the effects? These are the individual and collective challenges we face. As James Lovelock puts it: 'It all depends on you and me. If we see the world as a living organism of which we are a part — not the owner, nor the tenant; not even a passenger — we could have a long time ahead of us and our species might survive its "allotted span." It is up to us to act personally in a way that is constructive.'

# 2. Working with the Grain: Sustainable Agriculture and Organic Gardening

## The Future of Food: Competing Approaches to Agriculture

> *Our inability to provide adequate protection for the world food supply is, in my opinion, simply another manifestation of the same philosophical error that has led to the global environment crisis as a whole: we have assumed that our lives need have no real connection to the natural world, that our minds are separate from our bodies, and that as disembodied intellects we can manipulate the world in any way we choose. Precisely because we feel no connection to the physical world, we trivialize the consequences of our actions.*
>
> Al Gore

The Prince of Wales's championing of ecological sustainability finds a significant expression in his views on agriculture, views which he has vigorously translated into practical projects on the Duchy of Cornwall estate and especially on its Home Farm at Highgrove in Gloucestershire. His most recent goading interventions in the field have concerned the genetically modified (GM) food question, to which we will turn later in this chapter. However, this debate is part of a larger ideological divide between reductionist scientific high-tech approaches and the holistic organic perspective adopted by the Prince.

Proponents of the agrochemical and biotechnological approach point to the remarkable acceleration in grain yields through use of higher-yielding varieties, irrigation, fertilizers and other agrochemical inputs, and argue that developments in biotechnology will enable even greater yields with less use of pesticides. However, all this will come at a cost that may not be affordable or even agriculturally appropriate to the poorest farmers. Moreover, the further yield potential is open to question: higher inputs of (polluting) fertilizer and (increasingly scarce) water are giving diminishing returns.

The last few years have seen the emergence of an approach now characterized as 'agroecological,' a term that implies sustainable agriculture while recognizing the inherent problems of the notion of sustainability. Theorists like Norman Uphoff propose that there is a continuum of practices and technologies between the 'likely-to-be-sustainable' to the 'unlikely-to-be-sustainable.' They see agroecological approaches as especially beneficial to those parts of the world where it is hardest to implement currently favoured policies. The core of the approach — and an underlying (no pun intended) theme of this chapter — is an ecological approach to the soil: 'the soil is regarded not as a repository for production inputs or as a terrain to be exploited and mined, but rather as a living system in which micro- and macro-organisms interact with organic and mineral materials to produce environments below and above ground in which plants, animals and humans thrive.'

This approach can be traced back to the origins of the organic movement in the work of Sir Albert Howard in India in the early 20th century. Howard's basic thesis was that the health of soil, plant, animal and human formed part of a connected chain, and that any weakness in an earlier link is carried forward to an impact on human health. He thought that the prevalence of vegetable and animal pests showed a failure of plant and animal health and that 'the impaired health of human populations (the fourth link) in modern civilized countries is a consequence of this failure in the second and third links. Most importantly, he stated that the failure of plant, animal and human health was attributable to the undernourishment of the soil. Hence his advocacy of the principles underlying Nature's agriculture:

> The main characteristic of Nature's farming can therefore
> be summed up in a few words. Mother earth never

attempts to farm without livestock; she always raises mixed crops; great pains are taken to preserve the soil and to prevent erosion; the mixed vegetable and animal wastes are converted into humus; there is no waste; the processes of growth and the processes of decay balance one another; ample provision is made to maintain large reserves of fertility; the greatest care is taken to store the rainfall; both plants and animals are left to protect themselves against disease.

Since Howard's time — and the pioneering researches of his contemporary Sir Robert McCarrison in India — the connection between diet and health has been scientifically established. It is acknowledged as a key factor in the development of heart disease and cancer. Howard himself was active in the new health initiatives of his day and was instrumental in establishing the close links between organic agriculture and holistic health. He forecasted that a new system of preventive medicine and medical training would arise so that 'the physician of tomorrow will study mankind in relation to his environment, will prevent disease at its source, and will cease to confine himself to the temporary alleviation of the miseries resulting from malnutrition.'

Howard was a key influence on Lady Eve Balfour and the founders of the Soil Association. She identified the common ground uniting their founders as:

1) The conception of the soil as a living entity.
2) The recognition that human activities must conform to Nature's fixed biological laws if they are not to end in self-destruction.
3) Desire to promote research to interpret more fully what these laws are and how they work.
4) A determination to resist attempts to disregard these laws ... from whatever quarter, and with whatever motives such attempts are made.
5) The belief that this can be best achieved by using all possible means to disseminate information concerning proved knowledge and in this way to expose exploitation, particularly the exploitation of ignorance.

The Soil Association was founded by a group of farmers, scientists and nutritionists in 1946 and has become the leading UK organization devoted to the promotion of organic agriculture as an alternative to intensive farming methods. As outlined in Sir Albert Howard's philosophy above, these pioneers observed a direct connection between farming practice and the health of plants, animals, humans and the environment as a whole. The Association unites all the links in the food chain, working with consumers, farmers, growers, scientists, food processors, retailers and policy makers. Its growing influence can be seen in some of the key recommendations of the recent Curry Report. Its work involves education, campaigns, policy advice, promotion of local distribution systems, certification and setting of standards, farmer support and market development. The Prince of Wales has been Royal Patron of the Association since 1999 and gave the Lady Eve Balfour Memorial Lecture on its 50th anniversary in 1996.

## The Prince's Philosophy of Agriculture

*The criteria for a sustainable agriculture can be summed up in one word — permanence, which means adopting techniques that maintain soil fertility indefinitely; that utilize, as far as possible, only renewable resources; that do not grossly pollute the environment, and that foster biological activity within the soil and throughout the cycles of all the involved food chains.*

Lady Eve Balfour

In his Soil Association lecture, the Prince of Wales set out what he regarded as a noble aim for the Association for the 21st century:

Our aim should be nothing less than to restore agriculture to its rightful place as one of the greatest and most important of all the enterprises in which human beings are engaged. Farming, if practised in its fullest sense — and not as another industrial process — is a unique fusion of science, art and culture. Good farmers understand how to work with the forces of Nature to the benefit of humanity, intervening without dominating or over-exploiting. Our intervention must be based on knowledge and science, but setting the balance between intervention and exploitation will always be an art.

The Prince sees our mode of farming as a reflection of broader social principles of stewardship (implying accountability) and continuity as well as of our overall attitude to the natural world. Farmers have a dual role of producing food and protecting or nurturing the countryside. In the Prince's view, these two functions need to be integrated in overall policy-making, as has recently been recognized by the UK Curry Commission and the review of the EU Common Agricultural Policy.

The centrality of agriculture in our national life is a recurring theme of the Prince's agricultural speeches. And by this he means agri-culture and not agri-industry, echoing the title of Jules Pretty's book. The roots of the word culture imply nurturing growth of plants and animals, which is by definition an organic biological process. The Prince's views on agriculture are underpinned by his overall understanding of the sacredness of the natural world, a perspective that was shared by Lady Eve ('there are no materialists in the Soil Association') and many of the founders of the Soil Association. A religious philosophy is strongly associated with the belief in a God-given natural order exemplified in the 'Rule of Return' (and reaping what you sow), which in turn implies the existence of natural limits and the need to work in harmony with rather than against Nature (often capitalized in such contexts). The Prince puts it like this:

> I am convinced that the natural world has bounds of balance, order and harmony that set limits to our ambitions. When we exceed those limits, or attempt to over-ride the complex, natural system of checks and balances, we will always end up, sooner or later, paying a heavy price. In some cases, as with fish stocks in the North Sea (and in many other parts of the world), we have made painful discoveries about where those limits are.

The arrestingly simple moral is that 'all our actions have consequences, and that mankind has a duty of stewardship for the natural world.'

The direction of UK post-war agriculture was set by the 1947 Agricultural Act which paved the way for the successful mass production of cheap food through financial incentives that effected a radical transformation in farmer's attitudes and, in the Prince's view, made many lose touch with their instincts and sense of proportion 'leading them to convert parts of the surrounding countryside into a virtually treeless, hedgeless desert.' The system was 'economic performance without environmental accountability; maximum production without consideration of food quality and health; intensification without regard for animal welfare; specialization without consideration of the maintenance of biological and cultural diversity. The signals we sent said what we wanted: cheap food and plenty of it... we can hardly blame our farmers now for their outstanding success in achieving those goals.'

However, the Prince thinks that there was a more deep-seated reason for this change of attitude, namely the predominance of modernist thinking:

> the central feature of this (progressive) thinking appeared to be that the past no longer had any relevance to the way we did things. The developments engendered by science would set us free from the shackles of the past, from the dead hand of tradition, and from outmoded concepts which prevented progress. In this scenario everything was possible; there could be no limit to what mankind could achieve now.

And, as the Prince has repeatedly discovered, those who like him questioned the wisdom of a headlong rush along this path were branded reactionaries or latter-day Luddites.

The other powerful current is the mechanistic philosophy of modern science, with the machine as the chief engine of constant progress. Our educational inculcation with this concept of linear progress has, the Prince insists, 'blinded us to the important fact, which our ancestors understood, that the whole pattern of nature rests on a circular function, driven by highly complex, interrelated systems. I believe this with absolute conviction and it is axiomatic to all my activities at Highgrove.'

While acknowledging the benefits of modern technology appropriately used, the Prince shares the scepticism of many about the adequacy of a mechanistic and linear approach to life, as expressed here by the American essayist and farmer Wendell Berry:

> our system of agriculture, by modelling itself on economics rather than biology, thus removes food from the *cycle* of production and puts it into a finite, linear process that in effect destroys it by transforming it into waste. Thus it transforms food into fuel, a form of energy that is usable only once, and in doing so it transforms the body into a consumptive machine.

Farmers are encouraged by the teaching in agricultural colleges to think of themselves in industrial rather than traditional and ecological terms and, when they come to the practice of farming, they are dependent on multinational companies and their representatives for advice on 'what expensive compound to put on which crop at which time.' So the farmer comes to rely less on his own judgement. Moreover, he finds himself on a treadmill whereby he must produce over a ton of grain per acre just to pay for his seeds, sprays and fertilizers before even starting to pay for his fixed costs. The net result is that 'the farmer has to produce higher yields to obtain the return to support his increasingly unsustainable system.' Higher external inputs may increase yields but this may in turn depress prices, so that the farmer's margin is eroded and yields have to be even higher to compensate. For the Prince, this spells out a logic of long-term unsustainability, and reinforces his belief that 'many aspects of traditional farming systems are the most sustainable in terms of mankind and his environment.'

It is important to stress that, although the Prince is a keen proponent of sustainable agriculture and its philosophy, this does not mean that he is opposed root and branch to modern technology. As in his other areas of concern, he actually adopts a *both-and* approach, a fact that is often lost on critics trying to portray him as a conservative extremist or a backward-looking dreamer. He believes that the overriding challenge is 'to take the best of hard-won traditional knowledge and apply it with the best of modern technology, used sensitively. This combination of tradition and appropriate technology is precisely what characterizes the agroecological approach already outlined in this chapter and this is strongly supported by the Prince, who hosted a seminar on 'Reducing Poverty through Sustainable Agriculture' in 2001.

In his speech on that occasion he argues that sustainable agriculture is an integral part of sustainable development, all the more so since the inputs are so expensive to purchase:

> I have always thought that the best place to start looking for sustainability is in the traditional farming systems which have stood the test of time. But, of course, they can be improved by the application of modern knowledge and equipment. The really remarkable thing, to me, is to see just how much improvement is possible, often by doing comparatively simple things ... The common features of sustainable approaches include making the best possible use of natural and regenerative processes, of local resources and of human ingenuity and teamwork.

This approach yields real environmental benefits in terms of clean water, bio-diversity, flood protection and landscape quality as well as a diverse and nutritious diet.

Nor need this approach be confined to developing countries. The Prince calls for a more integrated approach to the life and long-term health of the countryside that goes beyond the commercial process of producing a crop to include 'the quality of life and employment of *people*, the quality of the end product, the maintenance of soil fertility, and of water quality, the conservation of flora and fauna through the skilful management of habitat — in other words, that subtle blend of private interest and public good which, when all is said and done, must surely amount to what we describe as the "cultural" life of the nation.'

The Prince shares the widespread and well-documented view that the industrialization of agriculture has had unfortunate and seriously damaging side-effects on the environment. Traditional management has given way to specialization and intensification: 'We see the consequences of treating animals like machines; seeking ever greater "efficiency" and even experimenting (catastrophically, as we now know) with totally inappropriate alternative "fuels" — in the form of recycled animal proteins — with which to "power" them.' The concept of efficiency is a mechanistic one applied to economic systems, but it is a word that needs deconstructing, as the Prince observes: 'efficient for whom, and over what period? Is it really efficient to produce more wheat than we need, at four or more tons per acre, at three times the real world price, and then dump the surplus on the world market, thereby depressing the price even further — to the great disadvantage of third world producers?' This very issue was a bone of contention — especially in relation to sugar — at the recent Johannesburg Earth Summit. In the long run, unsustainable practices are the ultimate in inefficiency.

Reports from environmental and animal welfare organizations have repeatedly emphasized 'lost biodiversity, of ploughed up pastures and species-rich mixed farms turned into impoverished arable acres; of huge reductions in the populations of birds such as the skylark and song thrush, and of many of our wild flowers; of polluted watercourses and, in places, of depleted and eroded topsoil.' More exact figures are, since 1945, a loss of 95% of wildflower-rich meadows, 30–50% of ancient lowland woods, 50% of heathland, 50% of lowland fens, valleys and basin mires, and 40% of hedgerows. Furthermore, populations of nine species of farmyard birds have fallen by more than a half between 1970 and 1995. Worse still, we are told that 'dairy cows — with a natural life expectancy of twenty years or more — are now quite literally milking themselves to death by the time they are six or seven, worn out by producing more than their own bodyweight in milk every month, and suffering from a lethal combination of distended udders, lameness, chronic mastitis or infertility; despite the routine use of preventative applications of antibiotics and other drugs to control diseases, leading to resistance and the use of ever-stronger drugs.'

The Prince concludes that we need an entirely new set of guiding principles for the agriculture of the 21st century, based on a broad view of sustainability that also encourages farmers to take pride in their role as stewards of the land. This does not necessarily mean farming only organically, since there are other less intensive and environmentally friendly methods (such as Integrated Farm Management) that fall short of being wholly organic. Conversion to organic methods requires a strong degree of personal commitment and belief in the principles behind it. The Prince feels that it is more important 'to embrace a set of objectives which includes the revival of rural communities and economies; which stresses the virtues of health and naturalness throughout the food chain; and which will enhance the quality of life — not only for those who work in agriculture but for the millions of others who take pleasure and pride in the countryside.' As we will see below, the Prince has taken his own advice by developing a well-managed model of sustainable, natural farming at Highgrove.

## *Highgrove and the Duchy of Cornwall*

> *I have put my heart and soul into Highgrove — and I will continue to do so while I can. I have also put my back into Highgrove and, as a result, have probably rendered myself prematurely decrepit in the process .... All the things I have tried to do in this small corner of Gloucestershire have been the physical expression of a personal philosophy. When I was younger I recall the nascent stirrings of such a philosophy; I felt a strong attachment to the soil of those places I loved best — Balmoral, in Scotland, and Sandringham, in Norfolk. As far as I was concerned, every tree, every hedgerow, every wet place, every mountain and river had a special, almost sacred, character of its own.*
>
> The Prince of Wales, Duke of Cornwall

Prince Charles became the 24th Duke of Cornwall on the death of his grandfather George VI in 1952, and took over the chairmanship of the Prince's Council — the governing body of the Duchy of Cornwall — shortly after his 21st birthday in 1969. The Dukedom is the oldest in the country, and was established by the far-sighted Edward III in 1337 for his son and heir, Edward the Black Prince, as a means of ensuring the succession as well financial independence of the heir to the throne. A charter stipulated that only the eldest surviving son of the monarch can become Duke of Cornwall and must subsequently succeed to the throne. Since that time the Duchy has provided an income for successive Dukes, who do not receive any payments from the Civil List. The Duchy is effectively a family trust whereby the capital must be maintained intact to be passed on to the next Duke (Prince William), but the income is paid to the current Duke to meet all his personal and public expenses.

The Duchy is one of the oldest and largest landed estates in the country. Recent purchases, mainly in Hereford and Kent, have enlarged the total holding to around 150,000 acres in 25 counties. This means that the estate is much more spread out than most, although much of it is concentrated in the South West, with 70,000 acres on Dartmoor and 21,000 in Cornwall itself, including the Isles of Scilly. There are nearly 300 farms, most of which are let to tenant farmers and are often passed down the generations. This establishes a special relationship between the Duchy and its tenants, in whom the Duke takes a keen personal interest. He has aimed to make the tenants feel part of a family operation, having 'great faith in the landlord-tenant relationship as one of the more timeless methods of guaranteeing the care and management of the countryside because of its reliance on a mutually supportive system which recognizes some of the fundamental features of human nature.' The family farm represents a principle of continuity and is reflected in the Duchy's work on integrated rural land development and the maintenance of rural communities. For instance, the maintenance of a strong sense of community in the Scilly Isles has led to a policy of letting property to islanders rather than incomers, thereby reducing Duchy income.

The estate is publicly regulated by a number of Acts of Parliament so as to ensure efficient management and an income for future Dukes. This involves the submission of the Duchy's accounts to the Treasury every year and the Treasury's exercise of a supervisory role over the financial affairs of the Duchy, which in turn entails the need to justify capital expenditure on large outlays like the purchase of Highgrove itself and the development scheme at Poundbury. The Duchy, whose offices are in Buckingham Gate, is run by the Prince's Council, which includes four officers. The Chief Executive — currently Bertie Ross, who himself owns land in Galloway — holds the post of Secretary and Keeper of the Records. The senior officer bears the ancient title of Lord Warden of the Stannaries (from *stannum*, the Latin for tin) since the profits from tin mining were assigned by Edward III to the Duchy and provided it with a huge proportion of its income over the next 500 years. The current Lord Warden is Earl Peel, who succeeded Lord Ashburton, whose father had held the same position twenty-five years previously. Famous former Lord Wardens include Sir Walter Raleigh (1585–1603) and Prince Albert (1842–61). The Duchy employs regional Land Stewards to look after its interests in different parts of the country. It also owns residential and commercial property in a number of places, notably Kennington, and is managing an ambitious housing and community development at Poundbury outside Dorchester (see Chapter 5 for more detail).

The Duchy takes a long-term view in all its activities, appropriate to its own history and continuity. In the early years the Prince spent time working with his own tenant farmers in each of the Duchy districts in order to gain first-hand experience of life on the farm. Aside from milking cows, mucking out barns and driving tractors, he learnt a good deal about the complex web of relationships that provides the basis for a farming livelihood and about the enduring rural culture that underpins life in the countryside. The Prince realized that the practice of good husbandry and stewardship of the land was already an operating principle within the Duchy. Only later would it come to be known as sustainable development — balancing the economic, social and environmental aspects of life in ways that do not compromise the interests of future generations. In his 1991 speech to the Royal Agricultural Society, he pointed out how such practices had been applied in the past:

> in medieval times the importance of sustainability was recognized in a whole series of local regulations to prevent long-term damage to village resources.

Replacement trees were to be planted every year, and no manure was to be sold off the manor. Even the expression 'by hook or by crook' derives from the way that wood could be collected from trees — only by knocking or pulling down the dead branches with a hook or crook, and not by felling.

The Duchy bought Highgrove for the Prince in 1980. At the time it only had 340 acres (unsatisfactorily in three separate blocks), but the subsequent purchase of Broadfield Farm in 1985 and, at a later stage, other neighbouring parcels of land has brought it up to its current 1,083 acres (with a further 800 acres of shared farmed land). The Duchy Home Farm was moved to Highgrove from Cornwall in 1985, the same year in which the Prince took the decision with Sir John Higgs to experiment with organic farming, which prompted a certain degree of concerned scepticism among his advisers. The Prince's original intention had been to farm by conventional means, albeit in a biologically sustainable fashion that left strips around arable fields unsprayed and reduced the input of fertilizers and chemicals. The Prince explains the two key techniques of organic farming: 'firstly, minimizing the use of external inputs and replacing them with sound, natural, fertility-building rotations using legumes. Secondly, controlling weeds, pests and diseases in crops and livestock with good management and sound husbandry, rather than with pesticides and pharmaceuticals.'

A discretely placed 85-acre block of land near Westonbirt became the first to be earmarked for conversion to organic farming, with the enthusiastic support of the Prince's new farm manager David Wilson. He and the Farm Director Terry Summers took the advice of the Elm Farm Research Centre and devised a seven-year rotation consisting of red clover and grass for three years, followed by winter wheat, spring oats and spring beans. Then, in the seventh year, one of the cereal crops would be undersown with clover to begin the restoration of soil fertility. All went well for the first two years, and it turned out that the unfertilized cereal crops were amazingly free of weeds. They discovered that the annual weeds such as cleavers and chickweed grow to only a few inches high with a low nitrogen regime, whereas they would often grow as tall as the crop with multiple applications of fertilizer. The small size of the weeds meant that they were smothered by the growing corn. So the weeds, although still present, do not affect the crop. Moreover, the presence of cereal weeds benefits insects and hence local bird life. Although yields are lower, this is compensated by premium prices for organic crops.

The Prince himself explains that some interesting changes were noticed after conversion to an organic regime, notably an increased worm population, a visual sign that the soil microbiology is in a healthy state and is breaking down and utilizing organic matter to improve soil structure and fertility. He cites two particular fields that had previously appeared to be dead structureless soils and produced the worst yields on the farm. After three years of a clover/grass ley under an organic regime the ploughman remarked how the land ploughed like a different soil — full of worms and with a good structure.

The first Fourteen Acre Field at Westonbirt was grazed by sheep in the initial conversion year, then grew a reasonable wheat crop before being sown with wholly organic Troy beans in the third year. Then disaster struck in a number of ways: first the neighbouring rooks completely devoured the newly sown crop, which was then drilled again. This time the couch grass eventually got the better of the beans and smothered them and put the Prince and his advisers in a difficult situation. They could either sacrifice the crop, fallowing the field and destroying the couch grass by dragging it to the surface and leaving it to dry. Or they could apply a dose of the chemical herbicide Roundup and plant another cash crop, but in the process lose their organic status. The Prince chose the first option, and was vindicated the following year when the same field produced a crop of wheat that sold for £275 per ton, compared with £120 for conventional wheat, giving him a premium of well over 100% and a greater profit than he would have made from a conventional crop grown in the same field. In 1988, a further two 85-acre blocks were brought into the organic scheme and in 1990 the decision was taken to press ahead and make the whole farm organic, a process that was completed by 1997.

One unusual venture that was first tried in 1989 was the sale of thatching straw as a further increase in the premium of an organic wheat field. Organic thatching straw sold for around £450 per ton as opposed to conventional straw at £350 per ton. The Guild of Master Thatchers was able to confirm that organic straw lasted up to twice as long as conventionally grown straw, which sometimes goes rotten after twenty years, apparently because 'the cell walls have been weakened by fast growth caused by high nitrogen applications.' In 1989 the wheat variety Maris Widgeon — ideal for thatching — was being grown on the Home Farm. It had to be harvested by binder and laboriously stood up into the sheaves that dominated the cereal landscape before the advent of combine harvesters. Then the threshing — another labour-intensive task — was carried out in November and the fourteen ton crop was bought by the owner of a thatched house who had read about the process in a newspaper article.

Sir Albert Howard argued that Nature never farms without animals, which are needed to provide manure for the fields. The Duchy Home Farm is no exception and has a dairy herd of 160 Ayrshires, 90 Aberdeen Angus beef cattle and a flock of some 550 breeding ewes. In addition, there are 7 Pedigree Aberdeen Angus bulls and 17 Suffolk Rams. Reflecting the Prince's position as Patron of the Rare Breeds Survival Trust, the farm also has 30 Hebridean ewes, 6 Cotswold ewes, 2 Tamworth sows, 3 Large Black sows and 1 boar, 3 Gloucester cows, 3 Irish Moiled cows, 2 Shetland cows and 2 Suffolk Punch horses. None of these animals receives routine wormers, vaccines or antibiotics — the principle is one of prevention combined with the use of some homeopathic and herbal treatments, resulting in veterinary costs being reduced by half. All the winter farmyard manure is collected from the barns and left in long heaps in the edges of fields, where it composts and rots before being spread on the permanent pasture in early spring.

We have already remarked on the Prince's practical concern for landscape and wildlife, which he thinks have been harmed by the practices of conventional farming. Highgrove has provided him with an opportunity to reverse some of this damage. He has had half a dozen ponds dug out and frogspawn introduced. Miles of dilapidated dry stone walling have been rebuilt. Twenty acres of woodland have been planted: one contains native timbers traditionally used by furniture-makers (as advised by the furniture designer John Makepeace), while another — Preston's Folly — was thinned of conifers which were made into fencing posts, and broadleaf trees were planted instead. In due course, when the broadleaves are large enough, the remaining conifers will be felled. Twelve miles of new hedgerows have been laid, to the benefit of farm and wildlife alike. Hedges provide stockproof windbreaks, shelter, food and nesting places for birds, and a sanctuary for wild flowers that in turn encourage insects and butterflies. Two pairs of barn owls were introduced after a survey had found that they would have enough food — especially voles.

Another ecological innovation at Highgrove is the reed-bed sewage-treatment system, which has replaced an earlier septic tank unable to cope with a tenfold increase in throughput resulting from a large increase in staff and visitors. The advantage of the Highgrove system is that it ensures the conversion of nitrates, phosphates and ammonia that are left untouched by conventional means, and it corresponds to the Prince's philosophy of treating pollution locally rather than passing it on to someone else. Visitors can see that the water is clear at the outfall and the results have been measured. They will also find marsh marigolds and water plants designed to attract dragonflies. The Prince also insists that kitchen staff keep a separate bucket for organic waste to be composted for the garden.

It is easy to admire the success of Highgrove from a safe historical vantage point while forgetting the challenges that the Prince and his team faced and overcame. Given the initial caution and scepticism of his advisers who were worried about his image and that of the Duchy, it would have been much easier for the Prince to 'rip open a bag of fertilizer' instead of going through organic conversion. However, he explained, 'I wanted to prove that it could be profitable to produce good-tasting food from a healthy soil kept fertile by natural means — and I have.' Critics still say that it's fine for him — 'he does not face the same commercial pressures as the rest of us,' to which the Prince responds: 'It doesn't matter who I am; the point is that we did it at Highgrove. We showed how it can work.' And, as we shall see below, the proof of the pudding is in the eating.

Perhaps the most public recognition of the Prince's work for farming and the countryside came when, in December 2002, he was voted Farming Personality of the Year by *Farmers' Weekly*. The Prince called for a recognition that the countryside is not a factory and that farmers and farming are a precious part of our national heritage. More controversially, he also urged public bodies and supermarkets to source more of their food in Britain.

## *The Garden at Highgrove*

*Throughout the entire process of developing the garden at Highgrove I have striven to create a physical reflection of what I feel at a much deeper level. Although I wanted each area of the garden to have its own atmosphere, I hoped that, when they were linked together, the different parts might create an integrated experience that would warm the heart, feed the soul and delight the eye.*

The Prince of Wales

Ten years ago Charles Clover wrote that 'Prince Charles has made his estate a symbol of a changed attitude to the natural world at the highest levels of public life.' This is even truer today than it was then, and nowhere more so than in the Highgrove Garden. As the Prince has said, one example is worth a hundred speeches: 'I prefer action to words, which is one of the reasons why I decided that conversion to a fully organic/traditional system at Highgrove was essentially right, and perhaps action can speak louder than words.'

When he arrived at Highgrove in 1980, the Prince knew that he 'wanted to take care of the place in a very personal way and to leave it, one day, in a far better condition than I had found it.' He adds that this would not be too hard given that the place was pretty dishevelled and run-down! And, so far as the garden was concerned, 'there was not a sign of one. Amazingly, there was absolutely nothing around the house. It sat, stark and exposed, without a trace of any shelter and without a single flowerbed beside the house.' The Prince goes on to describe 'pretty dreadful square ponds, unkempt shrubberies, a rather terrible rockery and damp thickets.' Not a promising situation, but one with huge potential, which the Prince set out to realize by working in harmony with nature, as his head gardener writes in the recent book on the garden.

Visitors to Highgrove can now appreciate the subtle relationships between its structure and content, between trees, plants and monuments. The Prince explains the need for a series of features to anchor the garden in the landscape: hedges to provide form, vistas terminated by eye-catchers like imposing column bird or the dovecote built in memory of Sir John Higgs. Vistas can also be created through gaps in the trees, and each window from the house can have a view to catch and hold the eye, 'leading it through the subtle exploitation of foreground and background' so that house and garden are united in a seamless tapestry. The evolution of the garden has been beautifully described and stunningly illustrated in a book by the Prince himself and Candida Lycett-Green.

The principles of organic gardening exactly mirror those of organic farming on a smaller scale: create a favourable environment for the plants by feeding the soil with organic matter derived from both animal and plant sources; muck, in short. Such nourishment represents a preventative approach that renders plants more resilient and resistant to both disease and pests. Insect pests are controlled through building up a network of insect predators such as ladybirds — pests are not eliminated altogether (slugs are the hardest, as all gardeners know), but are kept within tolerable bounds.

The Prince received invaluable advice and help from a number of key gardening experts. The first was Mollie, Marchioness of Salisbury, who has been gardening organically at Cranborne and Hatfield since the 1950s. Lady Salisbury helped design a small rose garden on the south side of the house with a yew hedge surrounding it as a first step to creating a screen from the prying telephoto lenses of the press. The Prince had no initial master plan for the garden; it grew from inspiration, example, reading and visiting other gardens. Lady Salisbury then turned to the redevelopment of the kitchen garden, partly inspired by the elaborate box-bordered beds at Villandry, a château in the Loire Valley. This involved a complete bulldozer job before two years of reconstruction and years of dedicated work by Dennis Brown made it into the organic exemplar it is today.

One of the next moves was Lady Salisbury introducing the Prince to Professor Miriam Rothschild FRS, who, apart from being the world's most eminent scientific authority on fleas, is renowned for her skill in growing wild flowers. The Prince was keen to introduce wild flowers to the meadow area so as to create a contrast between the formal and the wild. The initial plan was modified by the introduction of a variety of bulbs such as tulips into the grass to create the Tulip Walk (6,000 bulbs are planted every year!), which is at its best in May. It then becomes a hay meadow, a quintessential part of England that has all but vanished, and which is cut in July after the wild flowers have seeded. There are now more than thirty species, although it is sobering to note that it takes over one hundred years to recreate the meadow pastures of the past, 95% of which have disappeared since the Second World War. This project is part of the Prince's contribution to the conservation of wild flowers and the restoration of the integrity of the countryside, which he hopes others will in turn choose to emulate. Amusingly, the mixture provided by Miriam Rothschild for the drive is called Farmer's Nightmare.

The next project was the lawn area to the west of the house, which needed hedges, later personally topiarized by Sir Roy Strong. The hedge has gradually encouraged an increasing number of birds, including green and lesser-spotted woodpeckers. Then a terrace was laid out, also on the west side of the house, with a fountain in the middle and low Cotswold walls surrounding it on three sides. The Prince chose and planted this all himself, selecting as many scented varieties as he could so as to attract butterflies (he had the same goal in mind for his thyme walk). He does admit to having made the — to gardeners — all too familiar mistake of planting smaller plants behind larger ones! In the later stages the Prince invited the well-known plantswoman Rosemary Verey to help him select the right plant for the right place, especially in the Cottage Garden. Her own garden at Barnsley is only a few miles away, so she had the added advantage of local knowledge.

Another later development was the woodland garden, which began as a tangle of undergrowth and a few scraggy trees. This contains a number of buildings and features, including a tree house built for the young princes by William Bertram — and perched in the boughs of an old holly tree. A fern pyramid is an arresting site on a carpet of autumn leaves. This and the 'Stumpery' — consisting of artistically arranged tree stumps — were the inspiration of Julian and Isabel Bannerman and were originally designed for the Prince's collection of hostas. The area also houses one of a pair of green oak temples, suitably inscribed with quotations from Horace and Shakespeare — 'Find tongues in trees, books in running brooks, sermons in stone and good in everything.' In the spring, the ground is covered with snowdrops, bluebells, grape hyacinths and other bulbs.

A relatively recent architectural addition is the Sanctuary — an intimate place for meditation and quiet reflection — built in 1999 to commemorate the Millennium and dedicated to the memory of the then Poet Laureate, Ted Hughes. The basic principles of the small building were conceived by the architect Keith Critchlow, an internationally recognized expert in sacred geometry and Platonism. All the materials are local: the gold Farmington stone columns, earth blocks from Highgrove clay and chopped barley straw, dressings in local stone, and Cotswold tiles. It was built by the same local firm from Berkeley who had constructed the Orchard Room. The interior contains richly carved designs of vegetables from the garden while the stained glass is illuminated with flowers and leaves. For the Prince it is an expression of the Divine in a natural setting, a place for solitude and stillness. It links his sense of the sacred with his passion for gardening and his love of classical proportions, which are the subject of later chapters. Indeed, as he has said himself, the love that he has put into the garden is itself a kind of act of worship.

In a move consistent with his interest in holistic medicine, the Prince arranged for three-quarters of an acre of land to be planted with medicinal herbs in the spring of 2000. The area was expanded to two acres in 2001. Forty-five varieties of herb have been planted, including echinacea, scullcap and marigold. The project was designed to help researchers at the University of Westminster establish which components actually make herbs effective, and to enable them to set benchmarks of quality and protect endangered species. Herbs at Highgrove is now planned to provide an advice and information resource for farmers interested in the herbal market, which is now estimated to be worth £240 million annually in the UK. Most of the 2000 crop was made into remedies for patients at the University of Westminster polyclinic, where the public can receive affordable complementary treatments from students.

The overall aesthetic sense of the garden is enhanced by the way in which buildings, ornaments, statues, shelters, benches and gates are interwoven with the natural textures and colours of the plants and trees. This is what the Prince set out to achieve and is reflected in the impression he wanted to create — an integrated experience that would warm the heart, feed the soul and delight the eye. It does just this, as any visitor will attest. A Japanese party wrote that Highgrove was an experience that opened their eyes to the meaning of the word 'garden' — and to something of the being of the Prince. Voltaire urged us to cultivate our gardens. The Prince has done more than most by creating one of the great gardens of England in the space of twenty years.

## Duchy Originals

The Prince of Wales' first initiative to add value to his own produce at Highgrove dates back to 1990. He commissioned some research into the feasibility of a small range of agricultural marketing initiatives, the aims of which would be 'to encourage responsible husbandry of the land and environmentally friendly manufacture' and to raise funds for the his charitable work. One suitable vehicle for this idea was a food and drink brand that could lead by example through the quality of its products. The first venture was the Highgrove Loaf. It was made from the Duchy Home Farm's first organic wheat crop and milled by the local miller John Lister at his seventeenth century Shipton Mill near Tetbury. A trial run of 41,400 loaves was baked by Rank Hovis McDougall and sold in a number of Tesco stores in the

South-East of England. It cost about a third more than a conventional loaf but sold well during the trial period.

The next and best-known product — the oaten biscuit — introduced the brand name Duchy Originals in November 1992. The Duchy Originals approach is to offer premium quality food, using the best ingredients available, to find the best and most appropriate manufacturers and to ensure that the packaging is environmentally sound. The oats came from the Home Farm and they had the miller, but finding the baker was a more difficult task, for which they had to go north of the border to Walkers, makers of fine shortbread. Around 200 production trials later — testing texture, appearance and taste — the oaten biscuit was born and is now a familiar sight, especially on cheese boards. The range of shortbread, gingered and lemon biscuits followed in due course and were part of creating a demand for premium-priced high quality products. The latest offerings in the biscuit line are tantalising chocolate-covered butterscotch and black pepper and chives biscuits for cheese.

Duchy Originals is now a leading organic brand with over fifty product lines and a turnover of £14 million in 2001-2, rising to £23 million in 2002-3 and £35 million in 2003–4, an annual growth rate of over 50%. The aspect of this growth that gives special pleasure to the Prince is the corresponding prosperity enjoyed by his suppliers, many of whom are family businesses. Products lines now include preserves, milk, soft drinks, bread, sausages, mustard, ice cream, honey and chocolate. All of the Duchy Originals range is made with organic ingredients and certified by the Soil Association, with the exception of the free-range bacon and sausages. The organic sausages and dry cured bacon are made with organic pigs reared on the Home Farm at Highgrove. A herd of free-range pigs in East Anglia provides most of the meat for the free-range products and meets the Duchy Originals' own welfare standards as well as not employing growth promoters or prophylactic antibiotics. Due to the small scale of organic pig farming in the UK, it is likely to take another two years to develop enough supply to replace the free-range products completely. Meanwhile, Duchy Originals is working to set up new organic pig herds which could fit into organic rotations on arable farms around the country. New product lines include canapés, preserves, lemon and apple fruit drinks, hand fried organic crisps, Stilton cheese and Cornish Cream. And in 2003, the Duchy Collection of garden furniture was launched. Each piece is made by hand in Herefordshire using native hardwood from sustainable woodland.

In his 2002 acceptance speech to Euronatur, the Prince was able to explain the background to sourcing some chocolate for Duchy products.

> When I visited Guyana three years ago I learnt that cocoa used to be a major cash crop for the country, but that the industry had been redundant for thirty years. I suggested to the President that he might think about re-developing it — using some of the old cocoa plantations — to supply beans for Duchy Originals chocolates.
>
> To my delight, he agreed and the project has worked out very well, so far. A small co-operative of 26 farmers and their families was set up and their beans have just received organic certification. I hope to be using them in Duchy Originals chocolate later this year — in time for Christmas. I certainly did not set out to create a 'case study in sustainable agriculture' with my venture in Guyana, but there is a virtuous circle which I intend to try to repeat elsewhere, and which I believe other food producers and retailers could follow.
>
> Our strong consumer brand is supporting the development of small, but locally significant, community projects. These projects are based on the most sustainable form of agriculture and help to maintain thriving communities. And the developed world consumer has the satisfaction, not only of eating exceedingly good chocolate, but also of knowing that their purchase has helped maintain a dignified and more sustainable lifestyle in the developing world.

Needless to say, the Prince is following up on his intention to create new virtuous circles. The Guyana Sugar Corporation, encouraged by the cocoa result, is now experimenting with growing organic sugar. A recent initiative — Organic Gardening for Schools, with the Henry Doubleday Research Association (of which the Prince is Patron), encourages schools to set up their own food garden and to explain the benefits of fresh, healthy food. The success of Duchy Originals is reflected in the fact that it has donated £3.5m of profits to the Prince's Charitable Foundation over the last ten years. The largest single donation from the Foundation itself of £500,000 was made to the farming charities helping families affected by the 2001 foot and mouth disease outbreak.

## GMOs — Seeds of Doubt?

*Modern man does not experience himself as part of nature, but as an outside force to dominate and conquer it. He even talks of a 'battle' with nature, forgetting that, if he won the battle, he would find himself on the losing side.*

E.F. Schumacher

The Prince of Wales's views on agricultural biotechnology have been headline news since he first articulated them in detail in 1998, although he was already expressing his concerns about genetically modified organisms in his 1996 Soil Association lecture, where he quoted a report from the government's Panel on Sustainable Development:

> The introduction of GMOs must proceed with caution to ensure that any benefits now are not made at the expense of the safety and well-being of future generations and their environment. Once released ... a GMO cannot be recalled: the action is irreversible. More than in other areas there is uncertainty about the long-term outcome of human actions and of human ability to deal with the consequences. Introduced genes may over time spread to other organisms with consequences that cannot necessarily be foreseen.

The same report warns that 'unfortunately there are many recent examples of failure to anticipate problems arising from the use of new technologies (such as CFCs, asbestos, pesticides and thalidomide). Potential consequences are more uncertain where self-replicating organisms are introduced into the environment.' All this amounts to a call for a measured application of the precautionary principle in this area, while the rhetoric generated by commercial pressures has tended to paint a picture of minimal risks and maximum potential benefits. However, one should flag up that the precautionary principle can be used as a political front for views that are intrinsically hostile to technology.

In his 1996 speech, the Prince argued that 'we have now reached a moral and ethical watershed beyond which we venture into realms that belong to God, and to God alone. Apart from certain medical applications, what actual right do we have to experiment, Frankenstein-like, with the very stuff of life? We live in an age of rights — it seems to me that it is about time our Creator had some rights too ...'

This kind of theological argument does not go down well with the science community, which understandably regards the Frankenstein image as threatening and abusive. Thoughtful commentators like Sir Brian Heap realize that provocative ideas presenting the genome as the secular equivalent of the soul are likely to stir up deep feelings. However, other scientists respond in kind to the Prince by branding the Prince 'anti-science,' accusing him of interfering in a way that slows scientific progress. Despite the good copy generated by such controversial confrontations, there is a deeper issue at stake here: should science be subject to any ethical limits outside its own scope? Can science 'play God' with impunity? The Prince recognizes the polarities in this debate but does not in fact align himself with 'the somewhat apocalyptic scaremongering of those for whom any scientific advance is anathema.' He is, however, calling for a scientific and ethical debate before any irrevocable decisions are made.

The Prince is arguing here from a theistic perspective in a predominantly rationalist scientific world where 'realms that belong to God' is a meaningless phrase: from a rationalist viewpoint, ethics can only have a humanistic rather than a transcendent basis. In an article for the *Daily Telegraph* in June 1998, the Prince set out his views on the GM question, views that he has elaborated since then but which remain substantially consistent.

He began by stating his agricultural philosophy, outlined in a previous section:

> I have always believed that agriculture should proceed in harmony with nature, recognizing that there are natural limits to our ambitions. That is why, some twelve years ago, I decided to farm organically — without artificial pesticides or fertilizers. From my own experience I am clear that the organic system can be economically viable, that it provides a wide range of environmental and social benefits, and, most importantly, that it enables consumers to make a choice about the food they eat.

The argument for consumer choice highlights the fundamental incompatibility of the organic and GM approaches: any contamination from GM crops automatically compromises organic status since one of the criteria is that the level of GM crops in the field is 0%. Recent experience of GM contamination of crops grown by organic oil seed rape growers in Saskatchewan, Canada, has led to the loss of nearly the entire sector. And lack of proper segregation in North America makes it very difficult for non-GM farmers to grow GM-free crops. The Prince continued:

> But at a time when sales of organic food are soaring, a development in intensive agriculture is actually removing a fundamental choice about the food we eat, and raising crucial questions about the future of our food and of our environment which are still to be answered. Genetically modified (GM) crops are presented as an essentially straightforward development that will increase yields through techniques which are merely an extension of traditional methods of plant breeding. I am afraid I cannot accept this. The fundamental difference between traditional and genetically modified plant breeding is that, in the latter, genetic material from one species of plant, bacteria, virus, animal or fish is literally inserted into another species, with which they could never naturally breed. The use of these techniques raises, it seems to me, crucial ethical and practical considerations.

Here we reach one of the nubs of the argument: is there really a fundamental difference between traditional and genetically modified plant breeding? Biologists involved in the research claim that there is none. However, the critical distinction is that conventional breeding does not involve 'horizontal gene transfer' (the 'deliberate insertion of specific genetic material using recombinant DNA technology') from one species to another via an artificial vector — usually a virus. To achieve this, the species' defence mechanisms need to be broken down. A further implication is that this technique may lead to an increased incidence of antibiotic resistance.

The Prince moves on to safety considerations, which are the largest public concern:

> We simply do not know the long-term consequences for human health and the wider environment of releasing plants bred in this way. We are assured that these new plants are vigorously tested and regulated, but the evaluation procedure seems to presume that unless a GM crop can be shown to be unsafe, there is no reason to stop its use. The lesson of BSE and other entirely man-made disasters in the cause of 'cheap food' is surely that it is the unforeseen consequences which present the greatest cause for concern.
>
> Once genetic material has been released into the environment it cannot be recalled. The likelihood of a major problem may, as some people suggest, be slight, but if something does go badly wrong we will be faced with the problem of clearing up a kind of pollution which is self-perpetuating. I am not convinced that anyone has the first idea of how this could be done, or indeed who would have to pay. [Moreover], these GM crop plants are capable of interbreeding with their wild relatives, creating new weeds with built-in resistance to the weedkiller, and of contaminating other crops. Modified genes from a crop of GM rape were found to have spread into a conventional crop more than a mile away. The result is that both conventional and organic crops are under threat, and the threat is one-way.

The Prince turns next to arguments about the use of pesticides and herbicides:

> We are told that GM crops will require less use of agro-chemicals. Even if this is true, it is certainly not the whole story. What it fails to take into account is the total ecological and social impact of the farming system. For example, most of the GM plants marketed so far contain genes from bacteria which make them resistant to a broad spectrum weedkiller available from the same manufacturer. When the crop is sprayed with this weedkiller, every other plant in the field is killed. The result is an essentially sterile field, providing neither food nor habitat for wildlife.

While there are some documented cases of reduced herbicide use with GM cotton, a survey of 8,200 field trials of glyphosate (Roundup) tolerant soya varieties showed not only a 6.7% drop in average yield but also the need for between two and five times as much herbicide! The recent Soil Association report highlights the problems caused by rogue plants left over from the previous year, so-called 'volunteers.' These may be engineered to be her-bicide resistant, so that *the whole new crop has to be sprayed with a more powerful chemical in order to eliminate the volunteer.*

Reduced use of chemicals is at the heart of the sustainability argument between proponents of traditional agro-ecological approaches and the promises of biotechnology, especially when applied to the emotive topic of future food security in the Third World. The Cambridge scientist Sir Brian Heap quotes the world's leading botanist, Professor Peter Raven, President of the American Association for the Advancement of Science that '[our current] level of production has been achieved only because we manufacture increasingly toxic pesticides with which we now douse our agricultural lands at the rate of 3m metric tonnes per year, and poison the environment with the nitrogen we fix (our output now exceeds the total derived from natural processes).' Raven continues: 'we also cultivate or graze most of the world's available arable land and rangeland, and harvest two-thirds of the world's fisheries beyond sustainability. Over the past 50 years we have lost about one fifth of the world's topsoil, a fifth of its agricultural land, a third of its forests and seen a dramatic increase in the loss of biodiversity.'

Sir Brian argues that 'if such trends continue the prospect of 'business as usual' is even more unsustainable and the prospects of feeding those who are hungry in less developed nations are threatened even further unless alternatives are discovered and adopted.' This means finding sustainable forms of agriculture that reverse the trend towards increased toxic loads. Sir Brian acknowledges that 'organic methods of production are one of the options but so far they have failed to feed the world because yields are too low to put much organic material back into the land and in less developed countries manure from livestock tends to be burned for fuel.' Agro-ecological innovations do, as we have seen, go a long way towards raising yields in a sustainable way, but they are arguably insufficient on their own. This is where Sir Brian sees a role for controversial second generation GM technologies to reduce pesticide and herbicide use (we have already seen some of the problems associated with this) and third generation technologies that can fortify crops with desirable micronutrients. The jury is still out on such developments, but the future of agriculture must in any event be a sustainable one. We may need to redraw the boundaries after a vigorous debate on the exact nature of sustainability in agriculture.

The Prince is rightly concerned about the spread of insect resistance as a result of new GM technology:

> GM crop plants are also being developed to produce their own pesticide. This is predicted to cause the rapid appearance of resistant insects. Worse still, such pesticide-producing plants have already been shown to kill some beneficial predator insects as well as pests. To give just two examples, inserting a gene from a snowdrop into a potato made the potato resistant to greenfly, but also killed the ladybirds feeding on the greenfly. And lacewings, a natural predator of the corn borer and food for farmland birds, died when fed on pest insects raised on GM maize.

An even more serious issue, according to Harvard biologist Stephen Palumbi, is that 'transgenic crops with insecticidal genes or herbicide-tolerance genes actually favour the evolution of pesticide resistance and herbicide-tolerance.' So they 'actually exacerbate the problems they are supposed to solve' and continually raise the stakes in the warfare against nature so that each new variety becomes more toxic. A recent report in *The Times* warns of pesticide-proof superbugs at the same time as calling for a new generation of insecticides!

There are real hazards in a science that declares open warfare against nature, especially when combined in an unholy alliance with the financial imperatives of big business. Distinctions between science, politics and business can become blurred, leading to widespread public scepticism about processes of regulation. Both science and industry share a reductionist ideology of genetic determinism and a corresponding exploitative mentality whereby nature and human beings are objects that can legitimately be used for monetary gain. Commercial muscle can create a profitable cycle of dependency that aims to increase corporate control over the world's food supply and distribution systems. Nature is to be patented and commodified wherever possible. It may be profitable in the short term to wage a chemical campaign against nature in the form of insects and pests — it drives the production of ever more powerful new insecticides and herbicides — but the long-term outcome can only be an increase in the toxic load which inevitably leads to increasingly destructive effects on human health. Only by recognizing the fluidity, dynamism and interconnectedness of nature can we formulate policies that lead to long-term sustainability and health.

The Prince warns of the dangers inherent in loss of biodiversity, itself the key to ecological stability:

> Despite the vast acreages which are likely to be involved, there is no official requirement to monitor genetically modified commercial crops to see exactly what is happening. Think of the agricultural disasters of the past which have stemmed from over-reliance on a single variety of a crop, yet this is exactly what genetic

modification will encourage. It is entirely possible that within ten years virtually all of the world's production of staple crops, such as soya, maize, wheat and rice, will be from a few GM varieties, unless consumer pressure dictates otherwise.

Finally, the argument often used as the ultimate justification for GM foods:

> We are also told that GM techniques will help to 'feed the world.' This is a fundamental concern to all of us. But will the companies controlling these techniques ever be able to achieve what they would regard as a sufficient return from selling their products to the world's poorest people? Nor do I believe that the basic problem is always so simple. Where the problem is lack of food, rather than lack of money to buy food, there may be better ways of achieving the same ends. Recent research has shown, for example, that yields from some traditional farming systems can be doubled, and even trebled, through techniques that conserve natural resources while making the best use of labour and management skills.

Here we return to the agro-ecological arguments at the beginning of this chapter and the fact that there are economic and political causes of hunger that are not susceptible to technological fixes. The Green Revolution of the 1960s and 1970s displaced many indigenous farmers by introducing hybrid seeds that depended on chemical fertilizers for their high yield. The seeds were then sold along with the requisite fertilizers, pesticides and herbicides Ironically, these increased costs were partially offset by government loans which were to be repaid out of the profits of the crop! Moreover, many farmers changed to cash crops for export to promote world trade, at the expense of food to be grown and eaten locally.

Despite very considerable increases in yield, the social and environmental costs of the Green Revolution have been very disruptive: more irrigation was required so huge dams (with a limited life-time) were built, which drove thousands from their homes and caused erosion of flooded areas. Then the chemicals have polluted groundwater and contributed to the deterioration of the soil. Moreover, the hybrid varieties were short-stemmed with large heads of grain, meaning that increased food was obtained but with correspondingly less straw and fodder for animals. Finally, the hybrid seed does not breed true, so that the farmer cannot retain seed but has to purchase it every year directly from the supplier. As the biologist Brian Goodwin observes: 'the overall result is a pernicious cycle of increasing ecological damage, dependency of the farmer, dislocation of normal farming practices that are integrated with one another, and debt.'

The GM revolution arguably serves to extend these trends of dependency and ecological damage to the benefit of the same corporations who brought about the Green Revolution and now produce a technical fix for the environmental problems associated with it. It is questionable whether this new approach can be expected to solve these problems of dependency, especially if so-called 'terminator seeds' are eventually introduced. These seeds actually prevent the seed from germinating again so that it absolutely guarantees that the farmer has to buy new seeds from the company every year. As the Prince said in another context: 'Representatives of twenty African states, including Ethiopia, have published a statement denying that gene technologies will "help farmers to produce the food that is needed in the 21st Century." On the contrary, they "think it will destroy the diversity, the local knowledge and the sustainable agricultural systems ... and undermine our capacity to feed ourselves.'

The Prince concludes with the most radical question, calling for a wide-ranging debate encompassing agriculture as a whole:

> Do we need to use GM techniques at all? Technology has
> brought massive benefits to mankind, but there is a
> danger, especially in areas as sensitive as food, health and
> the long-term future of our environment, in putting all
> our efforts into establishing what is technically possible
> without first stopping to ask whether this is something
> we should be doing. I believe we should stop and ask that
> question, through a wide public debate of the issues of

principle which cannot be addressed effectively through science and regulation alone. Is it not better to examine first what we actually want from agriculture in terms of food supply and security, rural employment, environmental protection and landscape, before we go on to look at the part genetic modification might, perhaps, play in achieving those aims?

As a result of his first forays into this area, the Prince set up a discussion forum on his website, which attracted more than 10,000 responses, following which he wrote a further article in the *Daily Mail*. More recently, in his Euronatur speech, the Prince has reiterated his concerns about the immediate threat posed by GM crops to organic farms, and has called for more research in organic farming, as recommended in a recent report by the Land Economy Department of Cambridge University. The report comments on the imbalance in research budgets and proposes that that 'a long-term research strategy for organic agriculture would aim at rectifying this imbalance and help to improve the efficiency of organic production, thereby making it more attractive and profitable.'

The future of agricultural biotechnology and the role of organic agriculture hang in the balance. In terms of scientific, economic and political muscle, the biotechnological approach outguns the agro-ecological or organic by several orders of magnitude. However, there is growing popular support for the organic approach — at any rate in the UK — and its corresponding ecological worldview. There is also a sense, articulated by the Prince, of an arrogant hubris on the part of the proponents of genetic engineering technology that may lead to unpredictable and undesirable — even catastrophic — outcomes. The press tends to frame the debate as expert science vs. anti-scientific Luddites, but this obscures the fact that there is considerable *scientific* unease about developments in biotechnology, especially on the part of independent holistic biologists who understand the sciences of complexity, non-linear systems and ecology. Such scientists seek, like the Prince, to find sustainable ways of living in harmony with nature. Science is not to be abandoned but rather reformulated in the holistic context of organisms that ultimately depend on the Earth and are inseparable from it.

## The Future of Rural Communities

This section is being written the day after the huge turnout — over 400,000 people — at the Countryside March in central London of October 2002. Although the central focus of the march has been the threat to fox hunting (about which the Prince feels passionately), the wider issues involve the decline of rural communities and the misunderstanding of the country way of life by townspeople; and, one has to say it, political opportunism in highlighting a cause that is guaranteed to rouse the urban voter — that is, the core Labour supporter — a fact admitted in private by the late Donald Dewar with respect to Scotland.

As we saw in the discussion of the Prince's philosophy of agriculture, he is concerned to maintain the rural way of life and infrastructure as an essential part of our cultural heritage, stressing that farmers have a dual role embracing both food production and stewardship of the countryside: 'turning the countryside into a theme park for urban dwellers is not the answer to their problems. Once you lose that remarkable culture you cannot replace it.'

The Prince hosted a seminar at Highgrove in February 1999 to discuss the problems of rural areas and to find solutions to the well documented concerns about the exodus of families and young people from the countryside. This led to the Rural Revival Initiative, which aims to develop solutions to rural isolation by acting as a catalyst for projects that would help improve life in rural communities. While inner city deprivation is well documented, rural exclusion is less well known. The Prince is concerned about the hardships many people on low incomes experience in rural areas and is keen to focus on finding solutions to the poor quality of life of many people in isolated pockets of the countryside.

One of the first initiatives was the Northern Fells Rural Project in Cumbria. At the launch of the two pilot projects, the Prince explained the rationale:

> I arranged the seminar because I was becoming
> increasingly worried about what I felt were very real, but
> often hidden, problems of disadvantage in rural areas.

Unlike in towns and cities, people in greatest need in rural areas tend not to live in easily identifiable areas. And they are certainly not easy to spot. Country people are, by tradition and perhaps because of their tradition, stoical and independent. They seem rarely to complain, choosing to compare their lives with the harsher conditions of the past than with the current standards of lifestyles.

By bringing together a group of people with knowledge and experience, the Prince wanted to see whether we could add some new impetus to a rural revival, and to find some practical steps to tackle the causes of rural disadvantage. The Cumbria project aimed to identify gaps in rural services provision and make real improvements to the lives of residents in Caldbeck and surrounding parishes. As part of a self-help campaign, he persuaded Ford to donate a minibus with wheelchair access to Caldbeck. In an area with little effective public transport, the minibus (driven by nineteen volunteers) takes people to and from doctors, dentists and clinics as well as to railway stations, coach stops or social and sporting activities. It helps people to visit friends and family in hospital or residential homes and can take people to relieve carers so that they can go out. This project is the result of a partnership between the Countryside Agency, Business in the Community, Voluntary Action Cumbria and Caldbeck Surgery.

The initial projects received financial support from a number of companies. The initiative was extended in July 2001 with the launch of the Business in the Community (BITC) Rural Action Programme in the wake of the foot and mouth disease (FMD) crisis.Here the Prince suggested that businesses can sign up to help in three ways — building enterprising local communities through support and advice, reviving market towns or committing themselves to buying food and other services from local sources. He reiterated his conviction that the future of the countryside is one of the most crucial issues of our time, pointing out that 'even before the disaster of FMD, average farm incomes were £5,200 per farm and last year alone 20,000 jobs were lost in agriculture. Behind these figures is a way of life and an entire culture at risk of collapsing.' The Prince continued:

If FMD has taught people anything it is that there is an intimate connection between the land, the animals and themselves. They visit the countryside because of its beauty, they eat food which is grown there and sometimes they even choose to retire there. So I happen to believe that each and everyone of us has a responsibility for it and the people who live there — in just the same way that I believe we have a responsibility for our inner cities, which is one of the reasons why BITC began. These are not someone else's problems — they are ours.

The Prince had some initial difficulty in convincing BITC to redirect some of their attention to rural communities, but his tried and tested method of 'Seeing is Believing' did the trick. He took four groups of business leaders to four rural communities in Wales, North Yorkshire, Cumbria and Shropshire, to show them the problems and then test their reaction. After a visit, John Roberts, chief executive of United Utilities expressed the view that 'rural communities face significant challenges in terms of social inclusion that are every bit as difficult and daunting as those found in inner cities.' He then asked the BITC team to 'create a package of initiatives which will make a substantial difference. And not just in the short-term as a quick fix — that helps no-one — but for the long term. This is about determined and sustained activity and I will be watching with the closest possible attention to make sure that it is working — and if it is not, why not?'

The Prince proposed a Partners in Rural Leadership Programme to being together fifty rural entrepreneurs and fifty leading business managers, and had another specific suggestion:

And why not encourage enterprise in another way? One of the features of life in the countryside today is a lack of services. For instance, there was a time when the pub used to be at the heart of village life, but now 40% of villages do not have one. At the same time, village stores and Post Offices are shutting at an alarming rate. So why not, I thought, make the 'Pub the Hub.' Put into the pub the Post Office and the store, and increase the income so giving the pub itself a more secure future. I know this can be done. There is a wonderful example in Suffolk of the White Hart Inn where Adnam's Brewery have supported the tenants of the pub to expand its services. And it is a great success with extra staff now being employed.

A second initiative, the Prince explained, is centred on market towns which were once the economic engines of rural life. Recently they have been in desperate decline with many of the problems of inner cities: crime, drugs and vandalism. So BITC has an initiative bringing together partnerships in market towns to deliver business skills to help in their regeneration. The third initiative is all about local sourcing. The Prince encouraged his audience to think of ways in which they could change their company policy to support their local rural communities. He was able to say that he had the support of major food companies for this initiative like Sainsbury's, SPAR and the Samworth Brothers. The fourth issue highlighted was affordable housing in rural areas, which he hopes to discuss with Housing Associations and the construction industry. For his final challenge, the Prince asked the 750 member companies of BITC to carry out a Rural Impact Assessment.

The Prince concluded by urging his audience not to underestimate the power which they had to make a difference so that the people born and bred in the country can find an economic future, whether on the family farm or running their own business. He hoped that BITC could make a substantial difference, reminding his audience that:

the British countryside is only as beautiful as it is because it has been cared for, and lived in, by these people with generations of experience and knowledge. The unique scenery, and the people who live amongst it, are one of this country's most treasured national assets. They are also a crucial economic resource, with so much income coming from tourism — and it has never been more threatened than it is today.

These words strike a national chord and take us back to the underlying concerns of the Countryside Alliance. For the Prince, the future of farming and the future of the countryside are intimately linked, as this chapter has shown, and form part of his more general concern for sustainable development both in theory and in practice.

# 3. The Healing Path: Towards an Integrated Medicine

*We now have the twin crises of deteriorating health and
deteriorating environments that threaten our quality of life.
These crises are intrinsically linked, and both are reflections of
the way we think about organisms and their interactions. If
humans are essentially to be understood in terms of genes and
their products, then illness is to be corrected by manipulating
them. The result is drug-based medicine and genetic
counselling or engineering. These can be extremely effective in
certain circumstances, but medical care based on this approach
focuses on illness rather than health.*

Brian Goodwin

## Some Landmarks in the Holistic Health Movement

The chances are that most readers of this book will have experienced some form of complementary or alternative (CAM) treatment. There are currently 49,000 CAM practitioners in the UK,
compared with 36,000 GPs. 20% of the UK population use CAM
and 5 million have consulted a CAM practitioner in the last year,
with an estimated 15–20 million having done so at some point.
75% of the public want access to CAM on the NHS and 58% of
GPs have referred their patients to CAM therapies. In 1998 there
were 22 million visits to the practitioners of six major therapies
compared with 14 million to Accident and Emergency departments in the same year. We now spend £1.6bn on CAM in addition to the £65bn spent annually on the NHS.

Public interest in holistic health over the last 25 years has
tracked the development of ecological science and organic agriculture that we have already described. The biologist Brian
Goodwin makes an explicit connection between our overall

health and environmental systems, in which the quality of food is the essential link via the condition of the soil. Pioneers like Sir Robert McCarrison, Max Gerson and Max Bircher-Benner forged the links between nutrition and health, which are now well recognized as a factor in a range of degenerative 'diseases of civilization' such as cancer and heart disease. Furthermore, Scott Williamson and Innes Pearce, who pioneered the first true health centre in Peckham, South London in the 1930s and 40s, were the first to demonstrate that the health of the organism — both in terms of the individual and family as a whole — was directly related to the health of the environment. They formulated a radical definition of health as 'a process of mutual synthesis between organism and environment.'

A central point running through this chapter is that there have been two distinctive approaches to health in the Western medical tradition. The first — that health is the natural order of things — underpins the philosophy of natural, complementary and alternative medicine. The second approach — that the role of the physician is to treat disease — is typical of modern (allopathic) medicine. The starting point of the holist is health, while that of the current medical orthodoxy is pathology or disease. In the first case, the wholeness of Nature and its healing force is highlighted, while the second concentrates on fixing what it regards as the defects of Nature by means of pharmaceutical drugs, surgery, radiotherapy, and, more recently, the prospect of gene therapy. These approaches reflect respectively a holistic philosophy of working in harmony with Nature on the one hand, compared with a philosophy of control that can involve waging war on Nature with ever more powerful 'weapons.' As with agriculture, this is not a war that we can win simply by raising the pharmaceutical stakes and thus exacerbating the now serious problem of antibiotic resistance, especially in hospitals. As we shall see, the current agenda is to find an integration of these two approaches to health and medicine.

The Prince of Wales has played a sustained pioneering role in the development of the holistic (now integrated) health movement since his seminal speech to the BMA in December 1982. At the 2001 Penny Brohn Memorial Lecture, the Prince recalled this occasion:

I thought I'd just briefly describe why I got so involved in this whole area. I'm so glad to find that Dr Caroline Myss says the same thing about the question of how you integrate the best of the old and the best of the new, which I think is so important: the best of the ancient aspect of our humanity, the inner aspect of it, and the best of what we have discovered in the last 100 years or so. I remember being asked to be president of the British Medical Association in their 150th anniversary year in 1982, going to the dinner and making a speech. Some of you may remember that all I did was to beg for a little bit more understanding about the need for a more holistic approach towards the way in which we carry out our health care. I quoted a certain amount from Paracelsus and at the end of it all I was absolutely astonished to find what a reaction it had caused amongst the medical establishment. All hell broke loose!

The Prince was undeterred. It was the start of what has been a continuous personal campaign ever since. The following year saw the foundation of the British Holistic Medical Association (BHMA). Then in 1984 plans were laid by Sir James Watt, President of the Royal Society of Medicine, for a series of colloquia on the relationship between CAM and mainstream medicine. Sir James recalled that the turning point in the series came on an evening when a complementary practitioner demonstrated greater diagnostic knowledge than the doctor speaking on the same occasion. When the talks were eventually published, the Prince wrote a foreword.

Meanwhile, the BMA was preparing its own initial report, which was released in the autumn of 1986 and immediately criticized by the BHMA. It is a measure of the rapid progress in the field that the 1996 report was so much more constructive. The 1980s also saw the establishment in the UK of the Research Council for Complementary Medicine (RCCM), which oversaw some early CAM research and provided a valuable forum for discussions on research methodology. The RCCM has produced a very substantial research database on CAM, which can be accessed on their web site. The Marylebone Health Centre, of which the Prince has been Patron since the early days, was set up by Dr Patrick Pietroni in 1987 in the crypt of Marylebone Church, and the Marylebone Centre Trust was established in the following year, as was the Hale Clinic in London, which the Prince opened.

The 1990s saw major advances in the field, notably in the United States. Pressure from Senator Tom Harkin led to the establishment in 1992 of an Office of Alternative Medicine in the bastion of orthodoxy, the National Institutes of Health, with an initial budget of $5m. This was greeted with much scepticism, and the OAM was referred to by some early detractors as the 'Astrology Office.' An important event occurred in the autumn of 1993 with the publication of an article by Dr David Eisenberg of the Harvard Medical School in Boston in the *New England Journal of Medicine.* Eisenberg and his colleagues found that Americans were making more visits to CAM practitioners than they were to primary care physicians. Even more significantly, Eisenberg calculated that they were spending some $14bn in the process, which is big bucks by any standard. The OAM has now become the National Center for Complementary and Alternative Medicine (NCCAM) with an annual budget of $100m. Medical schools are increasingly offering courses on CAM in response to student demand.

The peer-reviewed journal *Alternative Therapies* was established in 1995 under the executive editorship of the charismatic Larry Dossey MD. Dossey has made one of the most significant contributions to the holistic health field in a series of books beginning with *Space, Time and Medicine* in 1982. In 1995 he published a review of intercessory prayer research in *Healing Words,* which sold over 250,000 copies in hardback and helped spearhead the development of Spirituality and Health programmes now running in over ninety US medical schools. At Harvard, Herbert Benson pioneered the relaxation response and placebo research and has been instrumental in arranging a series of high profile conferences on mind-body medicine at the university medical school. *Advances,* the journal of mind-body medicine, was established as far back as 1982, and is still one of the leading forums of its kind. *The Journal of Alternative and Complementary Medicine — Research on Paradigm, Practice and*

*Policy*, now edited by Dr Kim Jobst, was also launched in 1995 and concentrates on researching the therapeutic value of non-traditional medical therapies.

Back in Britain, the Marylebone Centre Trust pursued its work in partnership with the University of Westminster with the establishment of the Centre for Community Care and Primary Health with its MA programme in 1993. Since the mid-1990s the University of Westminster has greatly expanded its degree programme to include courses in therapeutic bodywork, general practice and primary health, complementary medicine, health sciences, homeopathy and traditional Chinese medicine. The Polyclinic was opened by the Prince of Wales in 1998 to provide a range of complementary therapies at affordable prices and in a teaching environment. Its School of Integrated Health was established in 2000, and will shortly be co-ordinating a major research programme with government support. In addition, the School has a Department of Complementary Therapies and a Department of Community and Collaborative Practice. This combination makes the University the leading CAM centre in the country.

The Prince of Wales personally established the Foundation for Integrated Medicine in 1996, and its work will be described in more detail below. The Laing Chair of Complementary Medicine was set up in Exeter University, and a thriving education and research programme has burgeoned. Other universities like Derby are now preparing degree courses in CAM. A number of new magazines and journals have appeared, along with an abundance of training courses in all manner of complementary therapies. Some of these —such as osteopathy and chiropractic — are now officially recognized by Parliament, while acupuncture is expected to follow shortly. The House of Lords Science and Technology Committee published a wide-ranging report into CAM in 2000. The overall picture in North America and many European countries is of the informed public calling for increased access to CAM and voting with their feet. At the same time, innovations and reforms are beginning to work very slowly through the corridors of the medical establishment.

A good example of this is the setting up within the Royal College of Psychiatrists of a special interest group in Spirituality

and Psychiatry, which is described below. An earlier development in the same vein was the establishment back in 1973 of the
Scientific and Medical Network by a senior group of doctors,
scientists and educationalists concerned about the fact that scientific and medical training was so closely allied to the adoption
of a narrow mechanistic and materialistic philosophy. The
Network has around 2,000 members in fifty countries and provides a forum for discussion of issues at the interface between
science, medicine, spirituality and the new discipline of consciousness studies.

We have already referred to the prevalence of mechanistic
metaphors and approaches in the chapters on ecology and agriculture. In this chapter, we will see how the same framework has
been applied to medicine and has led to some spectacular
advances. However, the limitations of such a view are also becoming apparent in the medical field. For instance, the American epi-
demiologist Jeff Levin argues that the orthodox medical model of
the human being is deeply flawed since it is 'grounded in a conception of humans as spiritless beings [that] could only have
engendered the mechanistic, materialistic approach to conceiving
of health and treating illness. ' He concludes:

> In sum, at the core of the body-only medical model is a
> screwed-up view of what a human being really is.
> Therefore, before we can fix medicine — and any of our
> other social institution — we need to restore a more
> holistic perspective to our understanding of human life.
> We can never have a truly 'integrated medicine' until we
> have an integrated body-mind-spirit model of what it
> means to be human. Without the latter, we will never be
> able to acknowledge all of the myriad potential
> determinants of health.

Here Levin reaches the heart of the matter: that without an adequate model of the human being we cannot have a truly adequate medicine or health system. The current model insists that
our brains produce consciousness like a kettle produces steam,
and that the human being can be understood, as Jeff Levin
remarks above, on the basis of a body-only model. Powerful as

this model is, it is simply incapable of explaining even research in mind-body medicine that shows that our state of mind and emotions has a fundamental effect on our health and well-being.

## The Prince's Case for Holistic Medicine

*The art of medicine is rooted in the heart. If your heart is false, you will also be a false physician; if your heart is just, you will also be a true physician.*

Paracelsus

The Prince of Wales was installed as President of the British Medical Association on its 150th anniversary in July 1982. His speech on this occasion praised the dedication of doctors and mentioned two themes that he thought might characterize his presidency: the first was access to adequate healthcare by religious sects in immigrant communities — especially Sikhs; and the second the problems of discrimination faced by disabled people. He explained: 'bearing in mind the close involvement the medical profession has with disabled people, it would be splendid to feel that I could turn to the BMA for advice or help on this matter.' These concerns reflect some of the Prince's other work taken up in other contexts such as the Prince's Trust.

It was his second speech on complementary medicine in December of the same year that caused a much greater stir. It is hard to recall how entrenched attitudes were in those early days when many people now speak so readily of the prospects for integrated medicine. The Prince began his speech with a warning shot: 'I have often thought that one of the least attractive traits of various professional bodies and institutions is the deeply ingrained suspicion and outright hostility which they can exhibit towards anything unorthodox or unconventional.' This proved to be a prophetic statement in relation to later responses from the architectural and agricultural establishments to his proposals. Establishment experts tend to form a conservative secular priesthood guarding conventional wisdom and on the lookout for the signs of heresy. The Prince added that 'human nature is such that we are frequently prevented from seeing that what is taken for today's unorthodoxy is probably

going to be tomorrow's convention.' This too has proved
prophetic, as has his more sombre reflection that 'the unorthodox individual is doomed to years of frustration, ridicule and
failure in order to act out his role in the scheme of things, until
his day arrives and mankind is ready to receive his message; a
message which he probably finds hard to explain himself, but
which he knows comes from a far deeper source than conscious
thought.' However, such individuals may eventually have the
satisfaction of their instincts proving to be right in the end.

The Prince goes on to cite the experience of the sixteenth century physician Paracelsus, quoted above, remarking that,
although he is remembered for his unorthodoxy, he was in
another sense a one-man BMA complaining about the pharmaceutical abuses and quack remedies (such as viper's blood) of
his day. Indeed, 'in 1527, by an act of which I am sure today's
young doctors would be proud, he burned the famous textbook
of medieval medicine, the Canon of Avicenna, [an action] which
became a symbol of rebellion against pedantry and unthinking
acceptance of ancient doctrines.'

Far from thinking of Paracelsus as a charlatan, continued the
Prince, we could do worse than consider the principles on which
he operated before 'science became estranged from nature':

> Above all he maintained that there were four pillars on
> which the whole art of healing rested. The first was
> philosophy; the second astronomy (or what we might
> now call psychology); the third alchemy (or
> biochemistry); and the fourth virtue (in other words the
> professional skill of the doctor). He then went on to
> outline the basic qualifications for a doctor: 'Like each
> plant and metallic remedy, the doctor, too, must have a
> specific virtue. He must be intimate with nature. He must
> have the intuition which is necessary to understand the
> patient, his body, his disease. He must have the "feel" and
> the "touch" which make it possible for him to be in
> sympathetic communication with the patient's spirits.'
> Paracelsus believed that the good doctor's therapeutic
> success largely depends on his ability to inspire the
> patient with confidence and to mobilize his will to health.

The Prince quotes Dr George Engel — founder of the biopsychosocial approach — to the effect that modern medicine is predominantly mechanistic in its outlook, with 'the body as a machine, disease as the consequence of breakdown of the machine, and the doctor's task as repair of the machine.' He continues:

> By concentrating on smaller and smaller fragments of the body modern medicine perhaps loses sight of the patient as a whole human being, and by reducing health to mechanical functioning it is no longer able to deal with the phenomenon of healing. And here I come back to my original point. The term 'healer' is viewed with suspicion and the concepts of health and healing are probably not generally discussed enough in medical schools. But to reincorporate the notion of healing into the practice of medicine does not necessarily mean that medical science will have to be less scientific. Through the centuries healing has been practised by folk-healers who are guided by traditional wisdom that sees illness as a disorder of the whole person, involving not only the patient's body, but his mind, his self-image, his dependence on the physical and social environment, as well as his relation to the cosmos.

It is important to note that the Prince is here — as in agriculture — advocating a *both-and* and not an *either-or* approach here: the science *and* the art of medicine, curing *and* healing. His words might seem self-evident these days, but this was certainly not the case twenty years ago. The Prince's main contention was that 'the whole imposing edifice of modern medicine, for all its breathtaking successes is, like the celebrated Tower of Pisa, slightly off balance.' This is emphatically not to deny the undoubted benefits of modern medical science but to suggest that it needs complementing with a more qualitative, patient-centred approach beyond a fascination with 'the objective, statistical, computerized approach to the healing of the sick.' As we have already seen, it was this speech that initiated a major debate within the health profession about the role of complementary medicine and helped move the whole field forward in a significant way. In July 1983 and at the Prince's instigation, the BMA set up a working party to consider the feasibility, and possible methods, of assessing the value of alternative therapies, whether used alone or to complement other treatments. Practitioners and users of the alternative methods were asked to tell the BMA what treatments they used and explain how they were thought to work. As we saw above, their critical report came out in 1986.

## Spirituality in Psychiatry

> *The cure of the part should not be attempted without treatment of the whole, and also no attempt should be made to cure the body without the soul, and therefore if the head and body are to be well you must begin by curing the mind; that is the first thing... For this is the error of our day in the treatment of the human body, that physicians separate the soul from the body.*
>
> Plato

In 1991, the Royal College of Psychiatrists followed the example of the BMA and the Royal Institute of British Architects by asking the Prince, as their Patron, to make a speech at their 150th anniversary celebrations. The Prince warned his audience about what had happened on these other occasions and joked that he must need his head examining for coming all the way to Brighton merely to reveal his 'lamentable ignorance about the complex problems with which you have to deal in your professional lives.' And he added that 'by the time I have finished this morning, I dare say it shouldn't be too difficult to diagnose what is wrong with me, and no doubt you will then all argue furiously over the course of treatment to be prescribed. My guess is that you will recommend complete rest for another two weeks accompanied by a total abstinence from stress-inducing speeches ...!'

However, the Prince had some serious points to make. He expressed his sympathy and admiration for the work of his audience in 'what must be, at times, a literally soul-destroying task. As a profession your calling is to try and bring a measure of healing and comfort to the mental anguish and suffering of countless numbers of people.' He referred to the difficulties in defining mental health, to differences in approach between psychiatry and psychotherapy, and to the continuing and unfortunate stigma attached to mental illness. This extends in the media to an undervaluing of the achievements of psychiatrists, 'whose triumphs are, almost by definition, private and invisible to the public eye.' The task we set psychiatry, he went on to say, is a demanding one involving the most complex organ in the body:

> in the absence of anyone else, we would like you to solve all the problems of society. We confront you with the most complex problems, part biological, part psychological, part social and part spiritual, and expect you to unravel them, treat all the parts that belong to psychiatry and at the same time somehow make better all the parts that don't belong to psychiatry.

The Prince said that he was 'sure it would be helpful if more people understood that a psychiatrist's first problem is to decide how to reach out to a patient, how to make them feel understood, cared for, and safe.' Nor is this an easy task: 'just being with a patient who is frightened or frightening must be incredibly difficult and takes immense courage and dedication; the human contact can awaken shadows in the doctor's own psyche, testing that inner strength which has the most profound influence on the patient. To listen and share in someone's pain takes great bravery and it deserves recognition.'

Then there is the continuing discussion about the relative merits of the biological and psychosocial approaches to psychological problems. While understanding the pressures within the profession, the Prince felt that the 'chemical cosh' was resorted to on occasions when more time and understanding which could conceivably rescue the patient from his predicament. At this point the Prince revealed his true colours: 'having made my own views on over-reliance on medication known to the British Medical Association some years ago, and having spent time since then in encouraging what I prefer to call complementary practice, it will not surprise you to hear that I am concerned, for what it is worth, that the psychological approach to mental illness should not be forgotten or discounted.' Hence his welcome for the 'growing importance being given to listening and counselling skills in all branches of medicine.'

If drugs represent an approach of active intervention, then listening is a more sensitive process that can enable healing and spiritual growth:

> Sometimes there is a need for doing, but equally there are times for being with, for waiting, for being patient and for allowing spiritual healing to occur. There is a sense, too, in which suffering, if handled sensitively, can be transmuted into a positively redeeming process. I was talking recently to the wife of a Church of Scotland Minister who told me that as often as not she and her husband are left to pick up the pieces with people who have failed to respond to psychiatric treatment. She told me that she has only witnessed a true transformation in such people when they finally discover within themselves that transfiguring dimension we define (or perhaps I should say that some of us define!) as God. Above all, perhaps, students need to be taught that growth and healing are natural processes. Science can accelerate them, but it can also retard or prevent them.

This brings the Prince to the heart of his message, the need for a rebalancing within medicine, prompted by the motto of the College, 'Let Wisdom Guide':

> For what it is worth, I believe we need to be reminded occasionally that wisdom has a far more profound meaning than just the acquisition of knowledge in the modern scientific-materialist sense. Should we not be asking ourselves pretty carefully where scientific materialism has been leading us — and, indeed, what kind of society it has been creating? Is there not an imbalance that needs correcting; an abandoned element that requires rehabilitation? It is perhaps worth recalling that Jung himself told one of his associates that he did not

want anybody to be 'Jungian.' [He said:] 'I want people above all to be themselves. As for "isms," they are the viruses of our day, and responsible for greater disasters than any medieval plague or pest has ever been. Should I be found one day only to have created another "ism" then I will have failed in all I tried to do.'

The Prince reminded his audience of the sacred context of medicine and healing in Ancient Greece, and wondered if our systematic denial of the irrational forces had not magnified their power and effect. This raises questions about the meaning of illness:

It seems to me that the meaning that illness has for us is, to a large extent, conditioned by our view about the purpose and goal of the life we are given on this planet. In other words, for the materialist, enlightened self-interest would lead us to see illness as of no value and with no meaning, whereas someone with a religious view of Creation will need to think about it in a much larger frame than merely the restriction of the individual's ability to do all that he or she could. If wisdom is to be your guide then Shakespeare makes a few salient points when Macbeth speaks to the doctor about Lady Macbeth, thus:

*Canst thou not minister to a mind diseased,*
*Pluck from the memory a rooted sorrow,*
*Raze out the written troubles of the brain,*
*And with some sweet oblivious antidote*
*Cleanse the stuffed bosom of that perilous stuff*
*Which weighs upon the heart?*

The conclusion of the matter, the Prince said, was 'more needs she the divine than the physician.' He did not expect his audience to agree with him, but he went on to say: 'I believe that the most urgent need for Western man is to rediscover that divine element in his being, without which there never can be any possible hope or meaning to our existence in this Earthly realm.' He quotes the inspired lines from Wordsworth's 'Tintern Abbey':

*And I have felt*
*A presence that disturbs me with the joy*
*Of elevated thoughts; a sense sublime*
*Of something far more deeply interfused,*
*Whose dwelling is the light of the setting suns*
*And the round Ocean and the living air,*
*And the blue sky and in the mind of man;*
*A motion and a spirit that impels*
*All thinking things, all objects of all thought,*
*And rolls through all things.*

For the Prince this is an indication of the deep interconnectedness and interdependence of life, which leads to the need to look
at the whole person in a comprehensive context. The spiritual
vacuum of our time, he maintains, means that 'there are no foundations on which to build an acceptance of our own weakness,
respect for the unique worth of others, and a reconciliation
between those classed as mentally ill and the society in which we
must all live.' As an example, the Prince refers to the example of
depression and anxiety: 'one of the main causes seems to be the
lack of acceptance of suffering in a society which focuses on
immediate gratification. We find it hard to accept that there is a
need to adapt to loss, and to grieve, and we are intolerant of people who are emotionally distressed. Often their distress is made
worse because they do not have the inner resources and spiritual
development which would enable them to see that there is a
meaning beyond themselves.' Suffering is intensified to the
extent that life and illness are seen as meaningless — hence the
Prince's call for a rediscovery of the spiritual realm, the divine
within.

The Prince concludes by suggesting that 'any vision of a better future for people who are afflicted by mental illness must
have its roots in a better understanding of mind and body, and
in values that go far beyond the material. We will build a better
future for the mentally ill because we know what "better"
means, and it means radical change in society's assumptions.'
He calls for 'greater recognition, even among such an enlightened group as yourselves, that mental and physical health are
not simply about medical repairs':

We are not just machines, whatever modern science may claim is the case on the evidence of what is purely visible and tangible in this world. Mental and physical health also have a spiritual base. Caring for people who are ill, restoring them to health when that is possible, and comforting them always, even when it is not, are spiritual tasks. Training people for your profession and maintaining your professional skills are not simply about understanding and administering the latest drugs but about therapy; in the original Greek sense of healing — physical, mental and spiritual, and also about wisdom, in the ancient sense of understanding the true nature of our existence enabling those who are 'seeing through a glass darkly' then to see face to face. If you lose that foundation as a profession, I believe there is a danger you will ultimately lose your way.

The intervening period has seen a continuing debate about the relative merits of biological and psychosocial approaches, but also a growing recognition of the significance of spiritual factors in mental health. The Prince's championing of a spiritual approach was a factor in the formation of a special interest group in Spirituality in Psychiatry. The group now has over 700 members within the College, and publishes its own journal as well as holding regular meetings.

## The Prince of Wales's Foundation for Integrated Health

Although he continued to be active in the health field in the late 1980s and early 1990s as president or patron of some twenty organizations and hospices, the Prince's next ambitious personal initiative was the establishment in 1996 of the Foundation for Integrated Medicine (FIM), which is now called The Prince of Wales's Foundation for Integrated Health. The aim of the Foundation is to promote the development and integrated delivery of safe, effective and efficient forms of healthcare to patients and their families though encouraging greater collaboration between all forms of healthcare. In addition to an emphasis on safety and effectiveness, the Foundation's approach is patient-centred and comprehensive in the sense that patients should be treated as whole individuals. It also favours accessibility whereby all appropriate and effective forms of healthcare should be available to those who need them. The Foundation's mission is 'to enable individuals to promote, restore and maintain health and well being through integrating the approaches of orthodox, complementary and alternative therapies.'

Operating as a forum, FIM set out to develop good working relationships with healthcare institutions and professionals in pursuit of its aim. To this end, the Prince initially convened and chaired a seminar involving healthcare professionals from a wide variety of backgrounds, to review the situation and to discuss practical steps to improve communication and co-operation between all concerned in healthcare provision. As a result, four working groups were created to examine requirements for research and development, education and training, regulation and the delivery of integrated care.

The discussion document *Integrated Healthcare — A Way Forward for the Next Five Years?* was published in October 1997 and launched by the Prince with his Centenary King's Fund Lecture on Integrated Healthcare. Here he reflected back on his first forays into the field fifteen years earlier:

> For well over a decade, I have tried to encourage a more integrated provision of healthcare for the ultimate benefit of patients. I am personally convinced that many more people could benefit from complementary medicine as well as from a more personal and patient-centred approach in orthodox medicine. It is also clear from the enormous increase in the use of complementary therapies by the general public — largely paid for out of their own pockets — that I am not entirely alone in this belief. It seems to me that complementary medicine can sometimes bring a different approach and assist in unlocking the individual's inner resources to aid recovery or to help manage and live with chronic illnesses for which there is little prospect of cure.

He maintained that 'we have reached a defining moment in our attitude towards healthcare in this country among both the public and health professionals.' Why, the Prince asked, does integration in healthcare matter? His answer was that:

> I believe it matters because we cannot afford to overlook or waste any knowledge, experience or wisdom from different traditions that could be brought to bear in the cause of helping those who suffer. Over the past ten or twenty years tremendous advances have been made in biological and other scientific research, such that we now have the prospect of successfully treating conditions previously considered incurable. But clearly this alone is not fulfilling all our healthcare needs as large numbers of people are paying to seek help from complementary medical practitioners. We simply cannot ignore what is a very real social phenomenon.

Speaking about the report itself, the Prince pointed out that its subtitle ended in a question mark, which signified his hope that it would give rise to further consultations and debate. The report was the result of widespread consultation with all the main medical bodies and is an impressively detailed document. It still forms the basis of the current work of the Prince's Foundation for Integrated Health in the areas of delivery, education, regulation, research and development.

~ *Delivery* — the aim is to increase access to complementary healthcare. Most people have to pay directly for complementary treatment; the Foundation believes it should be accessible for all those who need it, integrated with conventional medicine.

~ *Education* — work on education is primarily aimed at developing a common basis for all healthcare education and training together with programmes of continuing professional development for all healthcare practitioners.

~ *Regulation* — the Foundation is working to encourage the complementary medicine professions to develop and maintain statutory or voluntary systems of regulation and has a five year plan of work, supported by a £1,000,000 grant from the King's Fund.

~ *Research and Development* — the prime objective is to increase the capacity for high quality and appropriate research into complementary and alternative medicine and integrated healthcare.

The current initiatives in all of these areas can be found on the Foundation web site.

## Steps towards an Integrated Medicine

A Medical Litany
*From inability to leave well alone;*
*From too much zeal for what is new and contempt for what is old;*
*From putting knowledge before wisdom, science before art,*
*cleverness before common sense;*
*From treating patients as cases;*
*From making the cure of a disease more grievous than its endurance;*
*Good Lord, deliver us.*

Sir Robert Hutchinson

Writing in 1997 about how he saw the current health situation in the UK, the Prince expressed the view that health should be defined as more than the mere absence of disease. He remarked that the enormous growth in the use of complementary medicine was an international phenomenon which 'reflects a growing concern with the use of more and more powerful drugs and a potentially rather impersonal approach to healthcare. There is a feeling not only among patients, but also among GPs, nurses and other mainstream health practitioners, that there needs to be greater integration and inter-professional collaboration in patient care and that we can each, as individuals, play a greater role in contributing towards our own health and well-being.'

Consistent with his balanced approach to healthcare, the Prince stresses the value of the dramatic scientific discoveries that have enabled Western medicine to make leaps in our understanding of the disease process, and how to treat it. He points out that serious illnesses and injuries that were once regarded as untreatable can now be cured, and new forms of treatment are being developed all the time. He is confident that this trend will continue. Yet we also know that new medical treatments and procedures can be costly to develop, and sometimes equally expensive in application. As medicine becomes more sophisticated and more ambitious, so the costs have tended to spiral. Hence the need to make best use of all our available resources. The Prince goes on to say that:

> That is where complementary medicine could have an important — indeed, vital — role to play, in supporting and complementing current orthodox medical practice. Often it seems that complementary medicine can bring a different perspective and fulfil a real human need for a more personal touch which, in turn, can help unlock the individual's inner resources to aid the healing process. The goal we must work towards is an integrated healthcare system in which all the knowledge, experience and wisdom accumulated in different ways, at different times and in different cultures is effectively deployed to prevent or alleviate human suffering.

He concludes:

> I believe that we have a unique opportunity to take stock and consider how we can make the very best use of all our precious healthcare resources. We must respond to what the public are clearly showing they want by placing more emphasis on prevention, healthy lifestyles and patient-centred care. Integrated healthcare is an achievable goal. It is one we cannot afford to miss.

In 1998, the Foundation held a conference to review progress since the publication of its report the previous year. The Prince reiterated the central theme of the initiative: 'to encourage a dialogue among the different branches and traditions of healthcare and to develop a closer, more effective relationship.' He added that it is not a question of orthodox medicine taking over, or of complementary and alternative medicine diluting the intellectual rigour of orthodoxy. It is rather about reaching across the disciplines to help and to learn from one another for the ultimate benefit of patients.

A further conference on *Professional Competence — Public Confidence* was held in 1999 to review the range of responses received from various healthcare organizations. Here the Prince commented on what he regarded as the most significant change since his first involvement with the field: 'the growing acceptance by sections of the orthodox medical and caring community of this approach — which combines the physical, mental and spiritual aspects of healing.' This led him to reflect on the need for further regulation of some complementary therapies so that people could feel confident that the treatment they were receiving was safe. Self-regulation of therapies is the most desirable option, but this may involve the creation of an umbrella organization for each CAM area. Regulation includes the provision of simple information about the therapy and a procedure for complaint should things go wrong.

In the same year the Foundation was involved in the Guild of Health Writers' Awards for Good Practice in Integrated Healthcare, about which the Prince wrote an article in the NHS magazine. There was a total of 81 entries for the award, of which — encouragingly — the majority were already working within the NHS: Homoeopaths, osteopaths, reflexologists, acupuncturists, T'ai chi instructors, art therapists, chiropractors, herbalists and aromatherapists were all working alongside NHS colleagues in acute hospitals, on children's wards, in nursing homes and especially in primary healthcare, in GP practices and in health clinics up and down the country. There were entries from integrated teams in physiotherapy, mental health care, maternity care and from specialist integrated teams focusing on cancer, AIDS, multiple sclerosis, epilepsy and postnatal depression. What the best projects demonstrated, wrote the Prince, was that integrated medicine — the collaboration of two seemingly opposed disciplines for the benefit of patients — was not only possible, but actually worked. Secondly, by dint of intensely hard work and innovation, many of the entrants had found ways to research and prove the effectiveness — and cost effectiveness — of complementary therapies.

The winner, *Complementary Therapies within Cancer Services* at the NHS Hammersmith Hospitals Trust, was outstanding for the sheer depth of its integration in offering massage therapy, reflexology, aromatherapy, relaxation training and art therapy to cancer patients at Charing Cross and Hammersmith Hospitals. The Prince explained that the service was literally embedded within the orthodox matrix and has engendered a very real degree of professional respect at every level. It is continuously evaluated and regularly audited and shows consistently increasing referrals from mainstream medical staff. He added that several pilot studies were underway but records indicate that complementary therapies have significantly decreased palliative drug use among radiotherapy patients.

The runner-up — this time in primary care — was the Glastonbury Health Centre, which set out to develop a model of a fully integrated NHS primary care service that could be replicated in other NHS practices. The idea of a GP practice offering complementary practices is not new — but the Glastonbury initiative goes far beyond this in providing a truly integrated service. Patients are offered courses of acupuncture, herbal medicine, homoeopathy, massage therapy and osteopathy in the same way as orthodox practices offer physiotherapy or medication. Glastonbury carried out an evaluative study on its CAM provision between 1994 and 1997. Using established tools, it found that 85% of patients referred to complementary therapies reported some or much improvement. There were also statistically significant improvements in general vitality, social functioning, emotional and mental health in roughly two thirds of patients. Complementary therapies were shown to be particularly effective for patients with shorter term or more severe conditions on referral, and in relieving pain and physical discomfort for patients with musculo-skeletal problems. The research also suggested that the therapies contributed to relieving social and emotional distress in patients with psychosocial problems.

Another entry from a team at Queen Charlotte and Chelsea Hospital showed that teaching mothers with postnatal depression to massage their babies not only enhanced mother-child bonding, but relieved the mother's depression. If, the Prince noted, one considers that postnatal depression can afflict up to 10% of women who give birth in the UK each year, it is clearly a major problem with possible affects on the mental health of both parent and infant. In some cases, the long-term consequences may represent a lifelong financial drain on the NHS and social services. Set against this the sum of £30 — the estimated cost of five lessons in infant massage with appropriately trained massage therapists, that could be provided in any baby health clinic or GP practice. It would not be a bad idea to extend this beneficial practice to all mothers as part of an overall strategy for preventing postnatal depression. These and many other submitted projects were written up in a book published by the Foundation entitled *Integrated Healthcare: A Guide to Good Practice* by Hazel Russo.

In 2000, the Prince spoke at the BMA Millennium Festival of Medicine, using the opportunity to update the BMA on his thinking since his initial speech there eighteen years before — when he had chided them for an overemphasis on technology at the expense of the human factor. Noting the emergence of antibiotic resistance as a major problem — already mentioned in the chapter on agriculture — the Prince warned that the speed of technological advance can easily outstrip ethical considerations and bring about unforeseen consequences. He celebrated some of these advances such as the CT scanner but felt that such progress should be accompanied by 'the rediscovery of the healing relationship with the deeply felt need for better support systems to enable healthcare professionals to maintain and nurture their capacity to communicate and care.' The Prince applies the same thought to medical education when he hopes that 'the human skills and intuitive abilities that are possessed by new medical students will be valued and nurtured by the latest training programmes so that their vision and commitment to caring can be harnessed alongside their ever-increasing scientific knowledge and technical expertise.'

In 2001, the Prince presented the biennial Awards for Integrated Complementary and Conventional Healthcare. These awards are open to complementary and conventional practitioners or to organizations working in partnership with conventional practitioners who incorporate complementary therapies into their practice. The shortlist of eleven for the 2001 Awards contained projects from many areas of the NHS including several primary care services, such as an integrated smoking cessation project at a Manchester general practice, improving public access to complementary therapies in Newcastle Primary Care Trust, and the integrated service at Marylebone Health Centre, London. Other projects include a menopause clinic in Sheffield offering homeopathy and aromatherapy, and a centre offering a special therapy for foot disorders. These awards were made again in 2003 and are set to continue in 2005. In January 2003 the Foundation published another consultation document, *Setting the Agenda for the Future,* which will form the basis of its next five-year plan which was launched in May. The document reviews the original aims and progress made over the last five years with respect to evidence, standards, choice and access.

In the last year the Prince has turned his attention to the growing problem of allergies, citing a report from the Royal College of Physicians that 18 million people in the UK have an allergy and 12 million are suffering from one at any given time. The Prince points out that

> Allergies are also increasing in severity and complexity. While asthma and hayfever have increased two-to-threefold over 20 years, hospital admissions for anaphylaxis —a systemic form of allergy that can be fatal — have increased sevenfold over 10 years. In the UK, 34% of 13- to-14-year-olds now have active asthma, the highest prevalence in the world. I am told that the high figures are most likely to be explained by lifestyle factors including diet, exercise, smoking in parents, exposure to chemicals and a lack of protective factors in early childhood (exposure to bacteria and other micro-organisms that boost immunity) and overuse of antibiotics.

The Prince suggests that ' factors associated with our Western society, such as over-eating, lack of exercise and an obsession with hygiene, as well as our exposure to a myriad of chemicals from products whose effects we are only just learning about, are conspiring to weaken our defence against the environment. Our children are paying the price.' And the same applies to the enormous increase in child and adult obesity, about which so much has been written and which is closely related to modern conditions and lifestyles. Hence the Prince's argument that 'there is an urgent need to examine the way in which the Western approach to life and to the world around us is increasingly affecting our overall health. These [health] challenges stem from what I can only describe as an inherently unsustainable approach to the world around us and within us. In fact, we are now finding that the proverbial chickens are coming home to roost in terms of expecting something for nothing in the way we treat our environment and ourselves.'

## The Prince's Work with Cancer

*If there is any meaning in life at all, then there must be meaning in suffering. Suffering is an ineradicable part of life, even as fate and death. Without suffering and death human life cannot be complete. We had to learn ourselves and, furthermore, we had to teach the despairing men, that* it did not matter what we expected from life, but rather what life expected from us.

Viktor Frankl

The Prince has taken an active interest in cancer treatments since he opened the Bristol Cancer Help Centre in 1983. He is the Patron of the Centre as well as of Macmillan Cancer Relief and several other cancer charities. He launched the Macmillan Cancer Guide in June 1999. He draws on his own encounters with cancer patients to explore the fear, frustration, anxiety, vulnerability and confusion that many feel. What he finds depressing is that, despite the progress of the last twenty years and the greater openness in talking about cancer today, 'we still use the same terrifying words and images to describe it. Or should I say over-describe it.' He illustrates his point with an example:

I read of one young woman who, after her diagnosis, felt that people's attitudes to her had changed: 'I was written off as a dying person,' she said. But she was doing everything she did before. It's just that she had cancer too.
It was her friends who could not cope, not her. So, the stigma — the stereotypes — of cancer still exist. The

language of cancer simplifies what is complex and generalizes what is individual. And it can hurt people with cancer. It has been suggested today that we can start to change this by recognizing that cancer is not one disease but 200 different diseases, some serious, some not so serious. We all know that when we break a huge problem down into manageable pieces it begins to appear less daunting. So this seems like a practical step we can all take. It will force us to find new words and images to describe cancer. The simple stereotypes will not work any more and the archaic metaphors will gradually lose their relevance.

But along with that we can all question our attitudes to cancer and we can all make sure that we see the person, before we see their cancer. These diseases, serious though they are, do not actually deform people's personalities.

He encourages health professionals to take a lead here by seeing the person first, before they see the cancer. The publication and distribution of the Cancer Guide through the NHS is one way of sending the message that patient involvement is essential to effective care. However, there is also a need for more cancer experts, which Macmillan is addressing. The Prince concludes by calling for a rewriting of the rhetoric of cancer: 'the media could help us in this by using their immense influence to destroy the myths and misconceptions which block understanding and paralyse action. He also thinks that more can be done to give patients the knowledge and confidence to play a more active part in their treatment and care: 'there is still so much we need to learn about this disease and people with cancer can teach us a great deal. They are the only experts in their cancer.'

In October 2000 the Prince launched Loud Tie Day to raise awareness of the problem of bowel cancer, which affects 30,000 people a year in the UK, of whom nearly two-thirds die. The launch involved the longest, loudest tie ever seen in this country — 14 storeys high and 40ft wide — dropped in seconds down one of the tallest landmark buildings in the capital, the London Television Centre on the South Bank. The tie, bright red and covered in 6ft-high figures, each representing 1,000 people who will develop bowel cancer during the year, was painted by artists, people with bowel cancer and their friends. While the whole range of causes of the condition has not been identified, the Prince stressed the importance of lifestyle factors in prevention and commented that 'there is a major role for complementary medicine in bowel cancer — as a support to more conventional approaches — in helping to prevent it through lifestyle changes, helping to boost our immune systems and in helping sufferers to come to terms with, and maintain, a sense of control over their own lives and wellbeing.'

In 2001 the Prince — as Patron of the Charity Breakthrough Breast Cancer — supported Breast Cancer Awareness month by writing an article in the *Daily Mail*. 38,000 women in the UK are diagnosed every year, and the work of the charity seeks to work towards a future free of the fear of breast cancer. The Prince opened the Breakthrough Toby Robins Breast Cancer Research Centre in 1999, where eighty scientists are now working. In addition, he supported the campaign Kiss Goodbye to Breast Cancer, which has focused on the need for more research into the prevention of breast cancer: 'an integrated approach to combating breast cancer that encompasses research, complementary medicine and the critical area of prevention, is one that I wholeheartedly support.'

In a similar context, the Prince also hosted the first Penny Brohn Memorial Lecture by Dr Caroline Myss at St James's Palace. Penny Brohn was one of the founders of the Bristol Centre and a woman who outlived her original diagnosis by many years. On that occasion the Prince referred to the centrality of the process of healing and saluted Penny Brohn and her colleague Pat Pilkington for their courage in the face of a ferocious media onslaught. The Prince himself was once told that he was 'encouraging people to go there and die and to be twice as likely to die as otherwise.'

## Hospital Design — Building for Recovery

*I had a fast-growing conviction that a hospital is no place for a person who is seriously ill.*

Norman Cousins

In a speech at the NHS Estates Conference at The Prince's Foundation in November, 2001, the Prince explained that his interest in architecture and health care stemmed from the simple fact that he believes that our environment — which in this country is very largely man-made — has a profound influence over our physical, psychological and spiritual wellbeing. We shall develop this theme in a later chapter on architecture and heritage, but in this context hospital design provides a thematic link between the Prince's interest in health and his concern for architecture and design. The immediate context was a partnership between his Foundation and NHS Estates that is working on a very practical level, initially with five commissioning NHS Trusts in Lewisham, Sunderland, Salford, Middlesex and Wakefield. The Prince stressed that he had no illusions about the complex challenges that lie ahead, but he hoped that by working together with users, patients, the design team and other stakeholders it will find it possible to create health care buildings that truly stand the test of time.

The Prince began with a quip from Oscar Wilde who, when asked why he thought America was such a violent country, said that it was 'because your wallpaper is so ugly.' Behind this seemingly facile remark, argued the Prince, lies the contrast between the uplifting beauty of nature and the ugliness or soullessness of aspects of the man-made environment. And ugliness can be correlated with brutality and violence. The trend in twentieth century architecture has highlighted the mechanical, the impersonal and the functional at the expense of the human scale. The Prince quotes Sir Nikolaus Pevsner to the effect that 'the artist who is representative of this century of ours needs be cold, as he stands for a century cold as steel and glass, a century the precision of which leaves less space for self expression than did any period before.' This kind of sentiment is reflected in hospital design, as readers will no doubt testify from their own experience of being in such buildings.

The basic principle underlying the Prince's approach, as elsewhere, is 'to restore the "soul" — the psychological and spiritual element if you like, — to its rightful place in the scheme of things.' In other words, the Prince continued:

> as with the need in a new century to emphasize the pedestrian rather than the car as the central feature in the design of new settlements, so is there a need to place the

patient at the centre of hospital design. As the individual patient has a unique character, so should the building that provides the healing environment.

He goes on to suggest that:

in our restless search for new ideas for both building and health care, we have tended to ignore some of the more traditional, or timeless truths that can complement the remarkable progress in building and health care technologies and techniques. These help create the benign environments that will engender a sense of ease, harmony and, dare I say, health. There is little doubt, it seems to me, that in both the built environment and in health care, there is room for both the best of the inherited wisdoms and techniques and the best of new methods.

We have seen how the Prince advocates this *both-and* approach in agriculture and medicine more generally.

The Prince believes that the mutual influence between our physical environment and our deeper psychological or physical health has profound implications for the design of health buildings. In other words, hospitals are more than garages where mechanical repairs are carried out. Nowhere is it more crucial to design well, than in those places that are constructed precisely for curing our illnesses. Moreover, he says, it is now more widely acknowledged that 'many of the root causes of ill health are likely to lie with factors that are as much to do with our emotional, psychological and spiritual well-being as they are with our physiological condition.'

New surgical techniques, modern drugs, and developments in diagnostic skills, have all helped to give health and, indeed, life itself to millions who previously suffered or perished, and one of the main challenges in new building designs must be to cater efficiently for the needs of these new technologies and practices. Yet, argues the Prince, amidst this scientific miracle, there remain many elements of healthcare that continue to require a nurturing of the soul and the spirit, just as much as the body. Achieving the conditions for individual patients to help heal themselves is a crucial requirement in every kind of successful health care. It is precisely this need for a complete, or whole, range of sensory awareness that has increased interest in complementary, or holistic, healthcare, (which he prefers to call integrated healthcare) and which is also generating new interest in holistic building design. He joked that 'as soon as the word "holistic" is out of my mouth, I am aware that many people are overcome by a desire to tiptoe to the door and head for the bar to recover. Holistic is one of those words, rather like "sustainable," that has become freighted with unfortunate connotations of flabby thinking and antiscientific hogwash, as have phrases like "alternative therapy." So be it.'

Coming to the buildings themselves, the Prince remarked that 'one doesn't have to look very far to see how diseased much of our built environment has become. Worse still, it is very often health buildings, particularly some hospitals, that exemplify everything that is most damaged in our recent architectural heritage.' He commented that so many of the hospital designs of the 1960s and 1970s offer both a stark brutality from the outside and, very often, the inside too: 'designed in the hey-day of professional arrogance, they frequently present themselves to both the patient, the visitor and the passing public as colossal machine-like structures; intimidating, harsh and, like aliens from outer space at odds with their surroundings.' In other words, the design approach reflects underlying mechanistic assumptions in both architecture and medicine.

Challenging this point of view, the Prince argues, involves a thorough transformation in the practice of healthcare design and architecture, which:

> has itself been largely conditioned by the conventional notion of buildings being designed as 'machines.' Just as Le Corbusier considered that homes should be regarded and designed as 'machines to live in,' so too, hospitals became almost 'machines to treat people in.' In fact, it was precisely this approach, with its emphasis on mechanical and technological innovation, that left so many NHS buildings divorced from any integration with the natural processes and human scale that can, I am convinced, aid the healing process.

The irony of the prevalence of 'sick building syndrome' in hospitals was not lost on the Prince: 'How many people do you know who say they cannot bear hospitals? The atmosphere. The institutional corridors. The signage, the chairs, the sounds, the smells, the views into pipeworked courtyards from which arises a steam that turns your stomach.' This means that we now have an opportunity to realize that 'views, landscaping, light, proportion and atmosphere are not optional extras, they are as integral a part of a hospital as operating theatres and trolleys.' He suggested that the original definition of hospitality (from which hospital is derived) as 'friendly and generous reception and entertainment of guests, visitors, or strangers' might hold some inspiration for the future design of hospitals, health centres and clinics.

Sources of inspiration for the new design of hospitals can begin with the human body. Not only is it 'the standard of wholeness and perfection, and that has served as a template for architectural discipline, in diverse societies and cultures, for millennia. It is also the crucial subject of clinics and hospitals, suggesting a recovery of the sense of scale and proportion in the buildings themselves. Anticipating his critics, the Prince said that 'a belief in harmony and proportion doesn't mean that architecture has to speak Greek and Latin. Nor does it mean I want to see Doric operating theatres, Corinthian columned hospital wards or Ionic intensive care departments: how buildings are ventilated, illuminated, their access to nature and landscape, the texture of materials and the careful use of colour are all crucial ingredients. So, too, is the absence of clutter and noise. We live in a noisy world, and yet silence, peace and stillness are often the keys to recovery, perhaps the greatest of the natural healing forces.'

The external appearance of buildings also matters, including their setting in the townscape or landscape. The Prince observed that 'we seem to have almost entirely lost the ability to plan and design public buildings as truly dignified architectural compositions, that frame and articulate the land and townscape around them.' The original Maudsley Hospital in South London is a good example of the Prince's point that 'historically, such buildings took their place in a hierarchy of building types, and stood as landmarks that provided a clear sense of order to residents and visitors alike.' Next door, however, is

*As well as his many royal duties, Prince Charles is Patron or President of 363 charities, raising £100 million every year for his 17 core charities. Out of his concern for the countryside and its people Prince Charles gave £500,000 to farmers hit by the Foot and Mouth crisis in 2002. (Photo: Press Association)*

*The Prince saw Poundbury as an opportunity to put into action his ideas about building and town planning. (Photo: Press Association)*

*Since converting Highgrove Home Farm to an organic mixed farm, the produce is sold through Duchy Originals. The profits go to The Prince of Wales's Charitable Foundation embodying Prince Charles' principle of creating a virtuous circle. Prince William shares his father's passion for ecology and agriculture. (Photo: Press Association)*

*Performer and composer Sarah Bennett was named The Prince's Trust Young Achiever at the Pride of Britain Awards in 2003. (Photo: Press Association)*

*The Prince's Trust was his first national charity to be set up in 1976, to help disadvantaged young people. Here Prince Charles greets Blazin' Squad at Party in the Park in 2003. (Photo: Press Association)*

*The Local Reporting Awards celebrates reporters who write inspiring stories about disadvantaged youngsters and the people who try to help them. Sharat Hussain (left) and Mohammed Arif run a community sports scheme in Bradford. (Photo: Press Association)*

*Visit to Lent Rise Combined School in Burnham, Berkshire, which is a leading participant in a training scheme inspired by the Prince. The Education Summer School was inaugurated to rekindle confidence in the rightness of teaching quality literature texts and history.*

*Prince Charles first called for greater integration of complementary therapies into the NHS in 1982 and set up his Foundation for Integrated Health (FIH) in 1996. The Gateway Clinic in Lambeth which offers traditional Chinese medicine and dietary advice on the NHS won an FIH Award in 2003. (Photos: Press Association)*

*At the heart of everything the Prince does is his sense of the sacred and the spiritual. This watercolour was painted during a summer trip to Mount Athos.*
Copyright AG Carrick Ltd

*The Prince invited the Dalai Lama to give the L.M. Singhvi Interfaith Lecture at the Temenos Academy in 2004. (Photo: Press Association)*

the soulless 1960s Institute of Psychiatry, an instance of how 'more recent buildings have become segregated from their surroundings by car parks, pointless open spaces or inappropriate building materials and methods.' Only now, even the car park has been reduced with a further extension, which, it has to be said, is a slight improvement on the original entirely functional edifice.

The Prince concludes with an appeal to bring art and beauty into hospital buildings. He acknowledges that the value of art is widely appreciated in the world of healthcare, and he has seen some interesting examples of good work done to integrate art into the life of hospitals and clinics: 'but I would go further than this, and ask if we cannot truly integrate art into the very buildings themselves, since there can be no doubt that being surrounded by beauty is likely to assist our health, as indeed, a growing body of evidence seems to suggest.' He quotes the great arts and crafts teacher William Lethaby, that 'Art is the wellbeing of what needs doing,' adding that 'in that spirit, let us try and make this new generation of health care centres truly fit for the healing of both body and soul.'

Alan Milburn, then Secretary of State for Health, welcomed the Prince's initiative. He commented that 'the quality of the buildings is vital to the quality of the care patients receive in them. One million patients a week use NHS hospitals. One third of those hospitals were built before the NHS was created. One tenth date back to Victorian times. Many rightly feel that the neglect of NHS buildings, over many decades, is little short of a national scandal.' Milburn envisaged the partnership bringing in the principles of flexibility and designing hospital environments to support recovery.

Work is now being carried out in the five hospital pilot projects already mentioned. The team from the Prince's Foundation is working alongside the commissioning Trusts to develop a design vision and prepare project design briefs and specifications. The Foundation Team is addressing all aspects of good design, from accessibility and therapeutic internal environments through to urban and social integration.

## Integrative Medicine and Integrated Health

*Integrative medicine is neutral, accurate and acceptable in academic discourse and avoids the misleading connotations of both alternative medicine (which suggests replacement of the standard system) and complementary medicine (which suggests retention of standard therapies as central and primary).*

Andrew Weil MD

Integration — in one form or another — is the current buzzword when referring to the future of medicine and health. The use of the acronym CAM is giving way to the language of integration where CAM can play its part in a wider framework that includes the best of both orthodox and CAM treatments. Indeed the Prince was the recipient of the first International Award for leadership in Integrated Healthcare from Columbia University in late 2003. One of the foremost US spokesmen for integrative medicine is Dr Andrew Weil, who, as well as being the author of eight books and numerous articles, is director of the Program in Integrative Medicine of the University of Arizona. In an article for the *American Journal of Medicine,* Dr Weil begins from the 'economic crisis of unprecedented proportions' that is engulfing US healthcare and resulting from insurance systems breaking down because conventional medicine has become too expensive. One of the reasons for this state of affairs arises from the successes of medicine that have rolled back infectious disease to leave the more intractable chronic degenerative illness, 'a much more stubborn and costly problem.' In addition, there is an ageing population and a great dependence on technology. However, there is a growing demand for low-tech solutions. 40% of US citizens are using CAM (although most are still not telling their doctors!) and visits to CAM practitioners exceed those to primary care providers; and money spent is also greater.

Patients want greater empowerment, informed doctors and a wider view of the human being: 'they want physicians who are sensitive to mind/body interactions, who are willing to look at patients as mental/emotional beings, spiritual entities, and community members as well as physical bodies.' They also want their physicians who share their views about health and healing and who are aware of nutritional influences on health. The challenge, according to Dr Weil, is to 'sort through all the evidence about all healing systems and try to extract those ideas and practices that are safe, useful and cost-effective. Then we must try to merge them into a new, comprehensive system of practice that has an evidence base and also addresses consumer demands.'

The result will be a transformed system: integrative medicine is not simply concerned with giving physicians new tools such as herbs in addition to or instead of pharmaceutical drugs. Rather it aims to shift some of the basic orientations of medicine: toward healing rather than symptomatic treatment, toward a closer relationship with nature, toward a strengthened doctor-patient relationship and an emphasis on mind and spirit in addition to body. These shifts should make for better medicine in addition to greater satisfaction of patients.

To this end Dr Weil has been running a programme in integrative medicine at the University of Arizona College of Medicine in Tucson. It began with a focus on two-year post-graduate fellowships and has now broadened to include an internet-based associate fellowship for physicians who have completed residencies in primary care specialities and are interested in being academic leaders. The programme is operates an Integrative Medical Clinic for outpatients at the Arizona Health Sciences Center and has a waiting list of 1,000 patients! It also runs a research programme funded by a NIH grant.

The curriculum includes nutritional medicine, mind/body medicine, 'lifestyle medicine,' and spirituality and medicine. 'To call these fields "alternative",' writes Dr Weil, 'would be a great mistake. They should be an essential foundation in the training of all physicians of the future.' Other foundation courses include philosophy of science, art of medicine and healing medicine plus information on theory, practice, strengths, and weaknesses of major alternative therapies. The fellows do not become experts in other forms of medicine but are trained to know when other approaches may be useful. Finally, fellows are encouraged to develop own health and wellbeing so as to model health for their patients. Dr Weil considers it an indictment of the current system that students are unlikely to come out with healthy lifestyles.

As we have seen in this chapter the Prince of Wales's

Foundation for Integrated Health is working exactly along the lines suggested by Dr Weil, along with a great many partners in the health field. In May 2002 the Prince launched a new Integrated Healthcare initiative aimed at increasing access to complementary and integrated healthcare within the NHS with five projects in London, Bradford, Wiltshire, Newcastle and Bristol providing complementary therapies alongside conventional treatments. The Prince explained that these five integrated healthcare projects in primary care trusts around the UK 'will act as pilot studies to determine how best to deliver complementary therapies with conventional medicine. Another seven projects like the Glastonbury Health Centre, old hands at integrated healthcare, will provide expert advice and support. What we learn will be shared with all interested health professionals through an electronic networking system that will also circulate information about research studies and conferences.' This is encouraging news for the 75% of the population who believe that the NHS should be providing CAM treatments.

We can expect many such similar initiatives in the next decade. The Prince of Wales's pioneering contribution to the field was recognized by his receipt from Columbia University's Rosenthal Center of its first Award for International Leadership in Integrative Medicine in November 2003. Although the Prince sees that the practices of orthodox and complementary medicine can be brought together as integrated healthcare, it is clear that the corresponding philosophy must be more than reductionist materialism: we cannot bring about a transformed system on the basis of the limited mechanistic approach leading to an inadequate model of the human being. However, the analytical rigour and technical prowess of scientific reductionism can be carried forward into a wider human context that places greater emphasis on active partnership with patients and on their inherent self-healing capacities. This is expressed in the *both-and* approach advocated by the Prince that resolves the dichotomies analysed earlier in this chapter.

# 4. A Sense of the Sacred: The Prince as Defender of Faith

## Spirit in a Secular Age

*I have come to the conviction that the aesthetic and the historical elements, and the magnificent extension of our material knowledge and power, do not themselves form the essence of civilization, but that this depends on the mental disposition of the individuals and nations who exist in the world. All other things are merely accompanying circumstances of civilization, which have nothing to do with its real essence ... if the ethical foundation is lacking, then civilization collapses, even when in other directions creative and intellectual forces of the strongest nature are at work.*

Dr Albert Schweitzer OM

When the Prince of Wales insists, as he frequently does, on the need for a sense of the sacred, is anyone listening out there? Do we live in a progressively secular society where such spiritual sentiments are increasingly irrelevant to the business of life? Or are most human beings 'incurably religious' as Denis Alexander put it at a meeting in St Andrews University on Science and Human Values? In order to address these questions we need to make a brief diagnosis of our current religious and spiritual condition, which is by no means as simple as the secularization story suggests.

The conventional secular account claims that the advance of science has gradually rendered religion redundant: there are few if any gaps left for God to fill. Freed from the shackles of dogmatic superstition, the human being is liberated, but into the impersonal vastness of the universe — only to be assured that the whole process of life is ultimately meaningless. There is no doubt that evolution, geology and astronomy have exploded Archbishop Usher's careful calculation that the world was created in 4004 BC. There is equally no doubt that science has explained the physical workings of the universe in unprecedented detail. However, science on its own may not convey the whole story.

In spite of popular impressions to the contrary, rumours of the demise of God and a spiritual dimension have been greatly exaggerated. A BBC programme *The Soul of Britain* broadcast in 2000, provided some interesting results based on a poll of 1,000 randomly selected respondents conducted by the Opinion Research Business.

Which of these statements comes closest to your beliefs?

| | |
|---|---|
| There is a personal God | 26% |
| There is some sort of spirit or life force | 21% |
| There is something there | 23% |
| I don't really know what to think | 12% |
| I don't really think there is any sort of God, spirit or life force | 15% |
| None of these | 3% |

Some people say that all religions offer a path to God. Others say what they believe is the best path to God. Which of the following statements comes closest to your point of view?

| | |
|---|---|
| All religions offer a path to God | 32% |
| What I believe is the only path to God | 9% |
| There is a way to God outside organized religion | 33% |
| I don't believe in God | 26% |
| Don't know | 5% |

These results show that 70% of people believe in something, but only a quarter in a personal God. Similarly, a quarter (that is, a minority) are atheists or agnostics. In response to the second question, fewer than 10% of respondents believe that theirs is the only way, while 65% believe in a multi-faith or unorganized approach. This demonstrates the tremendous influence of the comparative study of religions in the last 100 years, along with interfaith initiatives and, arguably, the popularity of such world spiritual leaders as the Dalai Lama. Interestingly, these figures correspond with the findings of David Hay, which show that around two-thirds of the population have had a spiritual or religious experience. In addition, the near-death experience (NDE) has attracted much media coverage in the last twenty years. This too points to a spiritual component in human life. However, during this same period, church attendance has continued to fall. This means — as reflected in the above findings — that there is a large segment of the population for whom spiritual matters are significant but who do not adhere to conventional religions. Some of these people find a niche in new religious movements, others in traditions like Buddhism and Sufism, and still others more superficially in the plethora of practices recommended in the annual avalanche of self-help mind-body-spirit books. The emphasis here lies on meditation and personal experience; the intellectual origins of such practices can perhaps be found in early esoteric Gnostic groups with their emphasis on *gnosis* or direct intuitive knowledge of hidden realities.

If it is true that there is a spiritual renaissance quietly occurring in our time, then it seems to take two very different forms. On the one hand, as we have seen above, there are various forms of personal spiritual practice that are based on other traditions or are loosely called 'holistic' or New Age, and on the other there are evangelical revivals as epitomized in the Alpha Course that originated at Holy Trinity Church, Brompton in London. Each of these approaches tends to stress the heart rather than the head, but they are at complete loggerheads in every other respect. Indeed the two groups tend to regard each other's activities with deep suspicion: New Age (or even in some cases Buddhist) practices are treated as threatening and heretical, while New Agers view evangelicals as people who have submitted to authority and outdated dogma. So the answer to the initial question, is there anyone listening to the Prince's call for a revival of the sense of the sacred is an emphatic yes — around

70% of the population, a figure which one would never guess from the way in which the press, and especially a few scientists, react to his call.

## Living Traditions and the Perennial Philosophy

*What is missing in our age is the soul; there is nothing wrong with the body. We suffer from a sickness of spirit. We must discover our roots in the eternal and regain faith in the transcendent truth that will order life, discipline discordant elements, and bring unity and purpose into it.*

Sir Sarvepalli Radhakrishnan

The Prince of Wales has drawn inspiration over the years from a number of exponents of the 'perennial philosophy,' whose seminal writings are not widely known. Their writings have informed his critique of modernism with its loss of the sacred 'Centre' and soul, and the wholesale rejection of tradition. Seyyed Hossein Nasr makes it clear that the traditional criticism of the modern world targets the total world view, its premises and foundations, which it regards as wrong and false in principle. We have seen how the Prince's Reith Lecture focused on the recovery of a sense of the sacred, and how he criticized the dominance of scientific rationalism while calling for a more balanced approach.

The premises of modern science are based on a materialist understanding that systematically denies the reality of a spiritual or metaphysical dimension to existence. It is this premise that the Prince feels is culturally damaging as well as untrue. However, there is no reason in principle why a new science should not adopt a different set of assumptions, which would serve to open it up to inner realms of consciousness. The methods need not be any less rigorous as the current science.

A key notion for perennial philosophers is that of 'Tradition', which implies the transmission of knowledge and practice from one person to another. The important point is that its truth is subtly embodied in living exemplars — saints and sages —who demonstrate its spirit. Many people have a much more limited idea of tradition as something old-fashioned, but its true meaning lies in the continuity it establishes between past, present and future, as the Prince himself explains: 'Tradition is not a dead thing; it is, in fact, the only means by which we can experience a sense of belonging and meaning within a rapidly changing world. It is, ultimately, the only way of making sense of the past and the future through their subtle reconciliation in a kind of eternal present.' In the highest sense, Tradition is the handing down of a method of contemplation, which is itself a form of the cultivation of consciousness. Through such means, consciousness comes to be known as a fundamental reality, more fundamental even than matter.

## *The Temenos Academy — Arts and the Imagination*

> *Everything engendered in existence is Imagination — but in*
> *fact it is Reality. Whosoever understands this truth has*
> *grasped the mysteries of the way.*
>
> *Ibn Arabi*

The Temenos Academy was launched in 1990 as a teaching organization dedicated to the same central idea that had inspired the earlier *Temenos Review* (a journal devoted to the arts of the Imagination). In the words of the founder, the literary historian and poet Kathleen Raine, 'the Temenos Academy is an association dedicated to the teaching and dissemination of the perennial wisdom, which has been the ground of every civilization.' Scholars and teachers, committed to what is now generally known as 'the perennial philosophy' — the learning of the Imagination — were invited to lecture and hold study groups. From the outset the Academy was housed in the Prince of Wales's Institute of Architecture in Regents Park, where it was hoped that some of the architecture students would attend the lectures and thus absorb some of the philosophy that had inspired their predecessors for centuries. Dr Raine writes:

> Whereas in Shelley's words, 'the deep truth is imageless,'
> the Arts (from architecture, painting, music and poetry, to
> the songs and dances of the villages and the designs of
> textiles and pottery), have within every civilization been

the flowering of a vision of the Sacred, embodied in some tradition of spiritual teaching. The arts of the imagination flourish therefore in the Temenos — the precinct of that sacred centre, be that centre temple, synagogue, church, mosque, or the invisible sanctuary within the heart. Since knowledge is universal we seek to learn from all traditions. Within western civilization, Temenos follows the Platonic and Plotinian tradition from its pre-Socratic origins to the present day. Our purpose is to study the learning of the Imagination, both in the arts and also in such metaphysical teachings as are likewise the expression of traditional spiritual knowledge. We reject the premises of secular materialism, widespread at the present time, which deny the very ground of meaning and value. Therefore we look also for contemporary expressions in the arts and other modes of thought which are rooted in that unageing spiritual reality.

Dr Raine recalls that it was their mutual friend Sir Laurens van der Post who used to show the Prince copies of the original *Temenos Review*. She was invited to a dinner at Kensington Palace, where she explained the idea behind Temenos through a remark made by Dr A. K. Coomaraswamy that: 'It takes four years to get the best university education, but it takes forty to get over it!' She found that the Prince shared her 'commitment to those three fundamental Platonic values on which European civilization is founded, the Good, the True and the Beautiful, the sacred Tradition which has inspired European civilization in both pre-Christian and Christian centuries.' She remarks that it is 'essentially the same values that underlie Indian civilization as *satyam, shivam, sundaram* (being, knowledge and bliss),' and continues:

> We hold that not 'progress' with its ever-shifting values, but Tradition, is the mainstream of civilization. Tradition, far from being backward-looking, is a continual renewal from the living source of inspiration, permanent to human nature itself. Novelty and 'originality' are not progressive, and neither is the amassing of 'information,' which is not knowledge, and has no relation to wisdom, which is a

living principle. This tradition is to be called 'sacred' because it arises at all times from a living source, nor can it be stored in any form save as consciousness itself.

A highlight of the Academy's year is the annual Interfaith Lecture endowed by the former Indian High Commissioner to London, Dr L.M. Singhvi, who himself gave the inaugural lecture in 1998. The 2004 lecturer was HH The Dalai Lama, whom the Prince greeted personally as a long term supporter of the Tibetan cause. In addition, the Academy holds an annual concert to thank those who have supported its work. This has for the last few years been hosted by its Royal Patron, the Prince of Wales, at St James's Palace or Highgrove. At the 2001 concert, the Prince spoke of 'the vital role of the Temenos Academy in helping to keep the fast-dwindling remnants of sacred traditions alive in a world where fantasy is rapidly displacing imagination.' The Prince insisted that the 'real world' is within us and added that:

'Truth, Goodness and Beauty' in the outer, manifested world are only made possible through the inner, invisible pattern — the unmanifested archetype ... my life so far has been dedicated to re-integrating that archetype ... I believe the challenge of the new century lies in the urgency with which we address the need to re-integrate that abused archetypal pattern in our hearts so that — somehow — we can re-create the lost habitats of both the physical world and that sacred inner dimension which is God's mysterious gift to humanity.

The principles that underpin the work of the academy are:

~ Acknowledgement of Divinity.
~ Love of wisdom, as the essential basis of civilization.
~ Spiritual vision, as the life-breath of civilization.
~ Maintenance of the revered traditions of mankind.
~ Understanding of tradition as continual renewal.
~ The provision of teaching by the best teachers available of their disciplines, and of publications which set the highest standard in both content and design.

~ Mindfulness that the purpose of teaching is to enable students to apply in their own lives that which they learn.
~ Reminding ourselves and those we teach to look up and not down.
~ Governance of the Temenos Academy itself in the light of the above principles.

As Patron of the Academy, the Prince is in no doubt about the significance of its work:

> The work of Temenos could not be more important. Its commitment to fostering a wider awareness of the great spiritual traditions we have inherited from the past is not a distraction from the concerns of everyday life. These traditions, which form the basis of mankind's most civilized values and have been handed down to us over many centuries, are not just part of our inner religious life. They have an intensely practical relevance to the creation of real beauty in the arts, to an architecture which brings harmony and inspiration to people's lives and to the development within the individual of a sense of balance which is, to my mind, the hallmark of a civilized person.

## Islam and the West — the Deeper Connection

> *To forget the Spirit and settle for its earthly reflections alone is to be doomed to a world of multiplicity, to separation, division, and finally aggression and war. No amount of extolling of the human spirit can fill the vacuum created by the forgetting of the Spirit which kindles the human soul but is not itself human. It is necessary to realize the unity of the Spirit behind the multiplicity of religious forms in order to reach the peace that human beings seek.*
>
> Seyyed Hossein Nasr

> *What comes from the lips reaches the ears. What comes from the heart reaches the heart.*
>
> Arab proverb, quoted by The Prince of Wales

Much copy on Islam and the West has been generated since the terrorist outrage of September 11, 2001. Atheists and agnostics have used the attacks that occurred in New York and elsewhere to reinforce their argument that religion is inherently irrational and dangerous, while other commentators have contended that such actions are contrary to the spirit of Islam or of any other world faith tradition. There is no doubt that fundamentalism — the search for certainty through a return to the literal meaning of Scripture — is rife across a range of faiths, and that it can result in acts of violence that repudiate the very ethical basis of their founders. In the widespread scepticism of our age, one can appreciate the significance of Jung's remark in *Psychological Types* that 'fanaticism is overcompensated doubt.'

An important theme running through the debate is the tension between the traditionalism of Islamic culture and the (as many see it) corrosive effects of modern liberal culture. This is one of the aspects of the interface between East and West that has interested the Prince of Wales in the last decade, especially since three of the major exponents of the perennial philosophy — Guénon, Schuon and Nasr — are rooted in Islamic mysticism. The Prince's first major speech on this topic was given in October 1993 as Patron of the Centre for Islamic Studies in Oxford. The Prince used the occasion to make a plea for genuine mutual understanding, especially in view of Britain being a multi-cultural society in an increasingly interdependent world. The Prince pointed out that there are one billion Muslims worldwide. Many millions of them live in countries of the Commonwealth. Ten million or more of them live in the West, and around one million here in Britain. Our own Islamic community has been growing and flourishing for decades. There are nearly five hundred mosques in Britain.

From the perspective of mid-2004, it is poignant that the Prince then went on to express his outrage and despair about the systematic destruction by Saddam Hussein of the unique way of life of the Marsh Arabs of Southern Iraq. The supreme and tragic irony, he commented:

... of what has been happening to the Shia population of Iraq — especially in the ancient city and holy shrine of

Kerbala — is that after the western allies took immense care to avoid bombing such holy places (and I remember begging General Schwarzkopf when I met him in Riyadh in December 1990, before the actual war began to liberate Kuwait, to do his best to protect such shrines during any conflict), it was Saddam Hussein himself, and his terrifying regime, who caused the destruction of some of Islam's holiest sites.

... and now we have to witness the deliberate draining of the marshes and the near total destruction of a unique habitat, together with an entire population that has depended on it since the dawn of human civilization. The international community has been told the draining of the marshes is for agricultural purposes. How many more obscene lies do we have to be told before action is actually taken? Even at the eleventh hour it is still not too late to prevent a total cataclysm. I pray that this might at least be a cause in which Islam and the West could join forces for the sake of our common humanity.

The Prince is well aware of the many intractable and deep-seated problems that underlie many of the most war-torn areas of the world such as Bosnia, and of the underlying causes of such conflicts. However, he adds that conflict also arises, tragically, from an inability to understand, and from the powerful emotions which, out of misunderstanding, lead to distrust and fear.' He urges his audience that 'we must not slide into a new era of danger and division because governments and peoples, communities and religions, cannot live together in peace in a shrinking world.

The Prince argues that the common roots of Judaism. Christianity and Islam make for more bonds than divisions:

Islam and Christianity share a common monotheistic vision: a belief in one divine God, in the transience of our earthly life, in our accountability for our actions, and in the assurance of life to come. We share many key values in common: respect for knowledge, for justice, compassion towards the poor and underprivileged, the importance of family life, respect for parents. 'Honour thy father and thy mother' is a Quranic precept too. Our history has been closely bound up together.

However, much of that history has been one of conflict — for instance in the Crusades — which has generated the continuing fear and distrust. Islam has historically been regarded as a threat — 'in medieval times as a military conqueror, and in more modern times as a source of intolerance, extremism and terrorism.' His chief current regret, however, is that 'our judgement of Islam has been grossly distorted by taking the extremes to be the norm.' In fact, the Prince continues, the basis of Islamic law is equity and compassion, and we should study how the law is actually practised before jumping to premature conclusions. The same goes for the frequently publicized position of women in traditional Islamic societies like the Taliban in Afghanistan: 'women are not automatically second-class citizens because they live in Islamic countries. We cannot judge the position of women in Islam aright if we take the most conservative Islamic states as representative of the whole.'

The Prince reminded his audience that 'we in the West need also to understand the Islamic world's view of us. There is nothing to be gained, and much harm to be done, by refusing to comprehend the extent to which many people in the Islamic world genuinely fear our own Western materialism and mass culture as a deadly challenge to their Islamic culture and way of life.' Equally, he adds, 'the West's attitude to some of the more rigorous aspects of Islamic life, needs to be understood in the Islamic world.' Mutual understanding is a two-way process.

This 'would help us understand what we have commonly come to see as the threat of Islamic fundamentalism.' He elaborates: 'we need to be careful of that emotive label, "fundamentalism", and distinguish, as Muslims do, between revivalists, who choose to take the practice of their religion most devoutly, and fanatics or extremists who use this devotion for their political ends.' This is a point that has not been made in any of the commentaries in the last two years but which has its historical parallels going back to the Crusades and beyond. For example, Pope Urbanus absolved the crusaders in advance of the massacres they would perform, thus using religion for political purposes. In such cases the religious leader does not speak for Jesus, any more than Bin Laden speaks for Mohamed.

The Prince goes on: 'among the many religious, social and political causes of what we might more accurately call the Islamic revival is a powerful feeling of disenchantment, of the realization that Western technology and material things are insufficient, and that a deeper meaning to life lies elsewhere in the essence of Islamic belief.' This same spiritual malaise is present in the West, as we have seen above.

He also warns against simplistic interpretations:

> At the same time, we must not be tempted to believe that extremism is in some way the hallmark and essence of the Muslim. Extremism is no more the monopoly of Islam than it is the monopoly of other religions, including Christianity. The vast majority of Muslims, though personally pious, are moderate in their politics. Theirs is the 'religion of the middle way … if we are to understand this important movement, we must learn to distinguish clearly between what the vast majority of Muslims believe and the terrible violence of a small minority among them, which civilized people everywhere must condemn.

The Prince went on to outline the cultural debt owed by the West to Islam in terms of the preservation of classical learning in the Dark Ages:

> Not only did Muslim Spain gather and preserve the intellectual content of ancient Greek and Roman civilization, it also interpreted and expanded upon that civilization, and made a vital contribution of its own in so many fields of human endeavour — in science, astronomy, mathematics, algebra (itself an Arabic word), law, history, medicine, pharmacology, optics, agriculture, architecture, theology, music. Averroes and Avenzoor, like their counterparts Avicenna and Rhazes in the East, contributed to the study and practice of medicine in ways from which Europe benefited for centuries afterwards.

Islam nurtured and preserved the quest for learning. In the words of the tradition, 'the ink of the scholar is more sacred than the blood of the martyr.' Cordoba in the tenth century was by far the most civilized city of Europe. We know of lending libraries in Spain at the time King Alfred was making terrible blunders with the culinary arts in this country. It is said that the 400,000 volumes in its ruler's library amounted to more books than all the libraries of the rest of Europe put together. That was made possible because the Muslim world acquired from China the skill of making paper more than 400 years before the rest of non-Muslim Europe.

The Prince elaborated further:

Many of the traits on which modern Europe prides itself came to it from Muslim Spain. Diplomacy, free trade, open borders, the techniques of academic research, of anthropology, etiquette, fashion, various types of medicine, hospitals, all came from this great city of cities. Medieval Islam was a religion of remarkable tolerance for its time, allowing Jews and Christians the right to practise their inherited beliefs, and setting an example which was not, unfortunately, copied for many centuries in the West. The surprise is the extent to which Islam has been a part of Europe for so long, first in Spain, then in the Balkans, and the extent to which it has contributed so much towards the civilization which we all too often think of, wrongly, as entirely Western.

He concludes: 'Islam is part of our past and our present, in all fields of human endeavour. It has helped to create modern Europe. It is part of our own inheritance, not a thing apart.' More than this, Islam has something vital to contribute to the West: 'at the heart of Islam is its preservation of an integral view of the Universe. Islam — like Buddhism and Hinduism — refuses to separate man and nature, religion and science, mind and matter, and has preserved a metaphysical and unified view of ourselves and the world around us. At the core of Christianity there still lies an integral view of the sanctity of the world, and a clear sense of the trusteeship and responsibility given to us for our natural surroundings.' The West has lost this integrated view of the world: 'a comprehensive philosophy of nature is no longer part of our everyday beliefs.'

The Prince makes a plea for the rediscovery of an all-embracing approach to the world around us: 'this crucial sense of oneness and trusteeship of the vital sacramental and spiritual character of the world about us is surely something important we can re-learn from Islam.' The Prince is aware that critics will accuse him of 'living in the past, of refusing to come to terms with reality and modern life.' On the contrary, he continues, 'what I am appealing for is a wider, deeper, more careful understanding of our world; for a metaphysical as well as a material dimension to our lives, in order to recover the balance we have abandoned, the absence of which, I believe, will prove disastrous in the long term. If the ways of thought found in Islam and other religions can help us in that search, then there are things for us to learn from this system of belief which I suggest we ignore at our peril.' The Prince does not dichotomize these issues like his critics: he is always careful to present a balanced and comprehensive perspective — 'metaphysical as well as material, not metaphysical rather than material.'

The Prince returned to the theme of Islam and the West in a speech — *A Sense of the Sacred: Building Bridges between Islam and the West* — given at a seminar at Wilton Park, December 1996. The choice of theme was the Prince's own, and he began by admitting how difficult it was for us contemporary people to talk about it:

> But I am encouraged by the fact that, whenever I have
> summoned up my courage to speak about this subject in
> the past — even to groups of hard-headed, practical
> people like international financiers or property
> developers, it seems always to have struck an
> extraordinary chord, and captured a remarkable degree of
> attention. My belief is that in each one of us there is a
> distant echo of the sense of the sacred, but that the

majority of us are terrified to admit its existence for fear of ridicule and abuse. This fear of ridicule, even to the extent of mentioning the name of God, is a classic indication of the loss of meaning in so-called Western civilization.

The loss of an integrated view of the sacredness of nature has left us adrift in a meaningless universe, which the Prince regards as a serious situation. His proposal is that we have something to learn from those traditions, like Islam, which have not lost such a view and have retained a 'deep respect for the timeless traditions of the natural order.' His diagnosis of our situation is, like that of Schuon and others, that scientific materialism has assumed a monopoly of intellectual authority, which has unbalanced our culture and led to a dis-integration:

> Modern materialism in my humble opinion is unbalanced and increasingly damaging in its long-term consequences. Yet nearly all the great religions of the world have held an integral view of the sanctity of the world. The Christian message with, for example, its deeply mystical and symbolic doctrine of the Incarnation, has been traditionally a message of the unity of the worlds of spirit and matter, and of God's manifestation in this world and in mankind. But during the last three centuries, in the Western world at least, a dangerous division has come into being in the way we perceive the world around us. Science has tried to assume a monopoly — even a tyranny — over our understanding. Religion and science have become separated, with the result, as William Wordsworth said, 'Little we see in nature that is ours'. Science has attempted to take over the natural world from God, with the result that it has fragmented the cosmos and relegated the sacred to a separate, and secondary, compartment of our understanding, divorced from the practical day-to-day existence.

The Prince is right that science is now the primary intellectual authority and that some vociferous scientists have pushed religion to the margins, but the situation is not now as bad as he supposes here. For the Prince, the sacred is central and primary, and is reflected in his integral understanding of the natural world as a 'theophany' or manifestation of the divine. This is a position with a long lineage, even if not currently fashionable. The Prince thinks that 'we are only now beginning to gauge the disastrous results of this [materialistic] outlook':

> We in the Western world seem to have lost a sense of the wholeness of our environment, and of our immense and inalienable responsibility to the whole of creation. This has led to an increasing failure to appreciate or understand tradition, and the wisdom of our forebears accumulated over the centuries. Indeed, tradition is positively discriminated against — as if it was some socially unacceptable disease ...

The loss of wholeness also manifests as alienation, a loss of connection and a loss of responsibility. The Prince regrets the disdain with which tradition is treated, and suggest that a more integrated approach is needed, where natural science acknowledges its own limits:

> In my view, a more holistic approach is needed in our contemporary world. Science has done the inestimable service of showing us a world much more complex than we ever imagined. But in its modern, materialist, one-dimensional form, it cannot explain everything. God is not merely the ultimate Newtonian mathematician or the mechanistic clockmaker. Francis Bacon said that God will not produce miracles to convince those who cannot see the miracle of a growing blade of grass or falling rain. As science and technology have become increasingly separated from ethical, moral and sacred considerations, so have the implications of such a separation become more sombre and horrifying — as we see, for example, in genetic manipulation, or in the consequences of the kind of (scientific) arrogance so blatant in the scandal of BSE.

The Prince now comes to the 'bridge' of his title, signalling a new Renaissance with the revival of interest in sacred traditions:

> But there remains a need to rediscover the bridge between what the great faiths of the world have recognized as our inner and our outer worlds, our physical and our spiritual nature. That bridge is the expression of our humanity. It fulfils this role through the medium of traditional knowledge and art, which have civilized mankind and without which civilization could not long be maintained. After centuries of neglect and cynicism the transcendental wisdom of the great religious traditions, including the Judaeo-Christian and the Islamic, and the metaphysics of the Platonic tradition which was such an important inspiration for Western philosophical and spiritual ideas is finally being rediscovered.

The Prince then makes a direct statement of the heart of his spiritual philosophy:

> I have always felt that tradition is not a man-made element in our lives, but a God-given intuition of natural rhythms, of the fundamental harmony which emerges from the union of those paradoxical opposites which exist in every aspect of nature. Tradition reflects the timeless order of the cosmos, and anchors us into an awareness of the great mysteries of the universe so that, as Blake put it, we can see the whole universe in an atom and eternity in a moment. That is why I believe Man is so much more than just a biological phenomenon resting on what we now seem to define as 'the bottom line' of the great balance sheet of life, according to which art and culture are seen increasingly as optional extras in life.

The Prince appreciates that an essential innocence has been destroyed, and destroyed everywhere, but continues: 'I nevertheless believe that the survival of civilized values, as we have inherited them from our ancestors, depends on the corresponding survival in our hearts of that profound sense of the sacred and the spiritual.' Humanism is not enough, we need to plumb the depths of our being to find a sacred core of unity. The Prince argues that a rediscovery of an integrated view of the sacred can have important implications for healing, the environment and agriculture, as well as for architecture and urban planning. He concludes:

> The approaching Millennium may be the ideal catalyst for helping to explore and stimulate these links, and I hope we shall not ignore the opportunity this gives us to rediscover the spiritual underpinning of our entire existence. For myself, I am convinced that we cannot afford, for the health and sustainability of a civilized existence, any longer to ignore these timeless features of our world. A sense of the sacred can, I believe, help provide the basis for developing a new relationship of understanding which can only enhance the relations between our two faiths — and indeed between all faiths — for the benefit of our children and future generations.

In November 2001, the holy month of Ramadan, as he observed, the Prince launched London Muslim Centre Project at the East London Mosque with Prince Mohammad Al-Faisal of Saudi Arabia. The Prince's Foundation, through its Visual Islamic and Traditional Arts (VITA) programme, was involved in the project (see below), which provides a facility for the whole community. The Prince used the occasion to express his view that 'it is particularly important that we encourage our children to learn from and appreciate the many cultures that make up their personal heritage.' He again emphasized that Christianity, Islam and Judaism share many of the same spiritual beliefs and the key social values of 'compassion, tolerance, respect for family and the community, belief in justice and the search for greater wisdom and understanding.' He concluded: 'nobody has a monopoly on the truth. To recognize that is, I believe, a first step to real wisdom, and a vital blow against the suspicion and misunderstanding that too often characterizes the public relationships between different faiths.'

## The Prince's School for Traditional Arts

*All traditional art is profoundly and inseparably rooted in the innermost aspect of religion.*

Dr Martin Lings

The Visual Islamic and Traditional Arts Programme (VITA) was founded in 1984 by Professor Keith Critchlow at the Royal College of Art to specialize in the arts and architecture of Islam, but it has since extended its interests to include the traditional arts of other civilizations. It is now housed within the Prince's Foundation. VITA aims to convey an understanding of the sacred and to encourage the appreciation of the universal values that are fundamental to the art of the great traditions of the world. VITA promotes an awareness amongst its students that the beauty of form, pattern and colour as manifested in the various branches of Islamic art (or indeed in any traditional art), are not simply aesthetically pleasing or demonstrations of good design but represent a more profound universal order. VITA's perspective on art and architecture is that they are integrated into life as a whole. Artistic activity is 'neither a luxury nor a subjective psychological experiment; nor is it a whimsical exercise in nostalgia — it is a contemplative art [path] based on spiritual truths.'

VITA was responsible for awarding the first doctoral degrees at the Royal College of Art and has been a pioneer of practical post-graduate degrees at Masters and Doctoral level. On its transfer to the Prince of Wales's Institute of Architecture in 1993, the VITA programme was awarded validation for its degrees from the University of Wales. VITA is unique in the Western world in offering a programme that integrates a comprehensive understanding of the philosophy and practical skills of craftsmanship at post-graduate level.

With this in mind, the students study art from 'within': for instance through learning the practical skills of geometry, and simultaneously learning its significance as the language underpinning the sacred and traditional arts of the world, students are offered the opportunity to participate in the contemplative nature of art. They are enabled to realize through activity and participation — rather than observation and theoretical study — that the intricate and subtle patterns transcend the purely decorative realm and embody a profound and timeless beauty. Through their work, the students also perform a further service by making a practical contribution to the survival of the traditional arts. The course offers candidates from different cultures all over the world the chance to study and practise a traditional art/craft as a vocation and is by its very nature a creative form of international exchange.

The VITA Programme balances technique with beauty, the teaching of practical skills with the background and symbolic meaning inherent within the art produced by these skills. The course embodies the root meaning of the word 'educate' — that is, to 'draw forth' or 'bring out' latent talent and skills, rather than to 'push in'; this means that both staff and students work and discuss actively together. Craftsmanship, according to VITA director Dr Khaled Azzam, is both a process and a spiritual experience. Geometry is absolutely central as one of the four traditional arts/sciences of the 'Seven Liberal Arts' ('liberal' in the sense of liberating the soul from material concerns) and was considered as a universal language by Plato. Geometry as a basic matrix provides the link between all the sacred and traditional arts.

The course begins with the geometry of structure and space through an understanding of dimension. VITA also introduces students to the other three liberal arts: Arithmetic, Music or Harmony, and Astronomy or Cosmology — as variously interpreted by the Greek, Judaic, Islamic and Christian Traditions. Other skills include calligraphy in relation to the symbolism of the Arabic alphabet, painting methods and preparation of materials, tile- and model-making, Islimi or Arabesque with biomorphic forms based on the flowing patterns in nature and the geometric principles already learned, stained glass, icon or miniature painting, Japanese papermaking, lettering and stonecarving. The students also undertake an architectural project within the context of a course on Islamic architecture, and have to design a small sanctuary. In the second year, students work on their own projects that are exhibited to the public in June.

The exhibition catalogue gives each student a chance to explain their project and reflect on their experience of the course. One of their works is illustrated — pots, tiles, paintings, jewellery, carvings — and all convey that tangible sense of beauty and proportion to which we are inwardly tuned. They therefore feed the soul. So do some of the inspiring comments by students: 'Two profound notions I will forever take with me are Subtlety and the Centre'; ... 'One of the most valuable things I have learnt at VITA is how to actualize an idea — I have witnessed that, by using hand, heart and mind, a simple sketch can develop into a beautiful object'; ... 'It is Truth and Beauty which are the life force of traditional works of art — by working in a traditional and disciplined way I aim to reflect and embody these qualities in my vessels.'

VITA also runs community education programmes aimed at fostering links with ethnic minorities by encouraging them — and especially Muslim youth — to rediscover and reassess their cultural heritage within the context of modern Britain. There are special relationships with the East London Mosque, Mulberry School in Shoreditch (where a summer school is held for mainly Bengali A level art students), and Islamiyah School (where an arts curriculum has been designed). VITA has project links with universities and institutions around the world, notably in Jordan, Abu Dhabi, Lahore, and Karachi. Other VITA projects have included the Muslim Prayer Space in the Millennium Dome, interior design at Ar-Rum, a Muslim Centre in Clerkenwell, a building extension at the East London Mosque, the Carpet Garden for the 2001 Chelsea Flower Show (now installed at Highgrove), and a ceiling for a house in Queen Anne's Gate.

The VITA programme thus makes a significant educational and practical contribution to the cultivation of sacred traditions of art by keeping a flame alight and sending out its students to practise their crafts and enhance the beauty of the environments in which they work.

## The Prince as Defender of Faith

*In an age of secularism and cynicism it seems to me essential that all men of faith — those who acknowledge the existence of a higher dimension beyond the narrow, destructive confines of the egocentric world view — should come together in recognition of a common understanding of what is sacred and enduring in the human experience.*

The Prince of Wales

As heir to the throne, the Prince of Wales is also heir to the Sovereign's special role, dating back to the sixteenth century, as Defender of the Faith and Supreme Governor of the Church of England — the first title was granted by Pope Leo X to King Henry VIII, and the second stems from Henry's subsequent establishment of the Church of England. The Prince of Wales is profoundly attached to the traditional rites of the Church of England and especially to the *Book of Common Prayer*, which he described in 1997 as 'a most glorious part of our heritage and a book of prayer for the whole community.' The Prince asked: 'why does the Prayer Book matter, together with the numinous mystery of its language?' And his answer: 'because, as its very survival over the centuries has shown, its language and liturgy are sensitive to the profound human need for continuity and permanence, and have shown themselves not of an age but of all time.'

For the Prince, 'the genius of Cranmer's Prayer Book lies in the conveyance of that sense of the sacred through the power and majesty of the language of the Prayer Book that, in the words of the Collect, "Among the sundry and manifold changes of the world, our hearts may surely be fixed where true joys are to be found".' In this context, he reminded his Prayer Book Society audience that 'The Orthodox Church, for example, has never lost, abandoned or diminished the sacred beauty and symbolism of its liturgy. The great, overwhelming sadness for me — and I am sure for you too — is that we seem to have forgotten that for solemn occasions we need exceptional and solemn language: something which transcends our everyday speech. We commend the "beauty of holiness", yet we forget the holiness of beauty.'

This leads the Prince on to some observations about language that will reappear when we look at his views on education:

> If we encourage the use of mean, trite, ordinary language
> we encourage a mean, trite and ordinary view of the
> world we inhabit. Many people look in dismay at what
> has been happening to our language in the very place
> where it evolved. They wonder what it is about our
> country and society that our language has become so

impoverished, so sloppy and limited — that we have
arrived at such a dismal wasteland of banality, cliché and
casual obscenity. For many, it has been an absolute
tragedy to witness the abandonment of the idea of
English as something really to be learned by effort and
application, by long and careful familiarity with those
who had shown how to clothe their thought in the most
precise, vivid and memorable language. We had ended up
leaving ourselves open to the terrible accusation once
levelled by that true master of the banal, Samuel
Goldwyn: 'You've improved it worse!'

The Prince concludes: 'So, the Prayer Book's survival is, I
believe, a touchstone of our ability as a society to value its spiritual roots, its liturgical continuity, and its very identity as a
nation of believers.'

The Queen reminded us in her Golden Jubilee Christmas
Message how much strength she draws from the message of
hope in the Christian gospel, adding that she relied greatly on
her own faith to guide her through the good times and the bad:
'I know that the only way to live my life is to try to do what is
right, to take the long view, to give of my best in all that the day
brings, and to put my trust in God.' The Prince of Wales would
echo such sentiments, but he has made it clear that he regards
his potential remit as wider than the Church of England alone,
as we have seen in the previous section. It was his deep-rooted
belief in the importance of understanding the timeless role of
spirit and the sacred in a world increasingly dominated by a
materialist and short-term outlook which informed the Prince's
comment in 1994 that, 'I personally would rather see it [his
future role] as Defender of Faith, not the Faith.' The controversy
which ensued tended to obscure the Prince's explanation of his
deep concern that 'the whole concept of faith itself, or anything
beyond this existence, beyond life itself, is considered old fash-
ioned and irrelevant.' The multi-faith nature of modern British
society means that this thought applies to people in Britain of all
faiths.

As the Bishop of London observed in a sermon preached in
the Chapel Royal on the fiftieth anniversary of the Queen's

accession, the Queen as a Christian monarch embodies 'a vocational approach to life, lived, not as a consumer with personal gratification as the supreme good, but as a servant of God whose role is to strengthen the whole community.' Dr Chartres went on to remark 'for a Christian monarch, the whole community includes people of different faiths and none.' The monarch makes a free response to God's call in the Coronation service, and 'Christian monarchy embodies a life, a fully human life, lived in the presence and calling of God who dignifies all humanity.' The Prince of Wales would fully endorse this view of the monarchy as a vocation, and one that requires considerable personal sacrifice even if it has its corresponding privileges.

In recent years the Prince of Wales has demonstrated his respect for the other great faiths by visiting their holy places and places of worship, including a newly constructed Hindu temple in Neasden, north west London, and a new mosque in Northolt, west London, in 1996; the United Synagogue in St John's Wood, north London, in April 1998; and Buddhist shrines during his Asian tour in 1998. During an official tour of central Europe, also in 1998, the Prince acknowledged the importance of the Orthodox Christian tradition by visiting a number of important churches and monasteries on Mount Athos, a place to which he has made subsequent private visits on retreat.

In 2002, the Prince launched the Respect for Faiths initiative, designed to encourage interfaith good neighbourliness at a community level. It emerged from a discussion in 1998 about a 'way to celebrate the Millennium in a form which had a strong spiritual component; an idea which would have resonance and purpose with people of faith; an idea which could, perhaps, change attitudes. Something to encourage tolerance, respect and understanding.' The idea was raised again by the Chief Rabbi, Professor Jonathan Sacks in the autumn of 2001 in the context of finding a way in which the Faith Communities could celebrate the themes of community and service as part of the Golden Jubilee year. The simple central idea is 'to make a gift of time to someone of another faith — to share and learn together, to enjoy the company of people of a different culture, faith and experience.'

The initiative was launched at a time when examples of intolerance, national and international, abound. So the Prince observed that 'tolerance is an easy word to pronounce but it seems to be very difficult to enact in our lives. And yet it is such a tragedy that when the various faith communities have so much in common its members should so often be divided by the different ways we have of interpreting the inner meaning of our existence.' He reminded his audience that 'the founders of our ancient religions, after all, were those truly enlightened souls whose own lives were the most profound examples of how love and forgiveness, both on the outer and inner planes, are the only means of breaking the cycle of cause and effect — of hatred, vengeance and conflict — and of reconciling the opposites in our relations with each other.'

The Prince concluded:

> So, when we give a gift of time, let's remember that we are in fact united by a common bond of faith — faith in a sacred dimension beyond ourselves; faith in, for want of a better description, a divine 'essence' to the meaning of our existence; faith in the integrity of life itself.
>
> And this bond is something infinitely precious at a time in human history when we have already crossed the threshold into a world where faith itself is denigrated, where humanity is to be re-designed in Man's, not God's image, and Nature is to be re-engineered for the purposes of our own convenience.
>
> Faced with the ultimate consequences of such Promethean activities, I would have thought that all people of Faith — with a capital 'F' — have every reason to put their differences and intolerances to one side and to unite in defence of the Sacred.

As some commentators pointed out, there is a danger in extending respect and tolerance to the intolerable. The faith of the fanatic manifests as a dogmatic political ideology that favours self-sacrifice and martyrdom above all else. To this extent the fundamentalist fanatic is careless of the humanity of others, as terrorist outrages world-wide have demonstrated. Nor are such men open to dialogue: theirs is the only way to salvation; all other paths are mistaken and their followers doomed to perdition unless converted. And to the extent that such fanaticism is nurtured by ecclesiastical assurances of heavenly bliss for the perpetrators, religious leaders are guilty by association. In his destructive undertaking, the fanatical adherent brings his faith into disrepute by shattering the basic and irreducible spiritual order of Love. In his speeches on Islam and the West, the Prince has made it quite clear that he abhors such fanatical commitments and actions. His interest is in promoting the kind of openness, tolerance and dialogue that such approaches intrinsically deny.

At a deeper level the Prince is interested in what Frithjof Schuon calls the transcendent unity of religions. This means that each tradition needs humbly to acknowledge its own incompleteness and, as the Prince advocates, to listen and learn from what other traditions have to say. At the same time this dialogue enables traditions to appreciate the ways in which they all embody — even if they do not live up to — universal principles such as Love and Wisdom, as the Bulgarian sage Peter Deunov prophetically proclaimed:

> Love is necessary for the transformation of the world. It is the only force which can bring peace between the nations, each of which has a mission to accomplish on earth. Love is beginning to appear; goodness, justice and light will triumph; it is simply a question of time. Religions need to be purified; they all contain something divine, but this has been obscured by the repeated addition of human conceptions. All believers will have to get together and agree on one single principle: to make love the basis of any and every belief. Love and brotherhood, that is the common basis.

Perhaps the defence of faith is ultimately a defence of Love and Wisdom.

# Worldviews in Transition:
## Towards a Spiritual Renaissance?

*Man is not only an organism but is also the bearer of absolute value. As such, he is sacred and, regardless of sex, age, race and social status, cannot be used as a mere means for anything or anybody. Likewise, the great values of culture — science and technology, religion and philosophy, ethics and art — are a reflection, a realization, of the absolute values in the empirical world. As such, they cannot be degraded to mere instrumentalities for purely sensual enjoyment or utility. They are in themselves ends.*

Pitirim Sorokin

In his Radio 4 broadcast on January 1st 2000, the Prince reflected that the millennium was a time for both hope and renewal as we enter new phases of development. As we try to understand and explain the larger patterns of history and the decay and renewal of civilizations, we have been helped in the last eighty years by the publication of a number of sweeping analyses of the prospects for Western culture. Oswald's Spengler's massive tome *The Decline of the West* appeared at the end of the First World War, arguing that cultures, like organisms, went through cyclical phases of growth and decay. Arnold Toynbee's *Study of History* was published in twelve volumes between 1934 and 1961. He proposes key factors involved in the genesis, growth, breakdown and disintegration of civilizations, ending with reflections on the outlook for Western civilization. One of the great pioneers of such cross-cultural studies was Pitirim Sorokin, who was born in 1889 and was a cabinet minister in the 1917 Russian government. He had the singular but unenviable distinction of being sentenced to death by both the Tsarists and the Bolsheviks before being banished from the Soviet Union in 1922. He went on to become founding Professor of Sociology at Harvard. In his book *The Crisis of Our Age* he helps explain the tensions between science and religion and the transitional phase in which Western culture now finds itself. He distinguishes three main systems of truth and knowledge that correspond with three main supersystems of culture, which he calls ideational, sensate and idealistic:

*Ideational truth* is the truth revealed by the grace of God, through his mouthpieces (the prophets, mystics and founders of religion), disclosed in a supersensory way through mystic experience, direct revelation, divine intuition and inspiration. Such a truth may be called the truth of faith. It is regarded as infallible, yielding adequate knowledge about the true-reality values. *Sensate truth* is the truth of the senses, obtained through our organs of sense perception. If the testimony of the senses shows that "snow is white and cold", the proposition is true; if our senses testify that snow is not white and not cold, the proposition becomes false. *Idealistic truth* is a synthesis of both, made by our reason. In regard to sensory phenomena, it recognizes the role of the sense organs as the source and criterion of the validity or invalidity of a proposition.

Readers will readily understand Sorokin's argument that Western mediaeval culture (and indeed contemporary Islamic culture) was a preponderantly ideational culture based on faith and that the rise of science in the seventeenth century gradually replaced it with a rationalist sensate culture where the truth of the senses prevails. The Enlightenment ideal of reason has until now mainly been applied only to the evidence of the senses and mathematics, rather than to the integration of supersensory insights into a new science of consciousness.

Sorokin explains that a fully developed sensate system of truth 'is inevitably materialistic, viewing everything, openly or covertly, in its materialistic aspects ...the general tendency of the sensate mentality (is) to regard the world — even man, his culture and consciousness itself — materialistically, mechanically, behaviouristically.' This is exactly the position of modern science and philosophy and is clearly revealed 'by the fact that the terms "scientific" and "true", "unscientific" and "false" are synonymous.' Sorokin and the Prince both argue that the crisis in our self-image and the relativism of our value systems require a restoration of the spirit, a rediscovery of the sense of the sacred.

Sorokin also outlines in some detail the ways in which he sees contemporary sensate culture disintegrating, and he does not mince his words. Competent arbiters will be replaced by 'the qualified ignoramuses of the daily press ... by writers of best-sellers and of other varieties of cultural chewing gum ... The statesmen will be replaced by politicians ... and ... at the late stages of sensate culture, its "machinery of selection" will be picking mainly pseudo-values [for this read image] and neglecting real values.' He goes on, prophetically anticipating the worst excesses of post-modernism: 'The distinction between true and false, right and wrong, beautiful and ugly, positive and negative value will be more and more obliterated ... mental and moral atomism will grow and, with it, mental and moral anarchy.'

One widespread reaction to this growing moral relativism and spiritual uncertainty is a resort to fundamentalism, whether Christian, Islamic or Hindu. This corresponds to what Sorokin would call a new ideational phase of culture which is hostile to sensate science. The other more forward-looking avenue, which is gathering momentum as a grass roots movement of those termed as 'Cultural Creatives,' lies in what Sorokin calls an 'integralist conception of truth, reality and values.' A consequence of this integralist view is that social relationships should be guided by sublime love. Moreover, since truth, goodness and beauty are absolute values, they should not be relativized or degraded; nor can science claim complete freedom from control by goodness and beauty, hence it cannot and should not serve any malign purpose. The same principles apply to art as an embodiment of sacred principles, as we shall see in the next chapter. From an integralist perspective there should be no antagonism between science, religion, philosophy, ethics and art since, in the light of an adequate theory of true reality and value, they all serve the purpose of 'the unfolding of the Absolute in the relative empirical world, to the greater nobility of Man and to the greater glory of God.'

Sorokin adds: 'Our remedy demands a complete change of the contemporary mentality, a fundamental transformation of our system of values and the profoundest modification of our conduct towards other people, cultural values and the world at large. All this cannot be achieved without the incessant, strenuous, active efforts of every individual in that direction.' From this integralist perspective, the philosophy of the Prince of

Wales is a heartfelt response to our cultural crisis. Sorokin insists that previous societies have not been preserved from dissolution by practical and expert manipulation of economic, political, genetic or other factors, but 'mainly through the transmutation of values, the spiritualization of mentality, and the socialization of conduct and ennoblement of social relations effected through the medium of religion.' The kind of integrated spiritual philosophy advanced by the Prince fulfils Sorokin's criteria of an essential reorientation of values, a spiritualization of mentality and a consequent ennoblement of conduct. In 1996, the Prince saw some beacons of light in this respect:

> There is, I believe, a resurgence of spirituality across the world; small beacons of civilizing values in the face of the all-pervading materialism of recent times, which represent a yearning to improve the deeper quality of our lives and to restore those enduring cultural priorities which represent a moral fountain in a world dominated by consumerism. If the Millennium can be used to respond to those feelings and emotions, it will fulfil a need which will last well beyond the year 2000, and add immeasurably to the quality of all our lives.

The adoption of such a spiritual (and ecological) worldview is essential if we are to emerge from our current predicament. It implies a profound integration of head and heart, of rationality and intuition, beyond the tension of opposites. It is a quest for wholeness that is part of the intrinsic dynamic of life, death and growth and it is the task of each individual. If we do not choose such a path of harmony and balance, disasters may supervene and the path will choose us, instead. In this case the awakening will be ruder and the collective suffering more intense, but the spirit will be restored to its rightful place.

# 5. The Golden Mean: Architecture and our Cultural Heritage — The Prince's Foundation

*Beauty is the splendour of the true.*

Plato

*It seems to be becoming harder and harder in this age to stick to what we believe — or feel. We are told constantly that we have to live in 'the real world' — but 'the real world' is within us. The reality is that 'Truth, Goodness and Beauty' in the outer, manifested world are only made possible through the inner, invisible pattern — the unmanifested archetype.*

The Prince of Wales

The Prince of Wales's concern with the countryside and landscape is mirrored in his commitment to its counterpart in the built environment and townscape. The appearance of both town and country result from policies that reflect our overall outlook and values. The above quotation from the Prince makes it clear that he is a Christian Platonist at heart. Christian Platonism has a long history within the Church of England, with the Cambridge Platonists like Ralph Cudworth in the seventeenth century and Dean Inge of St Paul's in the twentieth. The Prince believes that it is the 'inner, invisible patterns' that ultimately produce 'order out of chaos, civilized values rather than barbarism, revealed Truth instead of misguided, arrogant eccentricity.'

In referring back to the great perennial wisdom of the ancients, the Prince recalls their injunction that the key to the human dilemma lies in the subjugation of the ego 'and the search for the impossibly difficult goal of *humility*.' He goes on: 'all the traditional arts stress the need for humility and, above

all, for harmony with the pulsating heart of the Cosmos —
whether in Architecture, Music, Literature or Art. The same
applies in Agriculture, Medicine and Education, where the need
for a rediscovery of Tradition has never been more urgent.' For
the Prince, this involves a passionate plea for the recreation of
physical habitats and the sacred dimension:

> Only through this re-integration and renewal, through the
> rediscovery of harmony and balance that lies hidden, and
> waiting to be found again, within living traditions, can we
> even begin to hope to meet the accumulating challenges
> and supreme dangers of this century and avoid what, I
> have come to the reluctant conclusion, are the otherwise
> inevitable catastrophes that await a world awash with an
> untold plethora of 'information,' but utterly devoid of
> knowledge and wisdom.

## Principles of Sacred Art and Architecture

> *Civilizations are invisible, just as constitutions, states, and*
> *churches are, and this for the same reasons. But civilizations,*
> *too, have manifestations that are visible. By exploring the*
> *range, in space and time, one can ascertain the spatial and*
> *temporal bounds of the civilization that [a] style expresses. The*
> *visible works of art that reveal so much about their civilization*
> *are merely expressions of it. They are not that civilization*
> *itself...* The most potent of the forces that move human
> souls is the spirit that blows like the incalculable wind
> who passage is audible but invisible.
>
> Arnold Toynbee

Civilization is a rather grand word, popularized by the series of
television programmes of the same name by Kenneth Clark over
thirty years ago. Lord Clark said that he could not define civilization in abstract terms, but that he knew it when he saw it —and
he was looking at it when he stood on the Pont des Arts in Paris
in his opening programme. Few would disagree. 'Civilization' is
also the word used by Arnold Toynbee in his monumental *Study
of History*, and it can be seen from the quotation above that he

defines it in terms of what one might call its 'spirit,' the underlying principle that is expressed in various visible forms. In his inspiring work, *The Face of Glory*, William Anderson argues that

> ... the constant factor in the origins of civilizations is the presence in societies of men and women who have achieved the inner transformation and who have through their example or through their own works brought about a significantly deeper transformation of art, thought and the interpretation of knowledge for their own and succeeding generations. They are the ones who are conscious, who have realized the full possibilities of their natures, and whose lives work a change in the climate of opinion through this subtle influence of their existence.

In other words, such people have responded to an inner call to embody and manifest higher spiritual principles. Nor do they regard art simply as a form of individual self-expression.

The most obvious point to make about the philosophy of sacred art is that it assumes the actual existence of an inner, spiritual dimension of reality of which works of art are a physical embodiment. Sacred art requires an understanding of symbols, and the sacred work of art is itself a symbol that offers us an opportunity for contemplation. It expresses the higher or finer through the lower or coarser and leads the contemplator back to the higher order reality of which the symbol itself is an expression, thus completing the circle of contemplation. Sacred art, according to Seyyed Hossein Nasr, 'has a sacramental function and is, like religion itself, at once truth and presence.' Sages — self-realized spiritual teachers — are the embodiment of the Divine Centre, which is why they too are 'truth and presence,' and form the axis of traditional societies or, more specifically, their point of contact with the Centre, with which the modern world has lost contact. Sacred buildings, too, are 'points where contact can be made with the Source of being.'

Sacred art is also a reflection of Divine Beauty and 'the knowledge of the sacred cannot be separated from beauty,' for, as Nasr puts it, explaining our initial quotation from Plato, 'since beauty is the splendour of truth, the expression of truth is always accompanied by beauty. Beauty is a central value — indeed an intrinsic expression — of sacred art and absolutely essential to understanding the Prince's aesthetic approach.

The implication of this Platonic view of beauty is that the created order as a whole is sacred because God is immanent within it as unity within diversity, the One behind the many; the world is a theophany, or manifestation of the Divine if we have eyes to see it in that way. Moreover, the experience of beauty can elicit happiness or even bliss, which is no accident since, as the philosopher artist Frithjof Schuon observes, 'beauty is a reflection of divine bliss and, since God is Truth, the reflection of His bliss will be that mixture of happiness and truth which is to be found in all beauty.'

A special aspect of beauty is order, symmetry, proportion — another preoccupation of the Greeks reflected in their geometry and philosophy from Pythagoras onwards. Proportion, according to the architect Keith Critchlow, is concerned with 'balance, harmony and relatedness between things; between body and mind, nature and humanity, illusion and reality.' Proportion extends to conduct as well, whereby the arrogance of *hubris* is followed inexorably by a fateful *nemesis*, as Sophocles and other Greek dramatists illustrate so clearly. It is from this Greek tradition that we derive the classical proportions of the Golden Section.

In summary, sacred art and architecture see the world as a manifestation of Divine Being. They are founded on a science of symbolic forms that includes the principles of proportion, unity and order resting ultimately on the Platonic identity of the Good, the Beautiful and the True.

## The Prince's Vision of Britain

*We live in a world of objects, in other words a world of mere existence. Our architecture shows it. In London we are witnessing the destruction of a great city — every great architect admits it. Ruthlessly torn down are the most beautiful eighteenth-century houses and in their places are put up battery-hen boxes, machines simply to make money in offices, so that London is fast becoming one of the most mediocre cities in Europe architecturally and where there is neither civic nor spiritual pride.*

Cecil Collins

The officers of the Royal Institute of British Architects were shifting uneasily in their chairs in Hampton Court Palace as the Prince of Wales stood up to deliver his speech at their 150th anniversary dinner in May 1984 — they had seen an advance copy that day and had tried to prevent it from being delivered (or rather detonated) — but the Prince was adamant, for reasons that he explains in the first quotation above. After a few interesting observations about the architectural interests of his forebear Prince Albert, the Prince came bluntly to the point: 'for far too long, it seems to me, some planners and architects have consistently ignored the feelings and wishes of the mass of ordinary people in this country.' This is perhaps not too surprising since 'architects tend to have been trained to design buildings from scratch — to tear down and rebuild.' They do not often meet the users of their buildings, the Prince went on, 'consequently a large number of us have developed a feeling that architects tend to design houses for the approval of fellow architects and critics, not for the tenants.' Hence the Prince recommends a community approach encouraging local participation: 'to be concerned about the way people live, about the environment they inhabit and the kind of community that is created by that environment, should surely be one of the prime requirements of a really good architect.' And in those days a particular concern highlighted by the Prince — and since remedied — was disabled access.

Coming to specific examples in London, the Prince mentioned Mansion House Square as a place where a community approach could have been used: 'it would be a tragedy if the character and skyline of our capital city were to be further ruined and St Paul's dwarfed by yet another giant glass stump, better suited to downtown Chicago than the City of London.' Such 'glass stumps' have proliferated, to the general detriment of the London skyline, which was one of the most beautiful in the world before the Second World War. The destruction sustained in the Blitz is one of the chief causes that made way for the kind of post-war developments deplored by the Prince. Much of the architectural heritage of great European cities was destroyed — the rebuild in Dresden, is, if anything, even more depressing than in parts of London.

In a memorable and much-quoted passage, the Prince brings his case right up to date by asking what plans were proposed for the National Gallery in Trafalgar Square: 'instead of designing an extension to the elegant facade of the National Gallery which complements it and continues the concept of columns and domes, it looks as if we may be presented with a kind of municipal fire station, complete with the sort of tower that contains the siren.' This high-tech approach, said the Prince, would be more understandable if one 'demolished the whole of Trafalgar Square and started again with a single architect responsible for the entire layout, but what is proposed is like a monstrous carbuncle on the face of a much-loved and elegant friend.' He added that it was ironic to wish to display early Renaissance pictures in such an incongruous setting. He deplored the lack of curves and arches that express feeling in design: 'why has everything got to be vertical, straight, unbending, only at right angles — and functional?' The Prince finished with a quotation from Goethe — 'there is nothing more dreadful than imagination without taste' — and hoped that the next 150 years 'will see a new harmony between imagination and taste and in the relationship between the architects and the people of this country.'

The shockwaves began to reverberate immediately. The press seized on the Prince's colourful imagery and the architectural establishment responded along the lines that influential people without professional training should not air their views in public exactly the sentiment that the Prince was criticizing! A variant of the same argument was that he was using his position undemocratically — 'a new, undemocratic hurdle in the planning process' — a vacuous criticism when one considers that 99% of the 5,000 letters received after the Prince's film *A Vision of Britain* in 1988 were positive. Others accused him of looking backwards rather than forwards, when he himself makes it clear that he looks both ways — in terms of the continuity of a living tradition. The main point is that with this speech the Prince launched a public debate that has continued ever since.

The Prince's next substantial architectural foray was in December 1987, when he gave a speech at the Corporation of London Planning and Communication Committee's Annual Dinner in Mansion House. The problem faced by Corporation planners was 'how to create commercial architecture as effective as the Mansion House, or the Royal Exchange or Sir Edwin

Lutyens' pre-war Midland Bank — worthy celebrations, I would have said, of the fruits of commerce.' The same cannot be said, continued the Prince, for Bucklersbury House, the Stock Exchange Tower or Paternoster Square. And now there were plans afoot to create a new development around the spiritual centre of London, St Paul's Cathedral. In the reconstruction years after the bombing of 1940 — when Churchill had said that St Paul's had to be saved at all costs — and 'in spite of all sorts of elaborate rules supposedly designed to protect that great view, your predecessors, as the planners, architects and developers of the City, wrecked the London skyline and desecrated the dome of St Paul's.'

'Not only did they wreck the London skyline in general,' the Prince continued, 'they also did their best to lose the great dome in a jostling scrum of office buildings, so mediocre that the only way you ever remember them is by the frustration they induce — like a basketball team standing shoulder-to-shoulder between you and the Mona Lisa.' Admittedly, he said, 'in Paris, the French have built some pretty awful tower blocks in La Défense, but can you really imagine them building those same towers around Notre Dame?' This is the point: in other European cities like Munich and Warsaw, some attempt was made to restore buildings to their previous condition, whereas 'here, even the street where Shakespeare and Milton brought their manuscripts, the legendary Paternoster Row, "The Row", the very heart of publishing since Elizabethan times, was turned into a concrete service road leading to an underground car park!' The Prince made his main point in the most forceful language: 'You have to give this much to the Luftwaffe: when it knocked down our buildings, it didn't replace them with anything more offensive than rubble. We did that. Clausewitz called war the continuation of diplomacy by other means. Around St Paul's, planning turned out to be the continuation of war by other means.'

Paternoster Square, the Prince explained, was one of the first CDAs — Comprehensive Development Areas — 'praised by architects, it became the model for schemes that have destroyed the city centre of Bristol, Newcastle, Birmingham, Worcester — the list is endless. "The Rape of Britain", it has been called.' However, the Prince continued, there was a second chance for Paternoster Square and this time other views than the experts can be advanced. The Prince's message was that 'that large numbers of us in this country are fed up with being talked down to and dictated to by an existing planning, architectural and development establishment' — the very people who were only yards away in the audience.

The Prince said that he had been invited to comment on the plans of the seven finalists but confessed that he had been demoralized even by the Competition Brief:

> [whose] 'overriding commercial consideration' (without which the Paternoster Square project will not be built)— and I am now quoting from the document itself — 'is to provide as much office space of the highest quality and efficiency, as is possible within the planning constraints' — that, and what is called a 'bold concept for retailing.' A bold concept for retailing! What a challenge!

Then he added, with withering scorn: 'I suppose Sir Christopher Wren was inspired by the same sort of brief. "Give us a bold concept for worship, Sir Christopher — and the most efficient praying area within the planning constraints.'

This brief left the architects with little scope and every incentive to cram as much onto the site as possible; but none questioned the logic and priorities of the brief. Moreover, the planning system is set up in such a way that the public themselves can take no positive initiatives but can only react to developer's proposals and oppose their grim tactical determination designed to wear down any opposition: 'there must be something wrong with a system which involves public opinion at so late a stage that the only course left open to the public is to obstruct the development through whatever means the planning system allows.' The Prince identified three major shortcomings: first, that 'control over the design of buildings next to major monuments is fuzzy and, in practice, unenforceable.' Secondly, 'the Department of the Environment does not encourage planning authorities to set firm aesthetic guidelines in development.' Hence, 'as things stand, they are only justified in rejecting a proposal if it is absolutely hideous; anything merely ugly must be allowed to get through.' Thirdly, measures adopted for preserving the skyline have simply not worked. Why not introduce a height limit, the Prince suggested. Summing up, he comments that planning legislation has allowed architects and developers the 'wrong kind of freedom' enabling them to impose their own ideas on a hapless public.

The Prince put forward his own ideas for the square, including a human scale, the reconstruction of the mediaeval street plan, the use of such materials as soft red brick and stone dressings with some classical ornamentation, and artists working with artists and craftsmen. Although some people will say that the Prince is not living in the real world of Big Bang and 24-hour financial dealing, he argued that business people themselves prefer places with some character and charm. Even if, he remarked, this is the age of computers and word processors, 'why on earth do we have to be surrounded by buildings that look like such machines?' So the Prince saw 'no reason, then, why wealth should not finance beauty that is in harmony with tradition, today as in the past, adding that 'the London of Wren's time was the greatest trading empire the world has ever seen... prosperity and beauty need not exclude one another.' Hence, the Prince concluded, 'this is a good time to reassert a sense of vision and civilized values amidst all the excitement and commercialism of the City.'

Once again the impact was immediate — 'rather an interesting row,' as the Prince put it — and unleashed an avalanche of 2,000 mostly favourable letters to St James's Palace. After a long and protracted series of negotiations and events, the eventual choice of plan fell on the more classical design of Peter Simpson. The Prince returned to the question of the City skyline — especially the height, scale and context of tall buildings — in a speech in December 2001, shortly after the destruction of the Twin Towers. In previous ages, observed the Prince, 'towers were almost entirely reserved for monuments with a special ecclesiastical or civic status.' Yet the 'skyscraper' in its modern form, he continued, is something very different. 'Most obviously, it is a building whose function is utilitarian and commercial, rather than civic or sacred; a so-called "statement building" that is self-referential, and fulfilling no communal purpose whatsoever.' Nor does it facilitate the creation of community, which is so central to the life of the city: 'in geometric terms, it has more in common with an up-ended suburban cul-de-sac than with the creative networked urbanism of streets and squares.'

The Prince is not against tall buildings in principle, but insists that they should be placed where they fit properly. Hence new towers should ideally stand together to create a new skyline rather than destroy an existing one. Drawing an analogy between people and buildings, the Prince observed: 'people need to "fit" into the public realm and this is why we always used to cultivate manners, modesty, and gentleness. The same should be true of buildings, although I fear that so much of the Modernist aesthetic is based on the notion of "standing out" rather than "fitting in".' His constructive suggestions included 'a requirement for buildings beyond a certain mass or height to be mixed in use, a home for a variety of businesses and residents as well, and capable of meeting differing needs over time.' He proposed that, 'at the base, new buildings should properly address the streetscape and help define a public realm that is truly public in form and function. Ground floors need to include shops, restaurants and other amenities that bring people into the building and help it integrate with the surrounding townscape.' He continues: 'let's have no more of the left-over spaces that so often masquerade as public amenity — what Thomas Wolfe entertainingly described as "a turd in every plaza"!' Finally, 'at the top of these new structures, let's see genuine artistry that truly reaches the hearts and souls of those who look on, rather than the overblown phallic sculptures and depressingly predictable antennae that say more about an architectural ego than any kind of craftsmanship.'

In the summer of 1988, the Prince's *A Vision of Britain* was broadcast by the BBC. This gave him the chance to express his views in some detail and to illustrate them graphically. The corresponding illustrated book came out the following year. Both film and book are engaging and encourage readers to look more critically at modern city architecture and make their own assessments. Early in the book, the Prince expresses his overall concern with architects and developers: 'their philosophical approach to the whole question of the design of the built environment as it affects people and the lives they live.' In other words buildings must keep people in mind and be based on humane principles.

He states his own credo when he says: 'I believe that when a man loses contact with the past he loses his soul. Likewise, if we deny the architectural past — and the lessons to be learnt from our ancestors — then our buildings also lose their souls. If we abandon the traditional principles upon which architecture was based for 2,500 years or more, then our civilization suffers.' Once again we see the Prince arguing for a continuity rather than a break with the past, as he does in agriculture and medicine.

The Prince was unsparing in his judgement of uncongenial plans and buildings. Faced with new plans for Birmingham's Bullring (the book contains pictures and paintings of its illustrious past), the Prince 'chose his words to be as inoffensive as possible,' describing them as 'an unmitigated disaster' and 'a planned accident.' Lack of vision meant that 'Birmingham's city centre became a monstrous concrete maze where only cars felt at home. People were bound to feel lost. Cars were placed above people and people were placed one above another on concrete shelves.' The Prince describes with some relish an occasion when he was invited to help demolish a sixties car park in Bow, remarking that 'it's harder than it looks to knock down modern buildings.' He reflects: 'As I hammered away at the car park, it occurred to me that this was a symbol of the whole sad legacy of 1960s housing — an up-to-date dinosaur that was born extinct. A colossal fossil. It was never alive, but it hangs on like grim death.' True to his organic credentials, but not without irony, the Prince remarked that 'crushed tower block, mixed with soil, makes a very good basis for growing roses.' As we know, much more of this unprepossessing tower block architecture is now either falling down or being demolished.

The Prince was scathingly critical of the 1951 South Bank development in London, describing the National Theatre as 'a clever way of building a nuclear power station in the middle of London without anyone objecting.' Mondial House in the City is an excrescence 'redolent of a word processor' and No. 1 Poultry' looks rather like an old 1930s wireless.' As for the British Library, 'how can you even tell that it *is* a library? It has no character to suggest that it is a great public building. And the Reading Room looks more like the assembly hall of an academy for secret police.' Finally, 'London's Royal Free Hospital looks like an office block. It is doubtless superbly efficient medically, but body and soul shrink when confronted with menacing architecture like this.'

The Prince sees himself as the champion of the traditional and human scale and is therefore opposed to inhuman modernism. In the book he puts forward 'Ten Principles We Can Build Upon,' which have since been elaborated in the Poundbury architectural design guidance and form the basis of any development undertaken by the Duchy of Cornwall. In the introduction, the Prince writes that he believes that 'we have suffered too long from the imposition of a kind of nondescript, mediocre, synthetic, international style of architecture which is found everywhere from Riyadh to Rangoon. Our own heritage of regional styles and individual characteristics has been eaten away by this creeping cancer, and I would suggest the time is ripe to rediscover the extraordinary richness of our architectural past, as well as the basic principles which allowed our much-loved towns and villages to develop as they did.'

## Ten Principles

1) **Place** — understanding and blending with the landscape setting. This includes protecting the land and ensuring that new buildings do not unduly dominate.

2) **Hierarchy** — the size of buildings in relation to their public importance, the relationship of buildings to each other the relative significance of their different elements, for instance front entrances. In our towns and villages, churches, public buildings, halls and pubs all have their scale and special sites. The deadening uniformity of modern blocks makes it hard to distinguish between a hotel, an office block and a hospital.

3) **Scale** — man is the measure of all things. Buildings must relate to human proportions and respect the scale of buildings around them. Each place has its own characteristic scale and proportion.

4) **Harmony** — each building has to be in tune with its neighbour so that it blends with the local and natural environment. Towns such as Bath, Edinburgh and Cheltenham exemplify the virtues of architectural harmony.

5) **Enclosure** — defined boundaries to development and defined areas such as squares and courtyards that can help

create a recognisable community of neighbours. Courtyards in places like Winchester, Oxford and Cambridge, cathedral closes and the Inns of Court in London are good examples of community-forming spaces, as are enclosed gardens.

6) **Materials** — using traditional materials that celebrate a region — flint in the Sussex Downs, timber in Herefordshire, thatch in the West Country. This will in turn encourage traditional craftsmen. As William Morris said, 'we are [their] trustees for those who come after us.' The standardized uniformity of modern building materials — concrete, plastic cladding, aluminium, machine-made bricks and reconstituted stone — created an overall mediocrity, 'a kind of architectural soap opera.'

7) **Decoration** — Modern functional buildings stripped of decoration give little pleasure or delight: 'beauty is made by the unique partnership of hand, brain and eye.' The rules of ornament are not usually taught in modern schools of architecture, but we can draw on the skilled craftsmen of Arts and Crafts movements. A re-education is required in this area, and is being encouraged by the Craft Scholarships at the Prince's Foundation.

8) **Art** — architects and artists used to work together — imagine the Sheldonian Theatre in Oxford without its sculpted emperors. There is no art incorporated in either the National Theatre or the more recent British Library. Both artists and architects need to practise life drawing and study nature.

9) **Signs and Lights** — hideous street lighting emanating an orange glare serves to reveal a plethora of advertising hoardings and unimaginative shop fronts. Good lettering greatly enhances a shop's appearance and it can be taught and learned. We are assailed by the size and scale of designs intended to attract our attention and easily forget the charms of more discreet signs that are still occasionally found on small country lanes.

10) **Community** — A sense of pride and the feeling that everyone contributes to the planning and organization of a place. Planning and architecture are far too important to be left to the professionals.

The Prince concludes that 'if we follow this course we can still remain modern, up-to-date and contemporary in terms of our technological approach to life, while at the same time satisfying intangible needs of the spirit.'

By the late 1980s the Prince had sketched the broad brushes of his approach, but he has returned to and elaborated some of these themes since that time. In April 1989 he opened the Build a Better Britain Exhibition as Patron of the Civic Trust. Here he spoke of the importance of our heritage of traditional designs and crafts:

> If we are to build a better Britain, which so many people seem to want, then we need to seek inspiration from the intuitive ability of our forebears to build in harmony with their surroundings and to express the essence of their humanity through the design and layout of their dwellings and public buildings — thereby creating a true sense of community and, above all, of belonging.

The Prince also objected, in the strongest possible terms, to the plans of the then President Ceaucescu to demolish up to 8,000 villages and move their inhabitants into faceless blocks of flats that are so shoddily constructed that they start to crumble almost as soon as they are erected. The Prince noted that 'the twentieth century has witnessed some strange aberrations of the human spirit, but few can match the activities of rulers who boast about their patriotism, and then systematically undertake the destruction of the cultural heritage of their people. The extraordinary cultural diversity of Romania is not only part of her natural wealth but a possession of inestimable value to all of humanity.'

In 1990, the Prince gave a speech — *Accent on Architecture* — at the American Institute of Architects' gala dinner in Washington. He reminded his audience that architecture is, or should be, for human beings, that it is the embodiment of a nation's values. Ours may be an age of vast wealth, he said, 'but it seems sometimes that the richer we get, the uglier we tend to make our surroundings.' He drew examples from the American tradition of architects like Frank Lloyd Wright (1869–1959) who worked 'with rather than against Nature.' The challenge, he said, 'lies in whether we can apply the lessons of the past, and a love of natural forms, to the development of office buildings in a city like New York or London in the 21st century.' Referring back to his encounter with the RIBA, the Prince joked that 'Choosing a theme has nearly ruined my health... apart from anything else, I don't want to create a diplomatic incident!' It is all very well, the Prince said, for architects to want their buildings to 'reflect the Spirit of the Age, but what alarms me is that the Age has no spirit. It is all matter, and therefore unable to endure.' The Prince puts this down to our conception of linear time and therefore linear progress, whereby the past is devalued in terms of the ideas of the present. This theme is also taken up by Lewis Mumford (1895–1990), who had recently died at the time of this speech, and to whom the Prince refers. In his *The Case Against "Modern Architecture"* Mumford analyses some of the preconceptions about modern civilization that are reflected in modern architecture, chief among which is the belief in mechanical progress. It was supposed that human improvement would come about mainly through an expansion of scientific knowledge leading to new technical inventions. And that 'traditional knowledge and experience, traditional forms and values, acted as a brake upon such expansion and invention, and that since the order embodied by the machine was the highest type of order, no brakes of any kind were desirable.' We have seen this same kind of tension in our discussion of GM food.

In 1990, encouraged by the support he had received from a growing number of architects and commentators, the Prince created a unique Summer School in Civil Architecture. A group of some twenty students had the opportunity to learn about architecture in a new way, in an intensive six-week spell in England and Italy. This initiative marked the beginning of the Prince's active and practical involvement in architectural education, which has continued ever since. In a speech at Villa Lante, Italy, in September 1991, the Prince remarked that the only problem with the venue was 'that the students find the environment almost too beautiful to work in!' They were asked to consider 'what makes architecture civil? What lifts it beyond the purely functional and material and invests the built environment with those features, principles and truths which in some extraordinary way strike a chord in our hearts and which give us a sense of well-being, of harmony and of appropriateness?' Only with these features and a connection to beauty through the inner life, said the Prince, can we claim to be heirs to civilization. He thought that each student would hope 'when they leave here [that] something of the timeless, ageless value and wisdom contained in the principles of traditional architecture will emerge in their subsequent work. That they will see their skills as being part of a link in that finely wrought chain which anchors us in both dimensions of past and present.'

The success of this, and a second school the following year, led the Prince to announce in January 1992 that he was creating a new organization to be known as The Prince of Wales's Institute of Architecture (whose activities have since been reconfigured within The Prince's Foundation). The intention was to teach the timeless basic principles of architecture needed to produce buildings of beauty which 'lift our spirits.' The Institute opened as a place for teaching, research and the exchange of ideas in October 1992. In his speech the Prince reiterated his principles and approach, relating it to his concerns about distortions introduced by the mechanistic worldview, which have already discussed in earlier chapters: 'In this scenario Man himself becomes a mere mechanical object and any notion of a metaphysical reality disappears altogether. The sense of humanity's uniqueness as a microcosm of the whole Universe is thrown out of the window, to be replaced by an egocentric world view which denies that all-encompassing sense of the sacred and stresses the purely rational.' Many people have an uneasy sense that something vital is missing from this view, which the Prince helps to articulate.

The Prince 'had often wondered why it is that I was not seduced by this conveniently logical, but utterly soulless philosophical approach,' noting that 'the pressures to yield to this concept of life have been and still are, to a certain extent, enormous. At best you are described as eccentric; at worst as a dotty crank... The temptation to conform,' he said, 'can be very powerful. So why haven't I? What is it that produces this overwhelming feeling — for it is only a feeling — in my heart that the whole Universe is based on the most profound principles which in themselves represent a giant paradox, but which for me inspire a continual sense of awe and reverence?' In a passage revealing his underlying mystical (in the non-pejorative sense of the term) approach, he continues, 'I confess that I don't know what it is, except that it comes from my heart and envelops my whole being. It is an awareness of something beyond the confines of Self and it becomes more evident when in the presence of great beauty.' The mystic, as we saw in the last chapter, is one whose 'eye of the heart' is open and who has an intrinsic sense of the unity and inner meaning of the Cosmos. In asking 'What is spirit, and how can its essence be restored to an appropriate place in the totality of our experience?,' the Prince explains his own view:

> I am no philosopher, but I can try to explain what I feel spirit to be. It is that sense, that overwhelming experience of awareness of a one-ness with the Natural World, and beyond that, with the creative force that we all call God which lies at the central point of all. It is, above all, an 'experience.' It defies conscious thought. It steals upon you and floods your whole being despite your best logical intentions. It lies deep in the heart of mankind like some primeval memory. It is both 'pagan' and Christian, and in this sense is surely the fundamental expression of what we call religion.

As we have seen in our discussion of the principles of sacred art and architecture, sacred mathematical and geometric principles were inherited by the Greeks from the Egyptians and, as the Prince remarks, 'the whole of European culture is based on our Graeco-Roman heritage, at the root of which lay what many consider to be these profound and, indeed 'sacred' principles. So the difficult question (and the task of the Institute) was 'how to restore the element of 'spirit,' as contained in such timeless principles, to its rightful position in the overall balance that I believe needs to be achieved in the education of an architect.' The Prince is careful to point out that this means an 'architecture of the heart,' an architecture that nourishes the spirit, which is 'not so much a traditional architecture, which resembles or apes the past, but rather a particular kind of architecture whose forms, plans, materials, are based on human feeling.' This will also include 'new [more sensitive and imaginative] forms of architecture, based on new materials, new ways of building, new forms of technology.' This, he hoped, is where his Institute 'might become a kind of crucible where the architecture of the 21st century can be forged.' The aim 'will be to produce practitioners, not just theoreticians. The Institute's curricular programmes will contain all the rigour consistent with the technical and economic demands of such a complex profession. But these will be placed within the wider context of our history and our culture and, indeed, other people's cultures and geographical locations.'

As with his philosophy of agriculture and medicine, the Prince emphasizes the importance of combining the best of past and present, of traditional and innovative, but based on time-honoured principles and knowledge.

## The Prince's Foundation — an Overview

*I passionately believe that the human spirit has a profound need for a sense of belonging and community. That quest for identity, something that is intrinsically of a human scale, is bound intimately to that which we build. The depressing spectacle of soulless housing estates, windswept industrial 'parks' and bland shopping malls both corrodes the human spirit and diminishes the natural environment.*

The Prince of Wales

The Prince's Foundation for the Built Environment is a charitable organization formed to extend the Prince of Wales's initiatives in architectural design, building and urban regeneration. It aims to 'improve the quality of people's lives by teaching and practising timeless ways of building and brings together The Urban Network, Regeneration Through Heritage, The Prince of Wales's Phoenix Trust, The Projects Team, The Prince of Wales's Drawing Studio and the School of Traditional Arts. It also houses the Temenos Academy, although the Academy is not a formal part of the Foundation.

The Prince's Foundation works to encourage a more holistic and humane approach to the planning and design of our urban communities — 'working to connect the art of building with the making of community.' It is the only institution in the United Kingdom that specialises in providing consultancy and education services for large-scale urban regeneration and development projects. Their approach is to foster a sense of community, pride of place, and good building and craftsmanship. As the Prince explained in 1999:

> My Foundation will give a very practical application to the idea of linking the best of the past with the needs of the future and will, I hope, make a real contribution towards creating better places in which to live and work. The Foundation works with a wide range of professionals and partners to assist in the development of places that can better meet the social, economic, environmental and spiritual needs of individuals and their communities.

The Foundation links ideas with practical action, drawing on a track record of academic study and research, a lead role in many urban development projects throughout Britain, and an extensive, broad-based network of professionals, individuals and communities. Based in its own unique building in Charlotte Road, Shoreditch, in London's East End, the Foundation has established an active centre for education, research and hands-on practical project work.

Initiatives which form part of the Prince's Foundation include:

*Development Projects*
Through the work of its Projects Team, The Prince's Foundation is playing a key role in the planning and development of over twenty large-scale, area-based development and regeneration projects throughout the UK, including urban villages. Working in long-term partnerships with Government agencies, councils, local communities and businesses, the projects team aims to demonstrate, by practical example, approaches to creating more humane and liveable neighbourhoods — mainly in existing urban areas, but also greenfield and brownfield situations. The Prince's Foundation's projects and education teams works closely together to develop and disseminate best practice in traditional approaches to urban development and to ensure the provision of relevant, practical training and wider capacity building for those concerned with improving the planning, renewal and stewardship of our urban environment.

**Urban Design and Architecture Short Course Programme**

This new programme of courses was launched in May 2004. The Prince's Foundation's history as a teacher of the building arts, a leader in urban regeneration projects and the hub of the Urban Network positions it as the natural link between the idea of good place-making and the practical techniques for accomplishing it. The annual course programme consists of 10 intensive modules designed to provide an understanding of the principles behind successful urbanism and architecture, along with rigorous education in the tools and techniques of good urban design. The programme is tailored to meet the needs of mid-career planners, urban designers, architects, traffic engineers, developers and members of local authorities who are involved in urban development and regeneration projects. Topics for 2004–2005 include The Order of Nature, The Languages of Architecture, Building the Future and The Culture of Building.

**Building a Better Patient Environment**

The Prince of Wales launched the Building a Better Patient Environment in partnership with NHS Estates in November 2001 (we have already mentioned this in the chapter on health). The programme aims to ensure the highest standards of design for the NHS's major programme of new hospital building. Foundation staff help to educate key representatives of NHS Trusts about the principles of, and need for, good design; the team are also providing practical assistance on delivering good quality design for a number of pilot projects.

**The Craft Scholarship Scheme**

In March 2002, The Prince of Wales presented the first of the Prince of Wales's Craft Scholarships. The Prince's Foundation launched the Craft Scholarship scheme in response to the acute shortage of traditionally skilled craftspeople that faces the building trade in Britain today. The Scholarships support people who desire practical training in the use of traditional materials and building techniques, whether these skills are used in the creation of new buildings or the conservation and restoration of historic properties.

## Initiatives in Regeneration and Heritage

The Prince's Foundation is deeply concerned with wider issues of urban regeneration and the role of heritage buildings in the built environment. The Foundation hosts an independent initiative working on these issues; Regeneration Through Heritage, which in turn works closely with another of the Prince of Wales' charities, the Phoenix Trust.

### Regeneration Through Heritage

This initiative was established in 1996 at the request of the Prince of Wales to promote the re-use of heritage industrial buildings, principally by assisting community-based partnerships to develop sustainable projects. It currently supports ten projects, with a total development value of £50 million, by providing skills and support on conservation, architecture and business planning. English Heritage and private sector companies fund the initiative.

### The Prince of Wales's Phoenix Trust

The Prince of Wales's Phoenix Trust is a charitable company that acquires, repairs and finds new uses for major historic buildings that might otherwise fall into decay or face demolition, for the benefit of the local communities in which they stand and the public at large. The Prince launched the Trust in September 1997, at Stanley Mills on the River Tay, near Perth. This group of redundant buildings was the Trust's inaugural project, involving conversion of two buildings into houses and flats. Other Phoenix Trust schemes include a nineteenth century water mill in Paisley, a twentieth century colliery in Wales and part of an ex-Royal Navy victualling yard in Plymouth. See *www.thephoenixtrust.org.uk*.

## The Prince of Wales's Initiatives in Teaching Art

### The Prince's Drawing School

The Prince's Drawing School was launched in 2000 to offer artists the opportunity to broaden and extend their drawing practice, especially through drawing from observation. The faculty consists of 35 artists who are experienced teachers from leading art colleges including the Royal Academy, the Royal

College of Art and the Slade. Over 400 artists a term attend classes at the studio and Shoreditch and out of house. A core part of the programme is the Drawing Year, an MA level course that gives young professional artists the opportunity to focus on drawing. See *www.princesdrawingschool.org*.

### The Prince's School for Traditional Arts - The Visual Islamic and Traditional Arts Programme (VITA)

The VITA programme (covered in a previous chapter) offers a unique opportunity to study both the theory and practice of Visual Islamic and Traditional Arts at higher educational level. The courses on this programme, which are validated by the University of Wales, enable Masters, MPhil and PhD students to explore the techniques and materials of traditional arts and architecture as well as covering the underlying philosophical and symbolic meaning of these arts. It is the only course anywhere in the world where students have the opportunity to study and practise traditional arts at postgraduate level. See *www.princes-foundation.org/traditionalarts.html*.

The Prince's Foundation moved from Regency Gloucester Gate, the original home of the Prince's Institute of Architecture to its own building in Charlotte Road in Shoreditch in 2000. The original mid-nineteenth century industrial building has been sympathetically restored and redesigned to house the various activities described above. The development is part of the revitalization of a number of empty and nearly derelict commercial buildings that have been transformed into artists' studios. Local architect Matthew Lloyd did most of the design work for the building. In keeping with the Prince's wishes, he used natural materials and traditional techniques, preserving some of the building's interesting features such as the cast-iron columns in what is now open exhibition space. The solid but elegant furniture and bookshelves in the library were made from pale ash grown at Highgrove and designed by Robert Kime, while the bookcases were built by Nicholas Coryndon. One interesting overall design feature is a ' non-electric natural air-conditioning system. The building as a whole is a fine expression of the ideals that the Foundation seeks to promote and additionally houses The Prince's Phoenix Trust, Drawing School and School of Traditional Arts.

As the Prince himself aptly put it: 'Architecture at its best does not, I feel, need to be grand or loud, but neither should it be mindless or soulless. Indeed, it is often the very modesty of well-crafted buildings that helps to create the best and most lasting sense of community well-being, urban order and vitality.'

## *Urban Planning — the Example of Poundbury*

> *Our cities don't need to grow uncontrollably. We must surely accept some framework of restraint which might restore a healthy balance to our urban environment, and restore equilibrium between buildings and Nature. These matters lead us to some of the central questions of our times. What does it mean to be truly human and what is a fitting way to house this human-ness? How much influence does the design of the built environment actually have on the well-being of human beings; on their sense of belonging and hence on the relationship an individual has with his fellow man — in other words, the community? And what, in the end, should be our relationship with Nature?*
>
> The Prince of Wales

The genesis of the Poundbury development outside Dorchester goes back to 1987, when the West Dorset District Council selected the 400 acres of open farmland on the western fringe of the town, owned by the Duchy of Cornwall since 1342, for development to meet local housing needs. The Duchy could simply have sold the land to a developer to produce another zoned housing estate — as they had done on a previous occasion — but the Prince of Wales as Duke of Cornwall saw an opportunity to respond to some of his RIBA critics like Richard Rogers, who pointed out that he had never built anything himself. Selling the land would have been both simple and easy to justify to the Treasury, who by law had to be convinced of its economic viability. However, the Prince was determined to 'break the mould and to ensure that such growth should recapture the organic form and sense of place of our historic towns and villages. Poundbury represented a challenge to achieve this without compromising its unspoilt rural setting. It also presented an opportunity to build a community which included a wide range of housing intermingled with economic activity.' The situation in Dorchester is a microcosm of the national challenge to satisfy the demand for an estimated extra 4.4m homes by 2016.

Much post-war planning and development in the United Kingdom has been characterized by *zoning*. Private and social housing have been segregated, while isolated out-of-town shopping areas and business parks have been created. This has in turn diminished the sense of living in a community, eroded the commercial vitality of towns and forced greater corresponding dependence on the car, a factor that has contributed substantially to the demise of local village stores as people travel to supermarkets for their weekly shop. Many cities, towns and villages are now surrounded by sprawling, suburban development which, more often than not, bears little relation to the heart and heritage of the original place — our local town of St Andrews is as good an example as any, with its rows of standardized new bungalows and council houses. Poundbury is the latest in a line of challenges to the current conventions of planning and development along lines championed by the Prince of Wales in his *A Vision of Britain*. It is the first new development in Britain where, with the help of architects, developers, and the co-operation of the local authority, the thoughtful principles of urban design in *A Vision of Britain* are being put into practice. Nor is this the first pioneering scheme undertaken by the Duchy — Edward VIII, while Prince of Wales, was involved in the development of its London estate in Kennington. The period between the original idea for Poundbury in 1987 and the beginning of construction in the autumn of 1993 was fraught with all kinds of complications and difficulties, which fall outside the scope of our narrative. A less determined individual would have thrown in the towel, but the Prince persisted in his vision. The significant landmarks of the development of Poundbury are these: the appointment of the Belgian planner and architect Leon Krier to produce a Masterplan for the site, the 1989 planning weekend in Dorchester, attended by the Prince himself, the revision of its classical ideals to put the emphasis on the local vernacular style and local materials, and the formulation of the scheme in a way that was both innovative and financially viable over the 25 year period of the project.

Instead of segregating uses, different types of property are mixed throughout Poundbury. Private and social housing (20% of the development) are intermingled and built to the same quality and designs so as to be entirely indistinguishable. Commercial buildings — from factories to offices — sit among residential areas, with shopping, community and leisure facilities. Here the Duchy has proved savvy about human nature by ensuring that commercial buildings are already in place and cannot therefore be objected to by incoming local residents. Streets are laid out around buildings to create interesting spaces and a natural control of car speeds. Indeed the overall design favours pedestrians and not cars, since there is an 'incident' (hump, blind bend, lamppost or such like) every seventy yards or so. The result is that cars creep around at about 20 mph. There is also a noticeable lack of large traffic signs and painted lines for exactly the same reason — they are rendered superfluous at such slow speeds. Indeed the only traffic sign in evidence is a *No Entry* sign about three inches across. Parking and services are mostly confined to landscaped courtyards at the rear so that it is rare to see a car on the street. Furthermore, residents sign up to an agreement promising that they will not park caravans or boats anywhere.

The architecture — using local and sometimes recycled materials — draws on the rich heritage of Dorset and, in particular, on the attractive streets of Dorchester itself. Poundbury is not just about architecture, but also about land use and integrated development. It is designed as an overall high-density urban environment to create an attractive, modern and pleasing place in which people can live, work, shop and play. Emphasis is placed on the quality of design and materials, landscaping, and attention to detail, all of which is spelt out in *Poundbury, Design Guidance*. The cartoon in the front shows a 'before and after' house with all kinds of unsightly excrescences in the second picture with a caption: *It couldn't happen here... ?* Certainly not, if the Poundbury guidelines are strictly enforced!

There is illustrated guidance on extensions, building materials, walling materials (including types of bricks allowed) and on lintels and arches. Outbuildings are regulated — 'prefabricated unit garages, flat-roofed plastic-sheeted timber or metal framed carports will NOT be allowed.' Roofs can be varied but within clearly defined limits of coverings, eaves, gutterings and over-hangs. Roof pitches may vary from 30 to 65 degrees, but 'pitches of 45 degrees should be avoided as they produce roofs that are "ineffably dull".' Unusually for new housing, there are open fires and therefore chimneys on each house, which should 'rise gener-ously above roofs… and should not appear inappropriately stout or dumpy.' Window designs are fortunately regulated to exclude plate glass and the hideous plastic eyesores to be found occasion-ally even on refurbished Cotswold cottages; and window panes are required to approximate the Golden Mean on the vertical axis. A range of permitted doors and porches is also specified, with all front doors giving directly onto the street. And since house builders provide a communal aerial system, no external aerials and satellite dishes are permitted. Lettering and shop signage specifications are clearly set out, with most elegant and pleasing results for the visitor who is not visually overwhelmed by large billboards and tasteless shop fronts. An amusing footnote to this design guidance was provided by a resident who was upbraided for putting an aluminium gas flue on the outside of his house. His solution — not an inexpensive one — was to commission a gar-goyle sculpture so that the effluent issues from its mouth!

Part of the legacy of Britain's industrial past dictated that fac-tories were traditionally located away from housing, but these days a good deal of local employment in West Dorset is pro-vided by the service sector or high-technology industries that can happily co-exist with residential uses and thereby reduce the need to drive to work. This integration and liveability in turn helps build the thriving sense of community so important to the Prince. The design of the community hall in the main Pummery Square is imaginatively based on a similar building in Tetbury, while the pub opposite has recently been bought and opened. The local shop and post office are due soon, both of which will provide residents with more chances to interact. The sheer variety of materials and designs within a traditional framework of design makes Poundbury unique among modern developments — no two adjacent houses are alike, and yet each blends into a harmonious whole. Interestingly, the cost of using high quality materials makes the houses only 10% more expen-sive, a price that people have shown themselves more than willing to pay since houses in Poundbury command a 15% premium on comparable housing elsewhere in West Dorset.

Sustainable development and enhancing the natural environment are two further key elements. Around a third of the 400-acre site will be landscaped with parkland and places for children to play. Native trees — often from Duchy of Cornwall nurseries — such as beech, plane, horse chestnut, ash cherry and white beam have been planted on all the streets and in the courtyards. In addition, householders are required to incorporate the latest energy-conservation features such as insulation, double-glazing, condensing boilers and water meters. Use of recycled materials is encouraged where appropriate. Services such as telephone, electricity and gas are housed in a single channel in the courtyards. Finally, all residents are members of a management company that maintains the common facilities, thus helping to generate a sense of community involvement.

Writing in *The Spectator* in 1998, the Prince commented that:

> Today, despite the early siren warnings of some sceptics, Poundbury is becoming a huge success: 140 homes are built and occupied and 150 people are working in new workshops and factories on the site. Moreover, it is about as far removed from the soullessness of many housing estates and business 'parks' as one could imagine. In short, it is becoming a place with its own spirit and identity, a proper part of the town of Dorchester, and not just a development.

Among sceptics converted after visiting Poundbury have been leading broadsheet journalists and a range of politicians, including the Deputy Prime Minister John Prescott, who remarked that 'what is being done here is very important work for this country's urban future.' Furthermore, the House of Commons Select Committee on Environment, Transport and Regional Affairs was sufficiently impressed by the principles which have guided the development at Poundbury and agree that the local vernacular should be respected in the design of housing, where this is appropriate. Poundbury — and Highgrove, as we have seen — is a physical embodiment of the Prince's vision. But it is not just a monument, it is a model of good practice for future sustainable urban development that has now been endorsed by the government in its plans for new housebuilding.

## Regeneration through Heritage — Urban Villages, The Phoenix Trust

*It has always seemed to me that the more social structures and technologies change, the greater is people's desire to retain and treasure the objects and places with which they are familiar. People instinctively feel the need for roots and landmarks in a rapidly changing world.*

The Prince of Wales

It will not come as a surprise to the reader that the Prince of Wales believes it important to preserve the best of Britain's built environment for the sake of future generations and as a cultural link with the past — he was President of the National Trust in their centenary year of 1995 and has recently become Patron following the death of Queen Elizabeth the Queen Mother — and also Patron of the National Trust of Scotland. However, it is not a question of preserving buildings merely for the sake of bricks and mortar, or, as he put it, 'the creation of a "theme park Britain" where we repackage our heritage merely for the benefit of tourists.' He believes that restoring and maintaining historic buildings can play an important part in the regeneration of troubled areas by creating assets for communities and generating a sense of community pride. He now has successful practical examples to prove this, as we shall see below.

Having taken part in discussions on the fate of the Royal Naval College buildings at Greenwich in the early 1990s, the Prince became interested more generally in the plans for buildings released by the Ministry of Defence and the Department of Health (particularly old psychiatric hospitals). The Prince was concerned that they should not simply be sold to the highest bidder but redeveloped sensitively for the benefit of local communities. The Prince made a presentation to this effect to a number of Cabinet Ministers. They were sympathetic to the general idea and Phoenix Trust (a charitable company) was subsequently established in 1998 to put the theory into practice. The Trust acts as a building preservation trust acquiring historic buildings at risk — such as abandoned mills, factories and dockyards — restoring and converting them to new and beneficial uses.

The Prince of Wales launched his Phoenix Trust at the disused Stanley Mills in Perth. Restoration of the riverside buildings, the most northerly cotton mills in Britain, became the first project of the Trust, and work started in June, 1998. The Trust concentrates its projects in areas that have experienced economic decline where community resources are often scarce. The projects provide a catalyst to local regeneration by generating job opportunities and acting as a focus for business and residential development. At a time when there is increasing pressure for new build and greenfield development the Phoenix Trust believes that it is important to show how these fine complexes of buildings can provide interesting places to live and work. The Trust acquires and develops historic buildings for sale and then recycles the income for further schemes. The Trust has also made a point of building partnerships with such organizations as English Heritage, Historic Scotland and the Heritage Lottery Fund.

The oldest part of Stanley Mills was built by Sir Richard Arkwright in 1786, to take advantage of water power from the Tay. The mills were closed in 1989 and the building deteriorated very quickly. The owner wanted to demolish most of it. But the Phoenix Trust, with National Lottery and other grants, acquired the two largest mills to create houses and flats. Work by the Trust has given others confidence to tackle the rest. A stunning building has been saved, given new life, and its original character preserved. Other active Phoenix projects include the Mills Bakery at the Royal William Yard in Plymouth, Anchor Mills in Paisley, Fort Gilkicker in Hampshire and Penallta Colliery in mid-Glamorgan. Penallta Colliery is situated in a former coalfield valley in South Wales, 14 miles due north of Cardiff. See *www.thephoenixtrust.org.uk.*

A related initiative is Regeneration Through Heritage (RTH), which promotes the re-usage of heritage industrial buildings for contemporary economic, cultural and social purposes, primarily through assisting community-based partnerships to develop proposals for the sustainable re-use of particular buildings of architectural merit. RTH is supported by English Heritage and the private sector. It currently supports projects in England and Northern Ireland, and is now seeking to identify further potential projects in all parts of the United Kingdom. RTH provides support to local partnerships that enables them to understand the characteristics of their building, develop appropriate proposals for its conservation and re-use, and undertake the technical work necessary for business planning and funding application purposes. Regeneration Through Heritage also operates a programme of study visits, seminars, conferences and will soon be offering an online directory of best practice (under construction).

In an article in *Perspectives* magazine in January 1996, the Prince set out his ideas on heritage: 'we must start by appreciating the unique heritage of our own country.' He continued: 'a society which sets its face against its past and only values what is new and exciting will never be a society that is at peace with itself or which understands itself. The past represents our memory as a society of who we are, whence we came, and the priceless traditions and knowledge which have accumulated over the centuries.' In other words, the past forms a key part of our national identity. Referring to the upcoming Millennium, the Prince pointed out that it provided 'the opportunity to execute works of art and to build significant public buildings which will be a genuine reflection of the deeper values of our humanity.' He called for the discovery of new and imaginative uses for fine old buildings to enhance the strength of communities and their traditions: 'celebrating the Millennium should not just be about building anew, but also about renewing the old ... we should be looking to use the Millennium to bring new life to the decaying and derelict centres of some of our great cities where the need to re-build the spirit of the local community is of supreme importance if a balanced and fulfilling city life is to be restored.'

In a keynote speech at a conference on 26th April, 1999, organized by Regeneration Through Heritage, the Prince said that many industrial buildings were as much a part of the national heritage as cathedrals, palaces and country houses: 'they represent the pinnacle of architectural and functional achievement during Britain's time as the workshop of the world.' Finding new uses gave pride back to communities, and brought new life back to inner cities instead of creating business parks on green fields. The conference was held at the restored former Great Western Railway Works, Swindon, Wiltshire, which is now a successful shopping and office centre. The Prince makes regular visits to a variety of heritage buildings, to draw attention to their potential value to local communities and to highlight successful restoration schemes.

Rather than demolish old factories and communities, the Prince suggests that 'a better way forward is to promote the process of re-inventing communities where people already live, and recognize the value of the investment both in people and the built environment which already exist, rather than abandon it.' The construction of new towns after the war was successful in so far as it improved the quality of life of their inhabitants with new facilities, but at the expense of the sense of community. 'The challenge now,' said the Prince, 'is to catch the popular imagination in the same way with a policy to conserve our precious countryside, use the resources in our towns and cities which now stand idle, and create new and exciting communities in the places where people already live.'

Current RTH projects include Conway Mill, a former flax mill in Belfast, Harvey's Foundry in Hayle, Cornwall, Houldsworth Mill, a former cotton Mill near Stockport, Mistly Maltings in Essex, Navigation Warehouse, a grain warehouse in Wakefield, Perran Foundry, a former iron foundry near Falmouth in Cornwall, Salt Warehouse and Warehouse no. 4, Sowerby Bridge, West Yorkshire, and Torr Vale Mill, a former textile mill in West Yorkshire. Space does not permit a detailed description of more than three projects — interested readers can consult the Prince's Foundation website for further details.

## The Prince's Foundation's Urban Network

Urban development initiatives were launched as the Urban Villages Forum in 1992 and achieved a radical shift in approaches to the built environment over the following decade. Many of the ideas originally proposed by the Forum, such as the principles of mixed-use mixed-tenure sustainable communities are now accepted as mainstream. The Forum brought together leading practitioners who aspire to build and regenerate successful towns and neighbourhoods in line with the key principles of good urbanism (embodied in the development of Poundbury), which include:

～ A fine grain mix of uses
～ Access to local services (and density sufficient to support them)
～ An integrated network of streets and public spaces
～ A mix of tenures, including integrated affordable housing
～ Architecture that respects its surroundings and is human in scale
～ Preservation and reuse of building heritage
～ Protection and enhancement of the environment
～ Community participation and ownership

One of the Forum's most recent major Urban Village projects was unveiled in early 2003 at Llandarcy in South Wales. It involves redevelopment of a brownfield site that had been a BP oil refinery complex. The Prince hoped that results at Llandarcy would meet the rhetoric and will represent a model of investment in longer term values involving the creation of communities, not just the building of structures: 'It is a chance to demonstrate that successfully making places means understanding that communities are living, breathing organisms that must be allowed to develop and evolve, and that the spaces and structures we create are crucial to that process.' The work of what is now called the Urban Network is currently integrated into the core programmes of The Princes Foundation.

The reader is now in a position to appreciate the full extent and influence of the Prince of Wales's contribution to architecture and heritage issues over the last twenty years. Since his first speech to the RIBA in 1984 he has campaigned indefatigably for traditional ideals to be considered in a modern context and has been involved in a wide range of pioneering practical initiatives. As we have seen, he has always kept people and localities at the forefront of his concerns, ensuring that his projects are community-building and landscape-enhancing. And his whole enterprise is underpinned by the Platonic trinity of the Good, the Beautiful and the True in an inspiring expression of practical idealism.

# 6. The Fulfilment of Potential — Education and The Prince's Trust

## The Prince's Educational Work

*Education is a higher word; it implies an action upon our mental nature, and the formation of a character; it is something individual and permanent, and is commonly spoken of in connection with religion and virtue*

John Henry Newman

The Prince of Wales cares deeply about the standards and quality of education, which he has called 'the number one priority for the future.' The Prince seeks to encourage and celebrate excellence, and at the same time — through various initiatives that will be highlighted below — to help the disadvantaged to get the best out of their education. He believes that the highest standards of education are a crucial means of helping young people to understand the world of which they form a part, the civilization and society they have inherited — and that such an understanding is the only genuine basis for safeguarding the timeless qualities of life for future generations.

The Prince made a major statement of his educational philosophy in the Shakespeare Birthday Lecture of April 1991. He recalled being unmoved by his first reading of *Julius Caesar* at school, but a performance of *Henry V*, in which he played the Duke of Exeter, made a lasting impression. The importance of Shakespeare to the Prince is reflected in his own selection that was published as *The Prince's Choice*, with a foreword adapted from this speech. For the Prince, great literature offers us the opportunity to learn timeless truths about the human condition that go beyond a soulless, mechanistic understanding of life:

'The truths he illustrates are universal. In this sense we can read not only a good story into all his plays, but also psychological insights and archetypes with all their engaging interplay.' Moreover, Shakespeare's language and culture is an inestimable part of our own cultural inheritance:

> For us all, roots are important: roots in our landscape and local communities; roots in our cultural and literary heritage; roots in our philosophical and spiritual traditions. If we lose touch with them, if we lose track of where we have come from, we deprive ourselves of a sense of value, a sense of security and, all too frequently, a sense of purpose and meaning.

Our roots give us a sense of identity and are vital to the continuity of culture. The Prince noted that French students have to study one of the great texts from the seventeenth, eighteenth and nineteenth centuries, while some GCSE courses contain no Shakespeare at all and new courses ask questions about him that do not require students to have read any plays. An overload of instant information is unlikely to make us wise, since 'wisdom comes through insight, and our greatest poets and literary geniuses are invariably the means by which we can obtain this insight into the workings of the Universe and into the timeless imperatives to which we, as individuals, are subject.' The Prince feared that the marginalization of Shakespeare 'seems to be symptomatic of a general flight from our great literary heritage' encouraged by experts who consider such study too elitist or insufficiently multi-cultural: 'there are terrible dangers ... in so following fashionable trends in education that we end up with an entire generation of culturally disinherited young people.' Not for the first time the Prince finds himself taking on the experts, who he feels are out of touch with the feelings of ordinary people. He regretted the number of illiterate and innumerate pupils still being turned out of state education while praising the dedication of the many teachers who work in trying circumstances.

The Prince also called for suitable vocational training for the less academic majority, which has become much more widely available since he spoke. In a speech delivered at the Skill City exhibition in November 2002, he said:

> We therefore need, I would suggest, a concerted campaign to raise significantly the status and desirability of vocational skills careers in the eyes of young people. We need to redress what I believe is an over-emphasis on academic and theoretical training for the minority and an under-emphasis on vocational training and apprenticeships for the majority.

In his conclusion, the Prince applauded the emphasis placed on the technical, the practical, the vocational and the commercially viable, but added: 'I would like to stress, again, that I believe that education is more than just training. After all, there is little point in becoming technically competent if at the same time we become culturally inept.' In a speech at the College of William and Mary in Virginia in 1993, the Prince made a similar plea for the nourishing of cultural roots:

> We need to preserve our sense of awe and wonder, not only for the achievements of science in our own day, but also for the heritage that has been handed down to us — for our natural environment, of the architectural glories left us by past generations, for the beauty of our language, for the inspiration of our history and the insights offered to us by great literature.

Nor should this heritage be the sole preserve of the privileged:

> Some say that children from poorer backgrounds should not be forced to study the work of writers from past ages because it will indoctrinate them in the habits of a hierarchical society. This approach amounts to telling these children that, because they are underprivileged, they must be deprived of the greatness of human thought and the beauty of human expression.

Following the Shakespeare speech in 1993, the Prince, as

President of the Royal Shakespeare Company (RSC) instigated and funded The Prince of Wales's Shakespeare School, to help support quality teaching of Shakespeare in schools. The School, which has since been run annually by the RSC, offers an intense course to 30 teachers from England and Wales, drawing on the resources of academics and educationists as well as those of the RSC itself. The School's main aims are to extend teachers' knowledge of Shakespeare's work, develop their critical awareness of rehearsal and performance, and extend the range of methods of teaching Shakespeare. The course is based on the premise that the process of teaching Shakespeare shares much common ground with that of directing his work on stage.

An HM Inspectorate report in 1997 said: 'It is clear that the course has had a considerable impact. All the teachers claimed the course had renewed their enthusiasm for the teaching of Shakespeare and developed their confidence in the use of more practical approaches which, in turn, had had a positive effect on pupils' learning.' The report concluded: 'the Prince of Wales's Shakespeare School makes a valuable contribution to the in-service training of teachers and all the signs are that it will help improve the teaching of Shakespeare in participants' schools.'

A recent initiative along the same lines is an Education Summer School for teachers of History and English, the first of which was held at Dartington Hall in 2002. In his opening speech, the Prince explained his view that the 1960s had abandoned the principles of the past as outmoded and had created a situation where young people 'will have a diminishing chance to understand their place in history, the significance of the culture and ideas which they have inherited, the nature of their own identity, and the distinction between the good and the bad, the creative and the mediocre.' So, he continued, 'in the field of education it seemed to me a particular tragedy that the crucial, shared link between generations — that "dialogue" which permits some kind of national, cultural and spiritual identity and an understanding of the values which underpin our pattern of liberal democracy — should be somewhat ruptured.'

The aim of the school was to inspire the teachers to enrich their teaching 'despite the unavoidably narrow straitjacket of the examination system.' The Prince thought that 'part of what may have gone wrong is that we have moved away from the idea of English as something really to be learned, by effort and by application, and by long and careful familiarity with those who have shown how to clothe their thought in the most precise, vivid and memorable language.' Any professional will tell you that practice — and a lot of it — makes perfect. 'In literature as in language,' the Prince continued, 'I would suggest that there are terrible dangers in following fashionable trends in education — towards the relevant, the exclusively contemporary, the immediately palatable.' He added that 'what is palatable is taught because it is the most accessible, but it may not be the most useful or, in a deeper sense, relevant.' The Prince concluded that 'in a world where the trite, the banal, the cliché and the commonplace are so dominant a part of our lives, we need ever more to cherish, and to preserve and celebrate the beauty, the solemnity and the harmony we inherit from the past.'

In June 2002, the Prince launched his Arts and Kids Foundation with a grant of £1 million from the Millennium Commission. The nationwide campaign aims to broaden the creative stimuli of today's youth by providing hands-on experience of all art forms such as dance, opera, theatre and the visual arts. The Prince believes that early exposure to the best theatre, music and other performing arts can help 'expand minds and fire imagination.' The eventual aim of the Foundation is to involve children of pre-school age in a wide-range of art forms that will include heritage sites, museums and galleries. It also plans to build partnerships with groups outside school, such as community art groups, youth clubs and after-school clubs to introduce children to and engage them in the arts. Powergen is the first corporate partner for Arts & Kids. It has pledged to develop reading initiatives over three years in a bid to re-energize modern-day storytelling.

## The Prince's Trust — Its Principles and History

*This sense of what is sacred has helped to shape my
understanding of the mysterious nature of the human soul; of
our shared humanity, and of the untapped potential of so many.
Perhaps it is this which lies at the heart of the work of my own
Trust. Over nearly twenty-five years The Prince's Trust has*

> *sought to find ways in which to help young people who are*
> *often hopelessly adrift in society and with nowhere else to turn;*
> *to help rebuild in them that sense of community and common*
> *endeavour which I believe are so necessary to enable our society*
> *to tackle effectively the wounds of despair and desperation*
> *which afflict so many of our fellow human beings.*
>
> The Prince of Wales

In a letter written to Tom (now Sir Tom) Shebbeare in 1993, the Prince explained that his activities of the previous fifteen years had been motivated by a desire to put the 'Great' back into Great Britain. He realized that his position enabled him to bring people together and act as a catalyst 'to help produce a better and more balanced response to various problems.' His was not a political agenda, but a desire to see people achieve their potential. Nowhere in the range of the Prince's activities is this passion for partnership and focus on realizing potential more evident than in the activities of the Prince's Trust.

The Prince's Trust was founded in 1976 and was in part inspired by the Prince's own experience of activities at his school Gordonstoun and in the Navy. The Prince was also following in the footsteps of his forebears — for instance Edward VIII, when Prince of Wales, raised more than £1 million in 1935 for King George's Jubilee Trust to address 'the urgency of the problem of youth.' As early as 1975 the Prince had identified the need for a new initiative aimed at disadvantaged young people between fifteen and twenty-five. A crucial principle was self-help, whereby young people could 'devise and carry through their own ideas and ambitions.' This would mean that 'their restless energy and talents may be canalized into constructive activities.' A further key principle was that of challenge and adventure allied to service: the activities would generate self-respect in participants as well as foster within them a sense of citizenship and concern for the common good.

The Prince's Trust has always laid great emphasis on trust. The Prince himself said at an early stage that 'No one was putting the trust in them [young people] they needed. If I was going to do anything, it had to be an operation that was able to take those risks: to trust young people and to experiment.' This meant giving grants as quickly as possible with the minimum of form-filling and red tape. Inevitably such a policy involved risks but the Prince insisted on such an approach: 'Occasionally things will go wrong. Occasionally someone runs off with the money. Well, that is just one of those things. But they won't all do that. And having taken the risks you find that we'll get enormously beneficial results.' Moreover, as Adam Nicolson points out in his history of the Trust, the Prince insisted that 'the important thing is that young people should run their own shows. They don't want to do things which are prescribed, planned and supervised.' In addition, the Trust has acted more as a 'release valve' or 'freedom machine' than a conventional charity, enabling young people to take off with their own energy. However, it has also recognized 'that, for all the virtues of self-reliance, there is no freedom without commitment and no growth without help.' The Trust pioneered the idea of 'self-realization through community service' at a time when such a concept was much less fashionable than today.

A similar approach was taken by the economist Mohammed Yunnus when he founded his Grameen Bank on the basis of micro-credit in Pakistan. He made small loans — a total of $27 in the first instance to forty women whose margins in local market were being unreasonably squeezed by unscrupulous suppliers and purchasers. No bank would lend such women money as the amounts were too small and they had no credit rating. Moreover, chimed the sceptics, they will run off with the money. They didn't, the loans made them self-sufficient and enabled them to repay the money and expand their business. The Grameen Bank is now an international operation and Mohammed Yunnus has received numerous awards for his work. A relationship of trust is enhanced by providing people with adequate human support in the form of mentoring — another central plank of the Prince's Trust approach — and a principle also applied by Mohammed Yunnus.

The Prince's Trust is now the UK's leading charity for young people and its driving passion is to turn untapped potential into real success. It now has over 10,000 volunteers, 800 staff and a turnover of more than £46 million a year. It offers a range of opportunities including training, personal development, business start-up support, mentoring and advice. These activities enable 14–30 year olds to develop confidence and skills, get into work and start their own businesses. The Trust focuses especially on those who are unemployed, under-skilled, within or leaving the criminal justice system or leaving care.

As of the end of 2003, the Trust had supported more than 480,000 young people over a period of 26 years. Specifically it has helped:

- 80,000 to improve their skills and job chances through the Team personal development Programme (9,300 in 2002–03)
- 58,000 to start-up in own business (current rate is 17 per working day — 4,359 in 2002-03)
- 20,000 through confidence building projects
- Over 185,000 through grants to individuals, young people's organizations and community projects
- Nearly 140,000 through school-based programmes

In the financial year 2002-3, the Trust supported more than 33,000 young people (up from 31,000 in the previous year). Amongst those, some 13,000 were unemployed, 11,000 educational underachievers, 2,100 with a care background and 2,650 were prisoners or ex-offenders.

The Trust began its activities in 1976, with 21 pilot projects funded partly by a fee of £4,000 given to the Prince by an American TV company for an interview about George III, and partly through other donations — including £2,000 from Sir Harry Secombe as a result, Secombe joked, of 'selling my mother-in-law to an Arab and for doing a special charity concert.' The Prince also contributed his severance pay from the Royal Navy — £7,400. Grants included one given to a 19-year-old woman to run a social centre for the Haggerston Housing Estate in east London, and for two ex-offenders to run a fishing club. Funds were also provided to hire swimming baths in Cornwall to train young lifeguards and for a self-help bicycle repair scheme. These early schemes did not generate much momentum, and the Prince had to persuade those around him who wished to discourage such social activity on the grounds that it might be seen as political. Moreover, the new Trust found it much harder to raise funds than the other already established Royal Jubilee Trusts.

The Trust took off during the 1980s, a period when there was a much larger pool of unemployed people and feelings ran sufficiently high to erupt into riots in 1981. Adam Nicolson observes that this unrest brought 'to much wider public attention some of the very problems which the Trust had been trying to address from the start. The spectre of an emergent underclass, of a whole layer of young unemployed people who felt they had no stake in a society which ignored and abused them, had become a central concern of public policy.' An emphasis on self-reliance allied to support from business (about which we shall say more below) enabled the Trust to advance its agenda. The business start-up programme was launched in 1982, the same year in which the first fund raising concert took place in Birmingham, raising £72,000. Rock bands helped, funded or even started by the Trust played alongside established pop stars including the legendary Status Quo. 1983 saw the first Prince's Trust Rock Gala at the Dominion in Tottenham Court Road, with Madness, Joan Armatrading, Phil Collins, Kate Bush and Pete Townshend. These fund raising rock galas continued through the 1980s. Candidates for these business start-up programmes were carefully selected and given the support of a volunteer mentor. One thousand businesses were started in the first three years, of which a remarkable 80% survived their first year. The current success rate after three years remains encouragingly high at 60%.

The Prince's Trust's ambitions, however, were greater than could be achieved without some Government support. A critical role was played by Sir Angus Ogilvy, who persuaded Lord Young, then Secretary of State for Employment, to match any funds raised for its young entrepreneur schemes. This proved rather more expensive than originally anticipated, especially when the Trust succeeded in raising £40 million in an appeal for the Prince's 40th birthday in 1988 — Lord Young had some explaining to do to Prime Minister Margaret Thatcher, but the Trust received its matching funds.

At this point the key ideas noted above — 'outward bound activities, self-realization through challenge, self-esteem through team membership' — began to be applied in all the Trust's activities. Week-long residential events were first held in 1985 at holiday camps around the UK, drawing hundreds of deprived young people. Camps continued annually for thirteen years, and in 1996 an international camp was held in France. A letter from a group in Greater Manchester in 1987 makes it clear that they had an unforgettable experience, a week of both work and fun: 'the atmosphere I experienced in itself was an experience to me, it was so warm and friendly, it was like being in another world for a week. It would be lovely if it could be like that always. Thank you from the bottom of my heart... ' The Prince was delighted and wrote back personally to the group. 1985 also marked the launch of The Prince of Wales Community Venture — an intensive 42-week programme, containing a mix of challenge, outdoors activity teamwork, and community care. This scheme later developed into the Volunteers Programme. Although 94 of the first 137 programme attenders found jobs, there was a high drop-out rate and the scheme — at £7,000 per person — was proving too expensive. The Trust was put on a firmer business and organizational footing in 1987 by the appointment of Sir Tom Shebbeare as the first full-time director and the arrival of Jim Gardner as Chair of Trustees. It is indicative that the Trust's spending rose from just over £31,000 in 1980 to £10 million in 1989.

In 1990, *The Prince's Trust Volunteers Programme* (now known as Team) was initiated. By 1995, ten thousand young people had completed the programme and by 2000 the figure had reached 50,000, of whom two-thirds subsequently moved on to employment or further training. The Team Programme is now funded by the Government as part of their welfare to work policy, and the Trust persuaded the Government to add a self-employment element to their 'New Deal.' *Study Support* was also launched in 1990 to provide under-achieving pupils with after hours study centres. This initiative was also taken up by the Government in 1997 and the current target is 8,000 such centres using funding from the New Opportunities Fund. The most strategic breakthrough of the 1990s was the acceptance that the Prince's Trust's activities were successful prototypes to be copied — imitation, as they say, is the sincerest form of flattery. The programmes, according to Tom Shebbeare, 'should be big enough to make a difference and good enough to be copied.'

In 1994 the first residential music school took place. This evolved into the nationwide *Sound Live* programme, teaching young unemployed about the music business. In 1996 the Trust held the first rock concert in Hyde Park for over twenty years. This event marked the start of a long-term strategy to establish a link between the Trust and young people's passions of music, fashion and sport (especially football). In 1998, a number of new initiatives were launched: mentors for teenagers leaving care; a scheme to target young offenders, 70% of whom had no qualifications to their name. Moreover, as the Trust's research established, an astonishing 90% of this young offenders group had been physically or sexually abused in childhood.

On the basis that progress could more easily be made by a younger age group, so called *xl clubs* were founded in the same year to motivate 15 and 16 year olds and keep them at school. Young people expelled from school or who themselves reject the system are three times more likely to enter a downward spiral towards a marginalized life of drugs, crime and prison. *xl* aims to prevent this from happening. Further programmes provided opportunities for travel and exploration in Europe and a partnership with VSO gave six month-long international opportunities for the Trust's disadvantaged clientele. Development Awards — originally one-off £100 or £200 grants — were shaped to incorporate ongoing guidance and support. Groups of young people can now apply for grants up to £15,000 to develop their own projects in their local community.

In 1999 the Trust reached a watershed with the amalgamation of the other Royal Jubilee Trusts into the Prince's Trust, which was then awarded a Royal Charter by the Queen at a ceremony in Buckingham Palace attended by hundreds of volunteers, young people and other supporters. The Prince told the assembled company: 'I know, without a shadow of a doubt, that young people can rise to the challenge if they are given the chance, and that they *can* be a success. And, if I had to sum up what the Trust's message is to the young people who need us, it would be, quite simply, 'Yes You Can.'' It was a powerful vindication of his original vision more than 25 years before.

Then in 2000, the Trust's organizational structure was revamped so that Wales, Scotland, Northern Ireland and each of the English regions now has its own fully-accountable Director and Council. And in 2002 the Trust announced a £5 million investment over three years to help the 30,000 young people a year who leave school with no qualifications and low basic skills. In order to keep itself informed of the changing aspirations, hopes and fears of the young, the Trust has commissioned a series of reports to ensure the continuing relevance of its programmes. Many of the original problems they aimed to tackle are still rife, so there is much that remains to be done.

## Core Programmes of the Prince's Trust

### Team Programme

This is a personal development programme enabling 16–25 year olds — the majority of them unemployed — to develop their confidence, motivation and skills through teamwork in the community. Young people join a Volunteers Team of up to fifteen participants at one of more than 300 locations around the UK. A Team comprises unemployed people including those on Government New Deal programmes, 16–18 year olds from Learning Gateway, people leaving care, young offenders, students and employed people sponsored by their employers. During the twelve-week programme, participants learn the importance of teamwork, spend a week at a residential activity centre, undertake a project based in the local community (for example, redecorating a community centre), complete a work placement, participate in a team challenge (usually involving disadvantaged groups — for example, taking a group of children with learning difficulties away on a short trip) and stage a team presentation, during which they recount their experiences.

Around 80,000 people have taken part since the Programme was launched in 1990. As a result of the Programme, over 70% of the unemployed participants find work or enter full time education or training while 90% of employers report improvements in the skills and attitudes of employed participants on their return to work. The Programme helps participants gain nationally recognized qualifications, improve motivation and self-confidence, assume some responsibility, develop teamworking and communication skills and raise their awareness of their local community and of how they can contribute to it.

## Business Programme

A recent report from the Trust — *Reaching the Hardest to Reach* — found that nearly 650,000 16–24 year olds were economically inactive and not in full time education, with a further 405,000 unemployed and not in full time education. This means that a staggering total of over a million young people under 25 are without work. The Trust offers low interest loans of up to £5,000 as well as grants and support to enable 18–30 year olds to start their own businesses under the guidance of a volunteer business mentor. All are unemployed or under-employed and have been refused funding by other sources. The Trust provides ongoing support in the form of mentors, self-help business guides and free telephone information lines. It is impressive that 60% of Trust-funded businesses are still trading in their third year of operation (nearly twice the national average), while many of those whose companies ceased trading enter full-time education or training. Highlights of the programme include the following:

- Over 58,000 18–30 year olds have been supported since 1983, creating more than 45,000 new businesses
- The top fifty businesses turn over almost £148 million and employ around 2,255 people
- £3,300 is the average cost of setting up and supporting a young person in business
- Nearly 5,000 young people received start-up finance and support in the last financial year
- 43% set up in the service sector, 23% in media, leisure and the arts, 11% in manufacturing, 8% in fashion and design in the last financial year
- Over 8,000 people are currently volunteering as Business Mentors.

The Prince's Scottish Youth Business Trust has replicated the business start-up idea in Scotland from 1989. Since the PSYBT began, more than 5,400 young people have started more than 4,500 businesses. The demanding first year of trading is survived by 82%, while 53% are still in business after three years. The total annual turnover of PSYBT supported businesses is

*A SUCCESS STORY*

— *in November 2001, Celina Nessa was living in East London, had been unemployed for six months and was on the New Deal unemployed programme. While helping at a youth club, she came across an advert for the Prince's Trust Volunteers programme. Celina joined a Volunteers' course at the Bridge Project in Tower Hamlets, with twelve other young people from a range of backgrounds. Nine were unemployed, two were employed volunteers from the Crown Prosecution Service, and one was from the Court Service. The programme included a work placement at the Employment Service and a visit to Arsenal at Highbury Stadium, where the group learned to write their CVs and complete internet job searches. At the end of the course the group enacted a skit and received their certificates from the Vice-Chairman of Arsenal, David Dein. Since the Volunteers course, Celina has completed a one-day-a-week work placement with magazine publishers Condé Nast, has been offered a six month placement with the Employment Service, has also taken her driving licence and now has a real sense of accomplishment and confidence in her future. She strongly recommends the course to others in her position wanting to gain skills and qualifications, and especially the experience of working in a mutually supportive team.*

over £80 million: the first year average turnover of individual businesses is £23,000, rising to £56,000 by year three. Over £14.6 million has been awarded, 87% in the form of low cost loans, and the remaining 13% (£1.9 million) in grants. The average investment by PSYBT is £3,600, in addition to the comprehensive aftercare support. 36% of the young people assisted are women, and the average age of a PSYBT recipient is 23. Nearly 80% were unemployed before receiving PSYBT support, and 18% left school without any formal academic qualifications. The PSYBT now works towards an annual target of 450 businesses a

**Mark Brann** *had been epileptic since the age of 17 and had real problems holding down a variety of jobs, losing 23 in three years. Understandably, he became frustrated and disillusioned. As he had always been fascinated by reptiles, he considered the feasibility of opening a small reptile shop but without a job there was no hope of saving the necessary start-up funds. He therefore contacted the Prince's Trust, who offered him a loan of £2,000 subject to a business plan and cash flow projection. Mark opened the Exotic Pet Centre with his mother doing the accounts while he ran the business. Such was the interest that Mark's cash flow was almost three times what he had forecast so he moved to larger premises. He is now building a regular visitor centre called The Forgotten World, which will be one of the largest reptile centres in the UK. Mark says: 'without the support of the Prince's Trust, I wouldn't be here now — it's as simple as that!'*

year. It manages a loan fund of almost £5 million and provides aftercare to over 1,000 businesses.

## Group Awards

The Prince's Trust Millennium Group Awards is the three-year joint venture funded by the Millennium Commission. Groups of three to twelve young people aged 14–25 are given cash awards of between £3,750 and £15,000 for community projects. There is also a corresponding international scheme of World Youth Awards where young people from different countries work in pairs for six months — over 900 people have participated in this. The Prince's Trust has awarded grants to over 2,000 young people participating in over 200 projects. Projects need to fall into one of the following categories:

~ EDUC8 — young people guiding others
~ Time Out — positive use of leisure time

∽ Where it's @ — new technologies to improve lives
∽ Eco-Planet — improving the local environment
∽ Harmonize — helping others to be part of the local community

Projects include a community radio station, a drop in centre, a community garden and a community website.

## Xl Clubs

These are a network of clubs within schools that encourage students to realize their potential by offering a focused guidance programme with tangible goals. The clubs focus on citizenship, community action and enterprise and are designed to build confidence and prepare participants for working life. For students 'at risk' of truanting and under-achievement at school, the clubs aim to improve attendance, motivation and social skills. They meet for three hours a week, partly in school time. Students are offered comprehensive support to help them into further education, including advice on interviews and application forms. Over 9,000 fifteen and sixteen year olds have participated since 1999, with 4,800 added in 2001–02. There were 700 clubs in December 2003 supporting 9,000 young people (up from 430 in September 2002) with a target of more than 1,000 by 2005. Clubs produce regular newsletters that can be downloaded from the web.

## Other Trust Programmes

### Development Awards

∽ Cash awards of £50–500 combined with advice and support to enable access to education, training and work. In addition, groups of young people can apply for grants of up to £10,000 to deliver community projects
∽ Over 8,000 young people have received these awards to date
∽ Over 30% of recipients obtain employment
∽ Another 60% proceed to undertake further education and training

*22-year-old* **Abby**, *from Northumberland, had been out of work for two and a half years before deciding to explore voluntary work overseas. She joined a team of eighteen young people from Thailand and the UK on a six-month exchange. Abby's goals before she left on the Thailand phase of the exchange were to 'experience a different culture and gain work experience and life skills.' Abby's experiences on the programme — which included eating a deep fried waterbug in Thailand — have made her look seriously at working abroad in a developing country in the future.*

*21-year-old* **Maryam** *from Milton Keynes, who had been unemployed for six months, wanted to join a World Youth exchange because she felt she 'would have a lot to gain.' Maryam also thought she'd have something to offer a cross-cultural programme like World Youth as, 'I am an Asian being brought up in a Western society.' She found her biggest challenge on the exchange was 'trying to educate people from Thailand that it's not only white people that come from England.' Despite the challenges, Maryam says that the exchange was 'an experience I will never forget.' In the future, she hopes to continue voluntary work in developing countries.*

## Sound Live

A 6-day residential course that develops a young person's musical talents. The course provides the chance to work closely with professional musicians and tutors as well as with other young participants. It covers playing new styles, playing in bands and specialist instrument tuition. It also helps a participant develop a career focus, through goal and action planning. The programme ends with a gig where all the participants perform. After the course, participants receive a further 6 months of ongoing support to help keep the momentum going and the

A SUCCESS STORY

— **Kelly Bridgwater** *was fourteen when she was recommended for xl by her school. She had no motivation and could not see the point of school. She really enjoyed the projects and felt supported by her group to gain the vital confidence in herself. Activities have included drama, rock climbing, canoeing and driving to study accident prevention. At sixteen, she has a folder full of records of achievement and is determined to continue her education. She has also made some really good friends on the course.*

support young people to achieve their goals. Since 1989  more than 4,000 unemployed young people have attended. 13% of unemployed participants obtain employment, 20% obtain full time self employment as band members and a further 30% move into further education or training.

## Mentoring For Care Leavers

This is a scheme to provide personal mentors to support and advise young people leaving care in the UK. These are among the most disadvantaged and vulnerable in society. They are more likely to be homeless or unemployed, and the majority leave school with no qualifications. Mentors help participants make the most of their possibilities for further training and education — and one in ten care leavers currently use Prince's Trust programmes. Participants are also eligible for the courses and development awards already outlined. In 2003, a further 500 mentors will be recruited, trained and maintained. Then there is a new initiative piloting personal development courses for young people still serving sentences, as preparation for their release.

  ∼ Since 1998 over 1,400 young people have been involved in a
    1:1 mentoring relationship

---

*A SUCCESS STORY*

*Joe was 22 years old, had been out of work for four years, was an ex-offender and was living in a probation hostel when he received a Development Award. His aim was to become a qualified roofer. When he applied to the Trust for help, he had found an employer who was willing to take him on and train him. But there was one problem: he had to supply his own tools, but had no income to buy them. The Prince's Trust provided Joe with support from a volunteer and a £300 Development Award to cover tools. Joe is now working and training to become a roofer. In his application he told the Trust: 'I just want the chance to build for the future, and I believe everyone should have that chance.'*

---

~ There are 42 mentoring partnerships projects throughout the UK

~ Through its partnership organizations the scheme has recruited and trained over 1,600 mentors

## Research Reports and Fact Sheets

The Trust publishes and updates a series of fact sheets on challenges facing young people. These include crime, ethnicity, homelessness, unemployment, parenthood, leaving care, disability, education and training, drugs and alcohol. These fact sheets outline current issues, discuss government policy and initiatives as well as presenting quantitative findings. This research enables the Trust to listen to young people and find out what they really think. As the Prince says, this enables the Trust to stay one step ahead of the game and respond more effectively to the needs and concerns of young people without becoming complacent and self-satisfied: 'However difficult the challenge, our aim must be to help those who are hardest to reach, be they young offenders, those who are psychologically disturbed or those without even the most basic skills.'

---

A SUCCESS STORY

— **Darren** *is 25 and lives in a YMCA hostel in London. He has been homeless and had drug problems in the past, and came on Sound Live in June 2000. Darren is mainly a rapper. After completing Sound Live, Darren was asked to do some market research for the YMCA, which led to him speaking at the Labour and Liberal Democrat party conferences last year. He made speeches to over 100 people on each occasion, talking about his use of drugs, homelessness, and what could be done to prevent some of the problems young people face today. He also talked about the work of the Trust, his experience in Sound Live and what his subsequent Development Award has enabled him to do. Darren is currently setting up an independent record label and has recently put down a number of tracks to be taken to major record companies. Darren has used his Development Award to pay for short courses in sound engineering and is keen to stay in touch with the Trust, particularly Sound Live, to identify and help other young people who attend the course.*

---

## SkillCity

The Prince's Trust is working with UK Skills on a joint venture to demonstrate and promote skills for young people. The first ever Skills Show occurred in July 2000, and was followed by another 'SkillCity' in November 2002, opened by the Prince of Wales. It attracted 80,000 young people to see — and perhaps have a go at — over one hundred vocational skills at a purpose built site at Salford Quays in Manchester. The Prince remarked on that occasion:

Many of our key industries are under pressure. Over the next four years, the construction industry alone will need to take on nearly 80,000 new recruits each year. The largest requirements will be for bricklayers, plumbers, electricians, carpenters and joiners. And yet more than two thirds of construction industry employers already have difficulties in finding and training people in just these skill areas.

The Prince was convinced that 'many of these skills shortages are caused by the fact that we are now encouraging far too many young people in this country to aspire to desk-bound and man-agement-oriented careers. At the same time, he continued, we are encouraging far too few to aim for those vocational careers which rely on practical skills and crafts — both modern (such as industrial electronics) and traditional (such as stonemasonry).' Hence the mismatch between skills and demand. It is ironic that a survey quoted by the Prince found that 30% of university graduates thought that they were overqualified for the jobs they were doing — and yet the Government is intent on expanding university provision still further.

*Route 14–25*

A new initiative designed to offer a tailor-made package of support for young people. It offers a single point of access to enable them to find appropriate education, training, business support and self-development. The major partner in this venture is the Royal Bank of Scotland, which is investing £3.7 million over three years. It has already been launched in Scotland, the North East and North West of England, and will extend to all other areas of the UK by 2004.

The foregoing account has identified the major milestones and achievements of the Prince's Trust, which are impressive by any standard. Not only has the Trust changed tens of thousands of young people's lives for the better, it has also contributed in no small measure to the overall social and economic progress of the UK, as James Morton has demonstrated in his book *Prince Charles —Breaking the Cycle*.

We have already seen how the Prince has approached the rebuilding of communities with his urban planning and housing projects run within the Prince's Foundation. We now move on to see how he has pursued a similar path in connection with business.

# 7. Responsible Action — Leadership, Business and the Community

*We must become the change we want to see in the world.*
Mahatma Gandhi

The Prince's Trust has long been supported by companies so it was natural for the Prince of Wales to work closely with businesses to further his passion for community regeneration and environmental sustainability. This chapter describes his involvement with a number of related initiatives — Business in the Community, The Prince of Wales's International Business Leaders Forum and The Prince of Wales's Business and the Environment Programme. Along with the Prince's Trust and the Regeneration Through Heritage programme of the Prince's Foundation, these initiatives work for common goals and create partnerships with companies, local communities and central Government.

## Business in the Community

*In my travels around this country it has become more and more apparent to me that when people feel excluded from their community and unable to make a contribution, the whole fabric of those communities is at serious risk. When that fabric starts to disintegrate then we all suffer — whatever our position. It seems to me the best way of starting to tackle the problems is to provide practical help which will encourage people to do something for themselves to regain their self-belief once again feel part of their community.*
The Prince of Wales

Business in the Community (BITC) was established in 1982 against a backdrop of very high levels of unemployment, collapsing traditional industries and serious urban rioting. Many people observed that although large companies were beginning to play a key role in sponsoring major sporting and cultural events, companies in the United States were much more involved with their local communities than their British counterparts. Sir Alastair Pilkington, who had previously set up the pathfinder Enterprise Agency in St Helens was chosen to chair a new organization promoting corporate community involvement. Sir Alastair thus became the Founder of Business in the Community, and insisted from the outset that BITC should be a genuine partnership between business, government, local authorities and Trade Unions.

The Prince's involvement with BITC dates back to 1985, when he received a letter from its chief executive Stephen O'Brien. Following an initial meeting, an extraordinary event was set up to bring together a group of leading industrialists with a number of black community leaders, who arranged the agenda. The outcome of the 24 hour seminar led to the Prince becoming President of BITC, a position he held until 2002. It is indicative of the Prince's commitment to this work that he attended over 450 BITC events over the following twelve years in addition to promoting it through letters and private meetings. Following a visit by the Prince to the old mill town of Lowell near Boston, BITC initiated a flagship project in Halifax, which became an epitome of good practice with its scheme to regenerate the environment and housing provision, while promoting confidence and employment in the process. This involved community architects and the close involvement of the whole community in the project. As Jonathan Dimbleby points out, the BITC emphasis on partnership championed by the Prince led to a fundamental shift in government thinking — the words community and partnership are common currency these days. Another early project initiated by the Prince through BITC was the creation of sixty inner city 'compacts' between local employers and local schools. It was not long before these became government 'education and business partnerships.'

Business in the Community is a unique movement of 700

member companies (including three-quarters of the FTSE 100), who are committed to continuous improvement of their positive impact on society. BITC is a business led organization involving 189 member companies in leadership teams that develop responsible business practice. It is the largest UK national organization of its kind with the capacity to translate company policy into local action, at the same time as connecting their global members with a network of international partners. BITC is a platform for dialogue that develops and shares best practice and collaborative action. BITC member companies employ over 15.7 million people in over 200 countries worldwide. In the UK its members employ over one in five of the private sector workforce, which makes them a powerful voice for responsible business.

BITC operates on the basis of five principles that form the heart of their strategy and the concomitant commitment to action entailed by membership:

~ Integrity
~ Inspiration
~ Integration
~ Innovation
~ Impact

In an article written for the *Financial Times* in 1997, the Prince wrote that his experience with Business in the Community had taught him three principles for engaging business with the community: 'the first is partnership. The power of partnership was first demonstrated when, in 1985, the example of Halifax, West Yorkshire, taught business leaders that, in co-operation with the local authority, they could help bring back employment opportunities to a declining milltown. That experience of persuading businesses to become involved in long-term, sustainable partnerships continues to be at the heart of Business in the Community's work.'

'The second principle,' continued the Prince, 'is the importance of encouraging business leaders to see for themselves the problems, opportunities and examples of best practice on the ground. More than 800 [now over 2,500] business leaders have taken part in my 'Seeing is Believing' tours in the past seven years. The practical results have been heartening.' The Seeing is Believing approach is a central plank of BITC policy and originated in a scheme proposed for its board to go on a field day to Hackney and Tower Hamlets in 1990. The Prince was convinced that practical face to face experience of inner city problems would have a galvanizing effect on business people committed to practical solutions. In the foreword to a book published in 1997, the Prince wrote that 'the experience of Seeing is Believing clearly changes the way business people think and feel about a whole range of community issues. Many confess to having been completely ignorant of the extent of social and economic problems faced by groups and individuals across the United Kingdom, some of which lie on their own doorsteps.' Following a visit in north east London, Tom Symes of Nabarro Nathanson 'came away feeling that it is an appalling waste to have a community which is located adjacent to the City of London, but so far from the wealth and employment creation opportunities that exist in the City.'

Groups have visited schools, housing estates and community projects. They have then been invited to report back to him personally on their impressions and plans for action. The 'heartening results' take many forms, for example providing training and work in some of the country's most deprived areas. Fifty of these can be accessed on the BITC web site, and in his article the Prince cites specific examples:

> Under the auspices of KPMG, the accountancy firm, 320 [now over 4,000] business leaders have been paired with headteachers across the country in a teachers' 'mentoring project' [*Partnership in Leadership*]. Regeneration partnerships have been formed in Great Yarmouth, Norfolk, following a visit led by Allen Bridgewater, chief executive of Norwich Union, and in Thanet after a visit led by Sir Martin Laing, chairman of John Laing, the construction company.

*Roots and Wings* is a mentoring initiative for young people at risk that was developed following a visit by Rudi Bogni of banking group UBS to Deptford Green School in south east London. Over 2,000 volunteers have now been involved in the programme.

In 1997, some 45 communities in the United Kingdom were identified by Business in the Community as places where business needed to be more involved in regeneration and these now form the basis for the Seeing is Believing programme visits. The Prince more recently extended Seeing is Believing to the challenges faced by rural communities, as we saw in Chapter 2.

'The third principle,' wrote the Prince, 'is the priceless value of that unsung hero or heroine, the community entrepreneur. Those communities which, against all odds, have succeeded in reversing a spiral of decline have done so, in my experience, because of local characters like Paddy Doherty in Londonderry who, in 1981, started to revitalize the bombed-out and rundown centre of his city. The results are spectacular.' The Prince explained that 'however inspiring the individual, our experience in Business in the Community shows that behind every budding community entrepreneur there needs almost always to be a network of business support.' Some senior business leaders like Sir Bill Castell of Amersham, Neville Simms of Tarmac, and Sir Neil Shaw of Tate & Lyle have been very active in working with community entrepreneurs.

In 1986, the Prince became Chairman of the Community Enterprise Awards. Speaking at the presentation of the 1995 awards he said that 'all over the country there are some remarkable groups of people working incredibly hard who are utterly determined to make a real difference to their communities. The whole object of these Awards is to reward and recognize all those unsung heroes and heroines.' The winners of the Community Enterprise Awards are a rollcall of these who have been the architects of community-led regeneration — Paddy Doherty of the Derry Inner City Trust, Tony McGann of the Eldonians and David Robinson of Community Links. As Paddy Doherty put it: 'To be successful, community development requires leadership, leadership that nurtures and excites.' In addition to recognizing and celebrating community entrepreneurs, the Prince developed the Local Investment Fund to support viable community enterprises. Over £1.2 million of loans have been agreed since the fund began in 1992 and a regional investment fund is now being launched in Merseyside with further roll-outs planned in the South West, Yorkshire and Wales.

In 1992, the Prince visited Second Harvest, a food bank programme, in Canada. As a result of this experience, he subsequently encouraged *Provision*, an Institute of Grocery Distribution initiative, to set up a national network to identify food and non-food supplies to make them available to charitable organizations providing meals for the homeless and underprivileged. This led in 1996 to *Gifts in Kind*, which was set up by Business in the Community and The Prince's Trust to deliver surplus goods to community projects. Over £3 million of goods including computers, toys, toiletries and clothing have been delivered to charities. *Gifts in Kind* is matched by gifts of time, as the Prince explains: 'companies serious about their management development use community assignments to stretch the skills of their young managers. Marks & Spencer, for example, places 300 staff a year on ten-hour assignments and full-time secondment.'

As the Prince said in 1997, 'obviously a great deal more remains to be done. I hope Business in the Community will go on striving to raise the quality of corporate community investment. We must encourage companies to involve themselves in the most disadvantaged communities and the most intractable issues and I hope that the work of Business in the Community — to change the mainstream attitudes of companies and to influence how they recruit, train, sell, purchase and invest — will go on.'

The last twenty years has seen a sea change in corporate attitudes to wider issues and the development of the concept of Corporate Social Responsibility (CSR). BITC has been in the vanguard of these developments, which have led to much higher expectations in terms of transparency and accountability. As Sir Peter Davis observed in the BITC 2001 annual report, consumer activism, riots, environmental issues and the anti-globalization movement have combined to make businesses look carefully at their broad responsibilities. This means that business performance is no longer assessed in terms of financial performance alone. And with the development of new indices — for instance the FTSE4Good ethical index — new types of benchmark and measurements are emerging. The pioneering work of BITC has set the trend in this direction and its influence will surely continue to extend.

## The Prince of Wales's International Business Leaders Forum

*Twelve years ago, when I founded my International Business Leaders Forum, there were all too many sceptics who thought our mission would never be taken seriously as part of the expected behaviour of business leaders. This was the simple, if somewhat controversial idea, that unless business operated in a responsible way in the face of the opportunities provided by the new market economies, and engaged in partnership to promote sustainable development, it would fail to win support and acceptance.*

The Prince of Wales

Drawing on the principles and his personal experience of Business in the Community initiatives involving business and community partnerships in the UK in the late 1980s, the Prince of Wales inaugurated the International Business Leaders Forum in 1990. This was the period immediately following the collapse of Communism in Europe, which precipitated a new spread of market economies. On the environmental front, the early 1990s saw a growing environmental awareness reflected in the first Earth Summit of 1992, which in turn began to focus the debate about the nature and consequences of the globalization process. The Forum acts as a focus for businesses around the world to work together in the global promotion and practical implementation of 'socially responsible business practices that benefit business and society, and which help to achieve social, economic and environmentally sustainable development in emerging and transition economies.'

The Prince of Wales initiated the Forum in February 1990 at a two-day meeting in Charleston, South Carolina, USA, with more than one hundred senior executives from the USA, Europe, Japan and Australia. Since then the Prince has chaired over forty meetings in thirty countries, often during official overseas visits. In addition he has led project visits and helped bring people together to plan practical action for the sustainable development of their communities. From an initial base of Anglo-American support secured at this founding meeting, the Forum became an independent multinational organization (registered as an educational charity) backed by some of the foremost business leaders in Europe, America, Asia and the Middle East.

At the end of its first year in operation, the Forum had five staff, five member companies, a small office in an attic in the City of London, and a turnover of less than £250,000. Thirteen years on it employs a team of forty staff working out of London and a further twenty associates around the world. It has over seventy international member companies and corporate partners, occupies an office and conference suite in London's Regent's Park, and has reached an annual turnover of some £3 million.

The Forum now works in over fifty countries. It has a particular interest in emerging and transition economies in Central and Eastern Europe and Russia, the Middle East, Southern Africa, Asia, Latin America and the Caribbean. The Forum's international member companies — from Europe, America and Asia — include Diageo, SmithKline Beecham, the Coca-Cola Company, Levi's, Price Waterhouse Coopers, KPMG, Norsk Hydro, Rio Tinto, BP-Amoco, BG, ABB, 3M, and Shell. Companies from Asia include Mitsubishi, Toyota and Honda of Japan. Chief executive officers, chairmen, and senior executives from fifty of the foremost global companies form the Board and Council of the Forum, providing leadership and funding.

An early initiative of the Forum was a meeting in Hungary to assess the relevance of corporate social responsibility in Eastern Europe as it emerged from the straitjacket of nearly fifty years of Communist rule. It rapidly became apparent that cross-sector partnerships were not enough and that there was a widespread need to build people's skills. Out of this need the 'Learning from Experience' project was born in which some ninety people from six Central and Eastern European countries took part. At a later stage this led to a specific programme for Hungary, Poland, Czech Republic and Slovakia, where 22 projects were funded, with involvement by thirty graduates from the original project. These include the Polish Environmental Partnership Foundation, the Czech Business Leaders Programme and the Levego Clean Air Action Group.

From the outset, the Forum has pursued three pathways:

~ In making the case that in the new world situation, businesses have a *positive role to play in development challenges*

through responsible core business practices and engage-
ment with society
~ In championing *cross-sector partnership and collective action* in
the networked society, where it is essential to combine
business skills and resources with community support and
public accountability
~ And in demonstrating that economic exclusion can only be
addressed through creating *'enabling environments'* in which
governments, international institutions and the media all
play a part.

As the Forum's activities have evolved, it developed and main-
tained its 'A-B-C-D' focus:
~ Advocacy of the case for business social responsibility and
partnership
~ Brokerage of partners
~ Capacity-building in training managers and partners for
leadership and action
~ Dissemination of ideas and good practices.

The Forum acts as a catalyst for projects chosen to demonstrate
good business practice, and works closely with international
institutions like the World Bank, and United Nations
Development Programme, the United Nations High
Commission for Human Rights, the World Health Organization,
the World Health Programme, the UNAIDS agency, and the
International Labour Organization. Many of these joint initiatives address capacity and institution building. The Forum has
launched publications with and through the *Financial Times* and
Time/Fortune. Over 11,000 business leaders around the world
have been involved in the activities of the Forum, largely
through its initiatives in brokering partnerships — particularly
those between the private sector, the public sector and the non-
governmental organizations of 'civil society' — to address the
challenges of development in new emerging markets.

The Forum has evolved as fast as its subject matter. In the
mid-1990s, for example, its focus on issues of business ethics,
social development and human rights was seen as rather radical
and ill-focused. Only six years later, these same issues could be

discussed comfortably in most boardrooms. The Forum takes the view that responsible business is about core business practices and standards, not just about philanthropy and community investment. It represents a strategic commitment in every business decision and operation, and one which encompasses every building block of business: skills, logistical capacity and people, as well as money. These days the framework is that of the 'triple bottom line,' which includes social and ecological along with the financial benchmarks.

The Forum runs several distinct programmes. Its *Values in Leadership* programme was launched to help develop a new generation of business leaders in two ways: by focusing on the role of boards and senior management teams in integrating social responsibility into their corporate strategy; and by influencing good practice in executive development within companies and business schools.

The Forum runs practical programmes in a number of areas:

~ Business standards and corporate governance
~ Education and human resource development
~ Human rights, labour standards and conflict prevention
~ Enterprise and economic development
~ Health development, workplace and environmental standards.

In each project area the focus is on three key factors: leadership in responsible business practice; innovation in cross-sector partnership; and the building of capacity and institutions.

The Forum is one of the World Bank's partners in the *Business Partners in Development* Action Learning Programmes which focus on the sharing of the best practice and partnership methods in natural resource conservation, water and sanitation, youth initiatives and road safety. It works alongside the UN Staff College in the *Partners in Action* programme to bring together UN staff and businesses around the world. A related initiative is the Forum's co-operation with the UN Secretary-General's office in promoting a 'Global Compact' to foster deeper links and co-operation between international agencies, the private sector and citizens' groups.

*The International Hotels Environment Initiative* (IHEI- *www.ihei.org*)
has been run within The Prince of Wales Business Leaders Forum
since 1992. Global hotel chains, with two million rooms, have been
involved in programmes to implement higher environmental standards in the industry worldwide. The Prince has taken a close personal interest in the programme, which he launched in London in
May 1993. There he argued that 'improved environmental performance can go hand-in-hand with improved economic performance, as travellers choose the 'green' option when making
bookings, and sustainability can save a business money in the
long-term as it works with rather than against the local community
and the environment.' He added that 'environmentally, socially
and aesthetically responsible hotel siting, design and construction
are, in my view, the foundation from which the industry should
develop in a more sustainable way.' This initiative was followed up
in 1995 by the *Green Hotelier* scheme and an environmental action
pack for hotels, and in 2000 by the hotel environmental bench-
marking programme. In 2001, IHEI launched a web-based bench-
marking tool (*www.benchmarkhotel.com*) allowing hoteliers to
measure energy usage, compare it with competitors and identify
where costs and environmental impacts can be reduced.

The *Youth Business International* (YBI) initiative (*www.youth-
business.org*) is a worldwide network of partner organizations
run by the Forum in co-operation with The Prince's Trust. Its
purpose is to enable the business community to help young people work for themselves by providing business mentoring and
access to finance. *The Resource Centre for the Social Dimensions of
Business Practice* is run by a consortium headed by the Forum
and is funded by the Government's Department for
International Development. It has been created to develop the
capacity, approaches and resources to advise business, the public sector and civil society on poverty elimination.

In response to concern over the growing 'digital divide' the
Forum has set up the *Digital Partnership* (*www.iblf.org/digitalpart-
nership*) as an international partnership with IT users and suppliers, educators and community leaders to bridge the large
skills gap in Information Communications Technology (ICT)
skills that currently exist in many developing counties. A pilot
initiative started in South Africa in January 2002 with support

from the World Bank and multinational companies. The country has an ICT skills shortage of around 200,000 people, so the programme will provide for the training of 200 Master Facilitators who will in turn train a further 10,000 e-facilitators.

One of the Prince's particular contributions has been in the conception of international INSIGHT programmes encouraging business and other leaders to visit examples of good practice, to see them for themselves. These are partly modelled on the Seeing is Believing programmes that we saw being used so effectively in Business in the Community. However, this programme is more extensive in that it also involves experience and cultural exchanges as well as a key role in building partnerships both within and between countries.

In 2000 The Prince of Wales's Business Leaders Forum marked its tenth anniversary with a series of events, and new campaigns to engage international chief executives and the global media in responding to the need to embed responsible businesses thinking — and the 'triple bottom line' of financial, social and environmental accountability — into all aspects of corporate strategy and operations.

In his message for the 2001 Forum Annual Review, the Prince said that there was plenty of work ahead. He saw 'little evidence that the globalization of business opportunity is being matched by an equal globalization of business responsibility.' He continued: 'nor do I see much evidence that rewards and incentives in the management of companies focus anywhere near enough on the contributions of companies to long-term prosperity, as distinct from short-term return. These are critical issues we need to address.' Looking to the future, the Prince said:

> I hope that through reviewing good practice, visiting examples of sound partnerships in action around the world, sharing business experience, making a commitment to continuous improvement in business practices, and working on initiatives to scale up experimental projects, all of us concerned with the long term prosperity our communities can make a greater impact on the thinking and practice of the managers and leaders tomorrow.

## Business and the Environment

In 1993, three years after establishing the International Business Leaders Forum and having recognized the crucial role business has to play in bringing about sustainable development, the Prince of Wales sought to establish a forum for senior executives where they could find the guidance and inspiration to make their own successful transition to corporate sustainability. The Business and the Environment Programme (BEP), which is developed and run by the University of Cambridge Programme for Industry, was first established in the UK in 1994. It expanded into Continental Europe in 1997, the USA in 2001, and Southern Africa in 2003.

The programme has brought together an exceptional range of leaders from all over the world: business, academic, political, NGO, public service, and institutional. BEP has generated a close-knit and continuing network of over 650 participants from over 350 organizations in more than twenty countries, with the potential and drive to influence the debate at corporate, public, and political levels. In bringing together key players in the sustainability debate the programme provides:

~ An international forum for business leaders, civil servants, and NGO representatives to address the challenge that sustainable development presents to business.

~ A peer network of individuals facing similar challenges, and who understand not only the economic and environmental implications of sustainable development but also the complexities of the wider social agenda.

~ Practical advice from business leaders and sustainability experts who have the necessary track record, as well as management experience, to help participants find benchmarks for their own organizations against leaders in their own industry, as well as other industries.

Each year forty-five delegates are selected to join the UK Programme at Madingley Hall in Cambridge, the European Programme at Schloss Leopoldskron in Salzburg and the US Programme at a selected location in the USA. As the Programme expands, new 'gateways' are planned for Latin America, Africa and Asia. Participants are selected on the basis that they have the necessary leadership authority in their own organizations to implement change at a strategic level. They enter the programme by means of a four-day residential seminar on the theme 'Sustainability and Profitability: Conflict or Convergence?' Seminars are led by a Core Faculty, which is chaired by a senior businessman and includes several distinguished academics and environmentalists. Contributors to the Programme are drawn from an international mix of business leaders, politicians, academics and other leaders in their field. The aim of the seminar is to give participants a deep, intensive experience in a constructive environment, which will help shape their attitudes, values, and aspirations with respect to sustainable development. The seminar acts as an educational gateway to the rest of the programme. Reports from regular meetings are posted on the web, along with case study examples and various types of learning materials.

During a lecture in 2001, the Prince cited two specific examples of the effect that the Programme had generated: 'A vice-president of a global car manufacturer has said that as a result of these seminars he has been much more self-confident in bringing up matters of sustainable development in front of the company's leadership team. He was able to speak with conviction and found that he was actually listened to. As a result he succeeded in making his company take major steps in addressing the global warming issue, and to be more open to dialogue with NGOs.' Another UK managing director of a global oil and gas company reported that 'the Programme had made a personal impact on him, and generated a commitment to embedding sustainable development and increased external transparency at the core of his company's long-term business strategy. This led the industry to start an open and transparent process for deciding what to do with accumulated drill cuttings beneath offshore oil platforms.'

The BEP thus reinforces the work of the Business Leaders Forum with respect to corporate environmental responsibility, with its Alumni network providing a powerful peer group of connections and mutual support. However, both social and environmental aspects feature in the debate on globalization and the role of business in shaping the future, to which we now turn. The next section brings us full circle to the concerns of the first chapter in which we examined the global environmental outlook.

### Globalization and Corporate Responsibility

*Without a global revolution in the sphere of human
consciousness, nothing will change for the better in our being
as humans, and the catastrophe toward which our world is
headed ... will be unavoidable ...We are still incapable of
understanding that the only genuine backbone of our actions
— if they are to be moral — is responsibility: responsibility to
something higher than my family, my country, my firm, my
success, responsibility to the order of being where all our
actions are indelibly recorded and where, and only where, they
will be judged.*

Vaclav Havel, Speech to US Congress 1990

If we ask the question, will our collective attitudes shift in time
to avert an ecological meltdown, the Prince is pessimistic while
at the same time working tirelessly to make sure that a more
optimistic scenario prevails. At a dinner for Business and the
Environment in March 2001 following a speech on 'Healthy
People, Healthy Planet' by Dr Gro Harlem Brundtland, he said
that, in his capacity as a dissident in society, he wanted to say
something highly provocative and unpopular:

I have long subscribed to the catastrophe theory that
humanity only wakes up to what it is doing to the
environment when confronted by global tragedies. For
example, you need only look at the way in which we have
managed our fish stocks. Cod stocks off Newfoundland
collapsed through intense over-fishing, and have still not
recovered after eight years. Yet even now, we are doing
the same to fish stocks off South Africa, in the North Sea,
and elsewhere, as if what happened in Newfoundland
was somehow not a matter of public record.

So I am afraid I end up believing that we will
inevitably see more catastrophe, and only then will
people realize what they have been doing to upset that
critical ecological and social balance on which we all
depend.

He continued:

> In this, as in all other matters, we need wisdom to
> understand the importance of balance. If you go beyond
> that point where things are still in balance, you will
> inevitably create an equal and opposite reaction. It is an
> unpleasant truth, but a truth all the same. It seems to me
> that there is a desperate risk that the forces of
> globalization are already dangerously out of balance, and
> I'll lay you a bet that in twenty years I'll be proved right!

In this speech to business leaders he makes the point that sustainable businesses imply sustainable societies and he does not let them off the hook:

> Of course we shouldn't over-estimate the capacity of even
> the largest and most powerful companies to achieve
> change. But nor should we *underestimate* what they can do
> when they put their minds to it. I am getting just a little
> fed up at hearing companies talk about what they can't
> do. The stakes, as far as I am concerned, are high enough
> that I would like them to try just a bit harder. Because if
> we don't build sustainable societies we aren't going to
> have sustainable businesses!

So the Prince suggests that partnerships — an approach successfully tried and tested in so many of his activities — are the way forward:

> As global companies experience the consumer-driven
> requirement to set higher standards for all their
> operations, I think they will find that operating in
> partnership with their stakeholders has a lot to offer, not
> least in setting standards and verifying performance.
> Building and maintaining such partnerships requires a
> high degree of openness, flexibility and willingness to be
> held accountable. As Dr Brundtland pointed out, 'the best
> partnerships are often those forged between unorthodox
> entities,' and I am increasingly hearing about forward-

thinking companies and NGOs working successfully together to tackle common problems.

The Prince does not claim that forging such partnerships is easy or necessarily popular with shareholders preoccupied with short-term returns:

> Making such partnerships work requires a degree of humility, some open-mindedness and, to return to where I started, the wisdom to see beyond the short term. These are the kind of qualities that we aim to encourage on the seminars run by my Business and Environment Programme, as well as a proper understanding of the meaning of sustainability.

Again the Prince insists that wisdom is a crucial quality in business as elsewhere, especially if there is to be a break with the 'business as usual' mentality:

> To be wise was once just about the ultimate personal quality, and essential for anyone responsible for a great enterprise, whether political, academic, military or commercial. Whatever you were doing, if your decisions affected the lives of others then being clever, and good at the job, were important, but not sufficient, qualifications. Wisdom would also be a non-negotiable part of the job description. But, more recently, I fear it has become rather an under-rated commodity.

So, the Prince asks, how would a wise business behave?

> A wise business will certainly be clever and able. But it will also take a broader, more holistic, view of what is really involved in creating wealth and long-term value. In doing so it will be more likely to meet the rising expectations of an increasingly affluent, confident and well-educated public.

This may involve taking an unpopular stand:

Even developments that you might think would be
wholly positive, such as developing fuel cells for cars,
building offshore wind farms, looking at alternatives to
peat use in gardens, developing hydrocarbon refrigerants,
or even just insisting on higher environmental standards
from suppliers, can provoke a reaction from the 'business
as usual' brigade. I know, because I've had more than my
fair share of it over the years! But wise businesses
recognize that making up their own minds about what is
right, and setting their own high standards, is the only
way to move towards sustainability in a world obsessed
with the short-term.

One of the main advantages, the Prince continued, is the creation and maintenance of trust, as well as the concomitant drive
towards a more ethical and sustainable future:

One of the key benefits of getting on the right side of
these issues is that companies who do so can build and
protect a vital long-term asset — trust. We all know
whom we trust and whom we don't, and that applies as
much to businesses as it does to individuals. But there
seems to be a lot of cynicism nowadays about the motives
of companies or institutions.

The Prince sees businesses in the forefront of progress towards
sustainability, but does not underestimate the problems for individual companies of a bold approach in this respect. One example of a far-sighted initiative supported by BP is the
International Futures Forum, which has been meeting in
Scotland to consider ways in which we can envisage and bring
about a sustainable future.

The Prince returns at the end of his speech to the nature of
globalization, an issue that has been the subject of much discussion within the Business Leaders Forum. He expresses his reser-
vations about the process:

I simply do not believe the assurances of those who tell us
that the forces it unleashes can all be constrained within a

framework of proper regulation. Globalization brings enormous problems for the developing — and indeed, developed — countries, whatever the commercial opportunities, and in many cases the lack of attention to sustainability will threaten the stability and long term prospects of fragile communities and countries. Unless we can find ways of achieving a much wider acceptance that responsible corporate behaviour includes the need to address these issues comprehensively, in partnerships with Governments and civil society, then I fear that the whole concept of globalization may ultimately prove to be so deeply flawed as to be unsustainable.

The Prince's concern is that business can become detached from the communities it serves. He makes it clear through his work with the Business Leaders Forum that he is 'not opposed to the concept of global business,' but he is worried about the short-comings of the business response to social and environmental responsibility. The globalization debate has become polarized in the last two years with the (mainly top-down) approach World Economic Forum on one wing and the (bottom-up, grass roots) approach of the World Social Forum on the other. Critics of cor-porate globalization simply do not believe that the current busi-ness as usual agenda is sustainable, leading as it does to growing disparities within and between countries and a search for the least regulated environment in which to do business.

In any event, the approach of the Business Leaders Forum is to address the backlash against globalization by 'working in partnership with public sector and civil society organizations to develop practical policies to address the social, environmental and economic failures in the globalization process.' This action will help create an 'enabling environment, providing the condi-tions for these practices and partnerships to flourish.' So this is not a 'business as usual' policy, but it remains to be seen whether such adjustments can make the existing economic sys-tem workable in the long term.

# 8. Conclusions: Timeless Roots and Radical Action

## The Prince's Principles

*As I have grown older I have gradually come to realize that my entire life so far has been motivated by a desire to heal — to heal the dismembered landscape and the poisoned soil; the cruelly shattered townscape, where harmony has been replaced by cacophony; to heal the divisions between intuitive and rational thought, between mind, body and soul, so that the temple of our humanity can once again be lit by a sacred flame; to level the monstrous artificial barrier erected between Tradition and Modernity and, above all, to heal the mortally wounded soul that, alone, can give us warning of the folly of playing God and of believing that knowledge on its own is a substitute for wisdom.*

The Prince of Wales

This statement by the Prince of Wales from a recent article in *Temenos* gives the fullest expression of his basic motivation and aspiration: that healing the soul and listening to her intuitive voice are the prerequisites to a wider healing of the divisions and collateral damage brought about by an exclusively rational and mechanistic understanding of life. Not all readers will fully agree with this diagnosis or agenda but most will acknowledge that modern life has resulted in undesirable imbalances that do require some correction or rebalancing.

All readers of this book have a philosophy of life, whether they articulate it or not. This will have been broadly challenged or supported by the contents of this book, depending on our starting points, especially in relation to the primacy of a materialist outlook, or a more spiritual approach, as encapsulated in the words summarized in this section below. Our personal philosophy is influenced, shaped and defined by many factors. We are born into a specific culture at a certain epoch in history. We are therefore embedded in certain ways of thinking and understanding the world, which we may in time accept, reject or attempt to refine and modify. We exhibit different temperaments that predispose us to adopt particular views, to affirm certain positions and to reject others. We argue about the merits of our views, some of us at home, some in pubs, some in academic seminars or in public debate. The Prince of Wales's prominent position means that his philosophy is exposed to public scrutiny and discussion. Many of the issues that he raises are essential ones that arouse strong passions one way or the other and about which the Prince expresses very definite views, as we have seen.

Our overall philosophy entails a worldview, which, as we have seen, translates into a view about the nature of human life. It has been the thesis of this book and the contention of the Prince of Wales that the mechanistic and materialistic outlook is limited and outdated, and is being gradually supplanted by systems based on spiritual, holistic and ecological principles. The Prince of Wales is in the forefront of this transition, articulating and embodying an integrated worldview in his philosophy and work that corresponds to a growing movement known as the Cultural Creatives who are harbingers of a new world system. His overall view corresponds to what evolutionary systems theorist Ervin Laszlo, President of the Club of Budapest, calls a sustainable Holos civilization that goes beyond its purely rational Logos predecessor. While the Prince's critics overwhelmingly tend to advance mechanistic and materialistic arguments, his supporters embrace similar spiritual, holistic and ecological principles. This struggle or 'paradigm war' should not be simplistically reduced to a dichotomy of modern science vs. traditional religion. The transition to a new worldview is occurring in science and medicine as well as in other areas such as psychology and the nature of spirituality itself, as we have seen in previous chapters.

These principles spell out starting points which are essential to understanding the Prince of Wales's philosophy: the centrality of the sacred, of wisdom and of spiritual vision; the significance of living tradition; and the practical application of spiritual insights to life.

## Sacred, Wisdom, Truth

The Prince's philosophy and its expression in his work are underpinned by his sense of the sacred nature of life and creation. The traditional spiritual embodiment of the Sacred is the Sage, whose very being as living presence emanates Wisdom and Truth. These qualities, along with love and compassion, radiate in all the founders of the great faiths and in a great many saints and mystics, known and unknown. The knowledge of the Sage is not just information or facts, but an inner intuitive understanding of the principles of life. It is the way in which they embody love and wisdom that naturally draws people towards them.

## Spirit, Soul, Heart

Commitment to the priority of Spirit, Soul and Heart follows naturally from the above. They represent the relatively neglected but vital inner dimension of the human being. The Sage is one in whom the 'eye of the heart' is open.

## Tradition

Tradition derives from a Latin word meaning to hand on. Traditions are transmitted through both knowledge and example, as in the relationship between sage and disciple, teacher and pupil. Living traditions represent continuity between the past and the present and are also embodied in institutions. Traditions can only be kept alive through constant renewal whereby the water of the spirit — or inspiration — continues to flow between the banks of the 'form.'

## Values, Education

The Prince makes an explicit connection between spiritual traditions and the transmission of civilized values. Indeed without such values we cannot claim to be civilized. These values are handed down through example, upbringing and education. Education is a key word because it gives people a chance to gain access to their cultural inheritance and to fulfil their potential.

### Heritage, Culture, Roots
We are all born and (if we are fortunate) educated into a particular cultural inheritance, which constitutes a large part of our human identity. Our roots lie in places and people that shape our growth. Our heritage is literary and artistic, spiritual and secular, economic and ecological. It is our birthright and it includes the countryside, wildlife, art and architecture, literature and philosophy, values and ideals. The Prince is concerned to maintain our access to our inheritance and, where necessary, to ensure its preservation.

### Stewardship, Conservation, Posterity
The obligation of stewardship derives logically from the Prince's views on heritage and tradition. We are guardians and stewards of our environment and culture, responsible for passing them on to future generations. Perhaps the best example of this in the Prince's own case is his stewardship of the Duchy of Cornwall, which, as heir to the throne, he is responsible for passing on in good order to Prince William.

### Balance
Many of us perceive that our lives are out of balance, especially that between work and life in general. There is a basic imbalance in the West, as the Prince sees it, between the inner and outer aspects of life, between the spiritual and the material, the intuitive and the rational, the ancient or traditional and the new or modern. In each case the latter is stressed at the expense of the former. The Prince is not advocating one at the expense of the other, as his critics frequently maintain, but the establishment of a new balance, of a complementary *both-and* approach rather than a dichotomous *either-or*.

### Integration
Integration follows on directly from the Prince's advocacy of a both-and approach. It applies to the individual and the commu-

nity in general as well as more specifically to orthodox and complementary medicine, traditional principles and modern technology,

## Harmony
Harmony is more than balance and integration. The word is derived from the Greek *harmonia*, meaning to fit together. Mathematically and musically the word goes back to Pythagoras with his monochord and golden section, and is expressed in all ancient Greek art and architecture with its emphasis on geometric proportion related to the ideal human form. The Prince also stresses the importance of going with the grain, of living in harmony with Nature.

## Beauty
Harmony naturally results in beauty, to which we intuitively respond. In his *Temenos* message the Prince links tradition with beauty and has frequently castigated modernist architecture for departing from these principles and promoting a soulless ugliness instead. The result is demoralizing in the widest sense since we are intimately affected by the surroundings in which we live. Our sensibilities are uplifted and inspired by beauty and correspondingly dulled and disturbed by ugliness.

## Goodness, Potential, Development, Opportunity
These words are put together as the Prince exhibits a basic attitude of trust in the goodness of people — especially young people — and cares about giving them every opportunity to develop their full potential and make a contribution to the community. This constitutes the basic policy orientation of the Prince's Trust.

## Service, Community, Consensus, Partnership
The motto of the Prince of Wales — and one wholly appropriate to the nature of his work — is *Ich Dien*, meaning 'I Serve.' The Prince understands service in the widest sense to include the duties imposed by his position. The sheer number of his charitable patronages — over 380 — bears witness to his sense of service. At the centre of his socially-oriented work lies the

importance of community. And this in turn is related to the building of partnerships and consensus within and between communities. The Prince's work is focused on enabling communities to help themselves.

### Responsibility
Self-help is an important step towards a sense of responsibility, which is in turn related to the enhanced sense of self-respect and self-esteem that comes from fulfilling one's potential and making a contribution.

### Nature, Biodiversity, Sustainability, Precautionary Principle
The Prince's attitude to the natural world is imbued with a sense of the sacred. This drives not only his work in organic agriculture and gardening, but also his wider concern for ecological issues. He has made many speeches in support of conservation, biodiversity, sustainability and the judicious implementation of the precautionary principle to issues such as climate change.

### Healing
The Prince's interest in healing is most immediately expressed in the work of his Prince's Foundation for Integrated Health. However, it goes much further and deeper than this. He sees that the damage wrought by a soulless, mechanistic outlook in agriculture (on the landscape) and especially in architecture (on the community) also requires healing.

### The Future
The Prince's constitutional position implies continuity. It gives him both a rootedness in the past and a concern for the future. While criticizing the excesses of modernism he is not simply advocating a return to a past idyll but the preservation of the best of the past and the present so that future generations are not culturally disinherited. This brings us back to the centrality of a living tradition, one that is not ossified in outdated forms but rather which inspires contemporary forms of expression. As Albert Schweitzer put it: 'As the trees bear the same fruit year after year, so from generation to generation all worthwhile ideas must be born anew in the thinking of mankind.'

## The Monarchy, Philanthropy and Values

*The English way of progress has always been to preserve good*
*qualities and apply them to new systems.*

Queen Elizabeth the Queen Mother

*The purpose of royalty is the headship of philanthropy, a*
*guidance and encouragement of the manifold efforts which our*
*age is making towards a higher and purer life.*

Prince Albert

It is a little known fact that the collective patronage of the British Royal Family extends to nearly 3,500 voluntary organizations. Frank Prochaska, author of *Royal Bounty*, describes the extent of their voluntary activity as having been on a 'unique, global scale.' He adds that this activity should be seen 'against the background of the waning of the crown's political power and the emasculation of those ancient ideas of nobility, which did not put a premium on social service. As the crown's political-cum-warrior traditions gave way to charitable patronage and active benevolence, kings and princes, rather reluctantly, took off their uniforms and donned middle-class dress to open bazaars and visit hospitals.' Elsewhere, Prochaska quotes Viscount Esher, an advisor to Edward VII, as saying that the crown had exchanged 'authority' for 'influence' in the course of the nineteenth century.

Prochaska traces the origins of royal charitable involvement back to George III and Queen Charlotte. Around 1789 — a fateful year for European monarchy — George III was giving away over £14,000 a year to charitable objects, which represented about a quarter of his income from the Privy Purse. Queen Victoria's charitable instincts were formed by her mother the Duchess of Kent, who had patronages of her own as well as taking on a further fifty on the death of the Duke in 1820. Prochaska estimates that Queen Victoria gave away around £650,000 to charitable purposes during her reign. The underlying motivations for Victorian philanthropy were a mixture of religious observance, civic duty and social advancement. It was morally laudable and socially respectable to engage in charitable works, but it was also a means of turning privilege into virtue, as Prochaska remarks, and, latterly, a route to gaining honours bestowed by the sovereign — a practice that has continued ever since.

The quotation above from Prince Albert shows his instinct for the changing role of the monarchy. One of the most influential books of the time was *Self Help* by Samuel Smiles, and Prochaska describes Prince Albert as 'Samuel Smiles with a German accent.' Smiles epitomized the voluntarist ethic of the Victorian era — that people had a personal duty to be charitable and that charitable works should be designed to enable people to help themselves. This attitude is exactly mirrored in the work of the Prince's Trust. Like Edward VII and Edward VIII when Prince of Wales, as well as Prince Charles himself, Prince Albert had to carve out a role for himself. This he did with energy and enthusiasm, involving himself in a range of philanthropic ventures in which he supported voluntary remedies and local small-scale projects as the best response to the problems of the day. In particular, he sought to reach the working classes and ameliorate their education and living conditions. A further interesting comparison with the Prince of Wales is Prince Albert's promotion of model cottages for the Society for Improving the Condition of the Working Class. He paid for a pair of these cottages to be put on display at the Great Exhibition of 1851, with a view to persuading developers and manufacturers 'to translate his ideas into bricks and mortar.' It is interesting to recall, too, that Prince Albert was an active Lord Warden of the Stannaries of the Duchy of Cornwall.

Both Edward VII and Edward VIII spent a long period of their lives as Prince of Wales, a title that Prince Charles has held for 35 years already. Edward VII's reputation as a playboy ignores the considerable amount of charitable work that he carried out with Queen Alexandra. After Edward's recovery from typhoid in 1872, serious consideration was given by Prime Minister Gladstone to the role he might play. Gladstone, interestingly, argued that philanthropy would not give him 'a central aim and purpose, which may, though without absorbing all his time, gradually mould his mind, and colour his life.' However, Edward did develop his charitable role and, by the 1890s, was carrying out around 45 charitable engagements a year. A notable achievement was the establishment of the King's Fund, which began as the Prince of Wales's Hospital Fund for London to commemorate the Queen's Diamond jubilee in 1897. The King's Fund still plays an important role in health today, and the Prince of Wales is its current president. With his own special interests in health, the Prince is carrying on a long family tradition of involvement in hospitals. During his reign, Edward VII was patron of about 250 charities and made contributions to another 250 causes a year.

Edward VIII was Prince of Wales during the upheavals of the First World War, the General Strike of the 1920s and the Depression of the early 1930s. He wrote about his role as Prince of Wales that 'the job ... as I tried to interpret it, was, first, to carry on associations with worthy causes outside politics and clothe them with the prestige of the Prince's high position; and second, to bring the Monarchy, in response to new conditions, ever nearer to the people.' Politics, as he writes, is to be avoided, and his concern was to identify with the interests of the people which in turn engenders loyalty. The implications of this contract of service for loyalty was noted in connection with Prince Albert in the late 1840s, when some radical socialists remarked that his philanthropic activities might upset their apple cart! Edward VIII supported projects for the homeless and unemployed through the Duchy of Cornwall but made his mark more through a series of goodwill tours that began in South Wales in 1919. He also played a leading role in the appeal for the King George V Silver Jubilee Trust in 1935 as a means to 'promote the welfare of the younger generation,' which has been such a central concern of Prince Charles.

A major theme running through Prochaska's book is the tension between individual voluntarism and collective or state provision of welfare. The Victorian project had concentrated on voluntary activity but their very considerable efforts had failed to eliminate social problems. The advent of the Labour Party provided a parliamentary focus for socialist collectivism that had been gathering popularity since the 1830s — but it had yet to be applied on the grand scale envisaged by Marx and Engels. Richard Crossman, a Labour Secretary of State for Health and Social Services in the 1960s, expressed the collectivist view of philanthropy as an 'odious expression of social oligarchy and churchy bourgeois attitudes. We detested voluntary hospitals maintained by flag days.' Later on, ironically, he confessed his amazement at the extent of voluntary contributions still made to NHS hospitals — there were over 1,000 of these, of which over seventy were bombed during the Second World War. The planning mentality reached its peak in Britain during the 1960s and 1970s, and was directly challenged by the views and policies of Sir Keith Joseph and Margaret Thatcher from the late 1970s onwards. The pendulum swung back towards voluntarism and self-help but in a new context where rights predominate over responsibilities. Much of the Prince's welfare work does reflect the principles of voluntarism, but the important difference is that self-help is now promoted in partnership with government. As Prochaska points out, the centralized state has also lost its plausibility as a panacea for social ills, just as voluntary charity had in the nineteenth century, so the way is open for just the kind of partnerships promoted by the Prince.

The publicity generated by the Prince's views on farming, the countryside and hunting during the autumn of 2002 revived the debate about his role and its relationship to politics, a tightrope that he has become accustomed to walking. Part of the debate centred on his regular letter-writing to ministers, regarded by some commentators as undue meddling or interference, the result of the Prince 'not having a proper job.' Others defended his right to express his views and those of the many people he meets. European Commissioner Chris Patten said that 'to regard a letter from the Prince of Wales as unconstitutional interference in public affairs seems completely ludicrous,' while former Conservative environment secretary John Gummer remarked that it is 'one of the great strengths of monarchy that the Queen and the Royal Family have had much longer experience of political matters than any minister.' After all, the Prince of Wales does see Cabinet papers.

In this context, St James's Palace stated: 'It is part of the Royal Family's role to highlight excellence, express commiseration and draw attention to issues on behalf of us all. The Prince of Wales takes an active interest in all aspects of British life and believes that, as well as celebrating success, part of his role must be to highlight problems and represent views in danger of not being heard.' But, the statement added, 'this role can only be ful-filled properly if complete confidentiality is maintained.' What the Prince has done in the public realm, as we have seen, is to stimulate public debate by expressing strong views on a range of issues, which in his present position he has every right to do. Precedent suggests that this situation will change dramatically when the Prince becomes King, when as a constitutional monarch he will be less free to make his views known. However, the role of the monarchy itself is likely to continue to evolve in response to changing circumstances.

As the Queen herself said in the weeks following the death in 1997 of Diana, Princess of Wales, the monarchy 'exists only with the support and consent of the people.' This support was strongly in evidence during the Golden Jubilee celebrations, but it constantly has to be earned anew. No member of the Royal Family can rest on past laurels, especially when subjected to unprecedented scrutiny by the press: the support and consent of the people effectively means the broad support and consent of the press. This is problematic when elements of the press have an underlying republican agenda. Since the near-abolition of the hereditary peers in the House of Lords, the monarchy remains the only part of the constitution based upon the hereditary prin-ciple and is correspondingly vulnerable.

In addition, as the theologian Ian Bradley points out in his book on the spiritual dimension of monarchy, the decline in respect, deference and loyalty has affected all our institutions and is in part due — ironically — to the very factors criticized by the Prince of Wales — the cult of novelty or the future, and a corre-sponding dismissal of tradition and history. A cynical, debunking mentality has been prevalent in the media at least since the late 1960s. This attitude helps to engender what Onora O'Neill called a 'culture of suspicion' in her 2002 Reith Lectures on Trust. It is assumed that people's underlying motives are base and selfish so people in the public eye lead a precarious existence as the press wait for an opportunity to expose their foibles. The positive implication of this exposure, however, is a greater demand for integrity in public life, which has been reinforced by a number of commissions, notably that headed by Lord Nolan. However, the creation of trust also requires the maintenance of discretion.

One of the great strengths of the monarchy is that it is a vocation, while becoming president is a personal achievement. And as Kathleen Raine observes: 'Just because the foundation of monarchy is *not* political it safeguards those freedoms and values that are the marks of true civilization.' The coronation is a sacred event and the monarch is ultimately answerable to God. As well as being Head of State, Elizabeth II is also Supreme Governor of the Church of England and Defender of Faith. The Queen's role thus combines secular with sacred functions. There has recently been some call for the monarchy to be secularized so as to reflect 'the spirit of the age,' but, as we have previously remarked, what concerns the Prince of Wales is that we may be living in an 'age without spirit.' Ian Bradley provides a different analysis when he proposes that 'as an essentially sacred institution, the monarchy is particularly well placed to lead the recovery of our lost metaphysical imagination and the resacralization of our secularized society.' The reader will have realized by now that this resacralization of culture forms an essential part of the Prince of Wales's work. Bradley sees the Prince as 'the supreme exponent of an essentially religious perspective on life in the prevailing climate of secular and scientific rationalism.'

The Queen and the Prince of Wales share a deep personal faith. As the Queen said in her 2000 Christmas broadcast: 'Whether we believe in God or not, I think most of us have a sense of the spiritual, that recognition of a deeper meaning and purpose in our lives, and I believe this sense flourishes despite the pressures of our world.' The Prince of Wales may wish to be known as Defender of Faith rather than Defender of the Faith (this is incidentally also a correct translation of the Latin) but there is no doubt that he aspires to the wisdom traditionally associated with kings and has promoted ideas of a spiritual renaissance based on a restoration of balance, order and harmony. Interestingly, an earlier understanding of kingship saw the king as a guardian of the cosmic order. Nowadays the king is — happily — not physically sacrificed by the people, but the role inherently demands service, sacrifice, loyalty, duty and responsibility.

The monarch — and to a lesser extent other members of the Royal Family — embodies these values both personally and symbolically. Herein, Bradley argues, lies the monarchy's greatest strength. But he also suggests that it is beginning to embody another set of values — 'healing, wholeness, openness, tolerance and vulnerability.' It is arguable that vulnerability is not actually a value so much as a state of affairs, while openness (which makes one vulnerable) certainly is. It is evident that the Prince of Wales does indeed embody the values of healing and wholeness in his vision and work, and it is equally evident that the future requires just such values alongside the traditional demands of service, loyalty and duty.

## Ahead of his Time

*In the world in which we find ourselves, technological advance is rapid. But without progress in charity, technological advance is useless. Indeed it is worse than useless. Technological progress has merely provided us with a more efficient means for going backwards.*

Aldous Huxley

The Prince of Wales is often charged by his critics of romantically yearning for a vanished past, implying that his ideas are out of date. As we have seen, he not only repudiates such a charge but demonstrates his concern for the future through his work. We quoted a passage in the introduction where he states explicitly that he is not interested in returning to the past, but he does passionately believe 'that we should learn from the past, accept that there are such things as timeless principles, operate on a human scale, look firmly to the long-term, respect local conditions and traditions, and be profoundly sceptical of people who suggest that everything new is automatically better.' In a recent article he has returned to this accusation of 'living in the past, or of wanting to return to the kind of past that can only be met in the imagination,' as a result of which he has been 'branded as a traditionalist, as if tradition was some kind of disease that had to be sprayed at airports.' He is told that he appears to want to go backwards into the 21st century, 'not, as some would have us do, blindly trusting in the technological utopianism of the high priests of scientific rationalism, but anchored in the mudbank of superstition and irrelevant spirituality.'

Part of the confusion arises from the Prince's insistence on timeless principles, which some people mistakenly identify with the past. However, the timeless is not in the past, it is a perennial source; the so-called ancient wisdom is in fact timeless and perennial — meaning that it is relevant to all times. What we need are new forms appropriate to our time. In the Platonic view which the Prince upholds, the spiritual essence or principle is unchanging — Love, Wisdom, the Good, the Beautiful, the True — but the forms that it takes will change with the generations.

The Prince takes exception to the one-sidedness of rationalism with its emphasis on the outer, the quantifiable, the measurable and its neglect of the inner dimension of life. The rational, he insists, is one aspect — albeit essential — of our nature, but human beings have a dual nature. The Prince believes that the human being is 'a microcosm of what lies at the heart of the Universe' and that 'the existence we find ourselves in — as part of this world and, in turn, the Universe — consists of a giant paradox. Hence everything in life has another side to it — good and evil, light and dark ... we are therefore confronted continually by opposites [and] one of the secrets of civilized existence is invariably the reconciliation of opposites, or the search for balance and harmony.' Referring to the proponents of our inherited wisdom, the Prince observed that 'they would want us to realize that true and lasting peace in the world only comes through the inner peace which every one of us can reach through the eternal struggle to reconcile the opposites in our lives.

Our Western drive towards power and progress has brought us face to face with ourselves, with the nature of life and consciousness itself. But power is not a principle to be pursued for its own sake, but rather a means to an end — so we have to decide what to do with it. Do we pursue our own or our national interest or do we seek the higher ideal of the welfare of the whole planet and its inhabitants? In a speech to the Académie des Sciences Morales et Politiques in 1992, the Prince noted:

> We are meeting, I believe, at a momentous period in
> human history. As a lately evolving species in the majesty
> of creation, we now have two unique qualities. We have
> the power to transform the very lifeblood of the earth,

and the wisdom to recognize and reflect on that power.
And yet, precisely at the time when the human spirit
should be opening out to embrace the dramatic changes
which are taking place in the scientific, intellectual and
sociological contours of our lives, life is still going on
almost exactly as it did before; indeed, our innate,
inherited wisdom tells us that there is a sense of
dislocation between our knowledge and the manner in
which we are responding to that knowledge.

It is this sense of dislocation that the Prince has sought to
address in his speeches and practical projects. There is a growing world movement of people who would like to see a future
based on harmony and co-operation rather than power and military domination. Such a vision represents our deepest aspiration, a world system based less on control, suspicion,
manipulation and fear and more on participation, trust and,
dare one say it, love. Utopian, perhaps, but if our practical
means are more consistent with our ends, there is a better
chance of creating a new kind of world.

What is the price of our one-sided pursuit of power and
progress? According to the Prince, it is 'the loss of balance and
harmony and the introduction of a harsh, brutalized, mechanistic view of the world and of mankind where everything is
reduced to the sum of its parts and we find ourselves, increasingly, as guinea pigs in a series of very uncertain experiments
conducted in the laboratory of Nature.'

As we saw in the opening chapter, there is another new science emerging, a science of wholeness and interconnectedness,
of which the Prince himself is aware: 'contemporary science is
revealing a world based on interconnectedness rather than separation, on relatedness rather than the distinct atomistic entities
favoured by the rationalists.' In the same speech he asks the
question: 'has anyone given serious thought to the political
implications of leaving behind the atomist view of human relations which has prevailed throughout the industrial era? If individuals must now be seen as unique but integral parts of the
whole, are not many of the economic and social premises on
which our models of progress today are based, seriously

flawed?' Precisely. Our political and economic systems are indeed still based on an old scientific metaphor, as Fritjof Capra makes clear in his book *The Hidden Connections.* We are now at a watershed where the old system is becoming unworkable but the new is not yet fully formed. And the new form will emerge from the grass roots rather than from any centralized government bureaucracy. It will be aligned with the fundamental insights of the new science involving wholeness rather than separation, relatedness rather than isolation, process rather than structure, community rather than either the monolithic state or the self-contained individual. The science of interconnectedness will be reflected in the politics of interdependence.

The Prince has supported the principle of sustainability since its inception in the mid-1980s and has taken an active part in promoting it ever since. He has applied sustainability to his own estates on the Duchy of Cornwall and has spoken up for principle in rainforests, timber and fisheries. He has also put sustainability at the centre of his work with business leaders, first with his International Business Leaders Forum and then, even more specifically, with his Business and the Environment programme.

The Prince was ridiculed in the early 1980s for his insistence on the importance of practical environmentalism (remember the first bottle bank at Buckingham Palace in 1980?) and organic agriculture. Undeterred, he converted Highgrove estate and garden to organic production and demonstrated the possibilities by personal example. Twenty years later the consensus is that the future of agriculture must be sustainable in any event, and that organic methods have an important role to play. There is a general realization that the environmental cost of current agro-industrial methods is too high and must be alleviated either through small-scale agro-ecological innovations and/or through third generation GM foods that do actually require fewer applications of chemicals. The Prince takes the uncompromising view that GM foods are entirely unacceptable in any form but the future may go beyond today's sharp dichotomies. However, one should not forget here the economic and political backdrop whereby a small number of giant companies are trying to assure their own future control of world food production in ways that are entirely inconsistent with the small scale, self-sufficient agro-ecological approach. There is no doubt that agro-ecological and organic methods are part of the future — and not just of the past — of agriculture.

Few people had heard of holistic medicine twenty years ago and the term 'integrated medicine' had not been invented. The Prince recalls how he pleaded with the BMA 'to adopt a more holistic, balanced and less mechanistic approach to the healing of the sick; to re-introduce elements of ancient wisdom and traditional therapies that had been thrown enthusiastically onto the scrap-heap of medical history and, once again, to rediscover the essential trinity of mind, body and spirit.' He confesses that he was not entirely astonished when 'the full weight of the industrialized medical Establishment descended upon me and, once more, I discovered how simple it is to be misunderstood and mis-represented.' However, 'nothing daunted, I have continued ever since to work at ways of establishing an integrated approach to healthcare whereby the best of orthodox, clinical medicine can be harnessed in tandem with the best of traditional "irrational" therapies.' The transformation of attitude took over fifteen years to achieve, but the Prince has been and still is in the forefront of the movement for integrated health.

Around the same time as his speech to the BMA, the Prince took on another group of expert 'industrial mechanics' in the form of the architects at the RIBA. 'Our technological competence,' he writes, 'is truly remarkable, but we make a terrible mistake if we equate our nature with that technology or, indeed, our buildings. Technology already dominates every aspect of our lives. We don't need to live in buildings that reflect that self-same technology and which, inevitably, dehumanize us by their very scale and lack of reference to human proportion.' The Prince's challenge has been to make architectural tradition a living thing by means of which we can 'experience a sense of belonging and meaning within a rapidly changing world.' Here the Prince has been active in urban planning and community regeneration, and in artistic and architectural education through the Prince's Foundation. He has also begun to realize his vision directly through the Duchy of Cornwall development at Poundbury. Once again scoffers have in the end been impressed by the Prince's efforts, and the Poundbury development is now considered a model worth emulating elsewhere.

'Mention that there might be a few timeless principles, well-tried principles that lie at the heart of the whole educational process, whatever age we live in, and you are instantly accused of being a highly dangerous, reactionary traditionalist.' Education has been another central concern of the Prince, who has argued against progressive ideologies that repudiate the past and bring a 'corrosive canker of moral relativism into the whole educational edifice.' The Prince's contribution in this field has been less extensive than in architecture, medicine or agriculture, and it has focussed more on the upholding of traditional educational values than on new initiatives. However, he has set up summer schools for the teaching of History and English, and especially Shakespeare. His Prince's Trust has also established *xl* clubs for school students to enable them to rediscover a sense of motivation and direction.

The value of the work of the Prince's Trust has been universally acknowledged by all those who know about it. It has an established track record of helping tens of thousands of disadvantaged young people each year. It pioneered a risk-taking approach to young people and was talking about participation, partnership and community long before these concepts became fashionable. Another measure of its success is the fact that Government has taken up so many of its programmes. In itself, the Prince's Trust has made a major contribution to national life, a contribution which has also been quantified by James Morton, although the real value is the difference that its programmes have made to the individual lives of young people.

Finally, the Prince has helped spearhead the relationship between business and the community as well as the development of the economic, social and ecological triple bottom line through his work with Business in the Community, Business and the Environment his International Business Leaders Forum. This work has dovetailed with that of the Prince's Trust and Regeneration through Heritage by helping rebuild and regenerate communities by giving them a new sense of identity and purpose as well as a sounder economic base for the future.

There is nothing inherent in the constitutional role of the Prince of Wales that makes any of this work inevitable. As one young person remarked, 'he didn't have to do it.' But there is an inner drive in the Prince that has inspired him to initiate a multifaceted programme based on his desire to restore the balance between inner and outer, the intuitive and the rational, the traditional and the modern. In doing this the Prince has remained true to himself and to his ideals in a way advocated by Dr Albert Schweitzer, who was awarded the Nobel Peace Prize in 1954:

> Grown-up people reconcile themselves too willingly to a supposed duty of preparing young ones for the time when they will regard as illusion what is now an inspiration to heart and mind. Deeper experience of life, however, advises their inexperience differently. It exhorts them to hold fast, their whole life through, to the thoughts which inspire them. It is through the idealism of youth that man catches sight of truth, and in that idealism he possesses a wealth which he must never exchange for anything else.

Schweitzer continues: 'We must all be prepared to find that life tries to take from us our belief in the good and the true, and our enthusiasm for them, but we need not surrender them.' The Prince has not exchanged the wealth of his ideals, to use Schweitzer's phrase, but continues to strive to attain them in new ways. Although he has many other charitable commitments he has not contented himself with existing forms but has set up three major trusts himself — The Prince's Trust, The Prince's Foundation and The Prince of Wales's Foundation for Integrated Health — within which a great variety of other projects are undertaken. Indeed the total number of the Prince's core charities is now seventeen, and Sir Tom Shebbeare has now taken over as Director of Charities to help them work more closely together. The Prince himself embodies the kind of balance of qualities about which he speaks and which characterize his work: the practical idealist, the radical traditionalist, the contemplative man of action. He is a man rooted in timeless principles and living traditions, whose actions address the problems of the present and point towards a more sustainable and humane future where we may succeed in living more closely in harmony with nature and with each other.

# Notable Dates in the Prince of Wales's Public Activities

The Prince of Wales is Patron or President of some 380 organizations, a few of which are referred to below.

## Environment

1970 Makes first speech on the environment.

1981 Institutes Buckingham Palace bottle bank

1983 Becomes Patron of Atlantic Salmon Trust

1987 Supports establishment of Brundtland commission, which coins the phrase 'sustainable development'. Gives major speeches to the Commission in 1992 and to Local Agenda 21 in 1995.

1987 Speech on dumping of toxic waste and the dangers of overfishing at the North Sea Conference

1990 Speech on sustainability Rainforests and Timber, Kew Gardens

1990 Speech on sustainable water use to the Institute for Water and Environmental Management

1993 Precautionary Principle Global Security Lecture, Cambridge University

1994 Speech at World Wildlife Fund conference on Timber

1995 Duchy of Cornwall woodlands near Liskeard certified as sustainable by the Soil Association

2000 Reith Lecture on Sustainability

2001 First of two lectures on the plight of the albatross in relation to longline fishing practices

2002 Receives Euronatur award in Germany

2003-4 Supports work of Marine Stewardship Council addressing the long-term issues in fishing and reiterates support for the albatross.

## Agriculture and Gardening

1980 Duchy of Cornwall buys Highgrove, which becomes the Duchy Home Farm in 1985.

1982 Becomes President of Royal Agricultural College

1986 Becomes Patron of the Rare Breeds Survival Trust

1988 Becomes Patron of the Henry Doubleday Research Association (HDRA) which looks after rare seeds.

1990 Decision taken to convert Highgrove to organic production, a process that was completed by 1997.

1991 Gives Royal Agricultural Society's Annual Lecture on the future of agriculture

1996 Gives Lady Eve Balfour Memorial Lecture to Soil Association, of which he becomes Royal Patron in 1999.

1998    Intervenes in GMO debate and establishes a forum on his web site.
1999    Establishment of Rural Revival Initiative
2001    Launch of Rural Action Programme through Business in the Community. Gives £500,000 to farmers hit by foot and mouth disease
2002    Voted Farming Personality of the Year by *Farmers' Weekly*

## Duchy Originals

1990    Introduction of the Highgrove Loaf
1992    Duchy Originals launched with the oaten biscuit
2002    Duchy Originals celebrates its 10 year anniversary
2003    Duchy Selections, a range of food made from sustainable and free range but non-organic sources, is launched.
2003    A range of outdoor furniture made with native hardwood from sustainable forests is launched under the Duchy Collections brand.
2004    The company's first £1million profit is achieved. To date, Duchy Originals has donated almost £3.5 million in profits to The Prince of Wales's Charitable Foundation.

## Integrated Health

1982    Speech on Complementary Medicine to the British Medical Association
1983    Establishment of Research Council for Complementary Medicine and British Holistic Medical Association. The Prince opens the Bristol Cancer Help Centre. The BMA sets up a working party on alternative therapies at the Prince's instigation, which produces a highly critical report in 1986.
1984    Plans made by Sir James Watt for a series of colloquia on complementary medicine at the Royal Society of Medicine
1987    Prince becomes Patron of Marylebone Health Centre and opens Hale Clinic
1991    Prince delivers a Presidential Address on spirituality and psychiatry to the Royal College of Psychiatrists. The College set up a special interest group in this field in 1998.
1996    Prince launches the Foundation for Integrated Medicine (FIM), which becomes the Prince of Wales's Foundation for Integrated Health in 2003.
1997    Publication of the FIM report on Integrated Healthcare, reviewed in 2003.
1998    Prince opens University of Westminster Polyclinic
2000    Plants medicinal herbs at Highgrove
2001    Gives speech on hospital design at the NHS Estates conference attended by the Secretary of State for Health, Alan Milburn. This leads to a collaboration between the Prince's Foundation and the NHS.

## Art and Architecture

1976    Establishment of the charity Arts and Business, of which the Prince has been President since 1988. The amount raised grew from £600,000 in 1976 to £100 million in 2002.

1984 Speech to the Royal Institute of British Architects
1987 Speech to planners in the City of London
1987 Work begins on planning Poundbury, the extension to Dorchester
1988 Makes television broadcast — *A Vision of Britain*
1990 First architectural summer school in Italy
1990 Major speech to American Institute of Architects
1991 First Summer School on Civil Architecture
1992 Establishment of the Prince of Wales's Institute of Architecture
1998 The Prince brings together his interests in architecture, building design and urban regeneration under the single umbrella of the Prince's Foundation for the Built Environment.
2000 The Prince's Foundation moves to its new premises in Shoreditch, East London. Launch of Prince of Wales's Drawing Studio
2000 Becomes President of Arts and Business
2002 Sets up the Arts and Kids Foundation.
2002 Launch of Craft Scholarship Scheme

## Urban Regeneration and Heritage Work

1992 Foundation of the Prince's Foundation for the Built Environment. Launch of Urban Network.
1996 Launch of Regeneration Through Heritage.
1997 Launch of Prince of Wales's Phoenix Trust at Stanley Mills in Perthshire.
2001 Launch of Building a Better Patient Environment
2001 Launch of Urban Development and Regeneration Short Course Programme
2003 Becomes Patron of the National Trust and the National Trust for Scotland; and of the Society for the Protection of Ancient Buildings.

## Religion and Spirituality

1993 Gives public lecture on Islam and the West as Patron of the Oxford Centre for Islamic Studies.
1996 Speech on A Sense of the Sacred: Building Bridges between Islam and the West
1997 Becomes Patron of the Temenos Academy
1997 Gives speech to the Prayer Book Society
1999 Builds Sanctuary at Highgrove
2002 Launch of Respect for Faiths initiative

## Young People and Education

1976 Founds the Prince's Trust
1982 Launch of Business Start-up programme
1986 Launch of Prince's Scottish Youth Business Trust
1988 Prince's Trust raises £40 million in appeal
1990 Prince's Trust Volunteer's Programme launched

1991 Becomes Patron of the Royal Shakespeare Company. Gives major speech on Shakespeare and education. Publishes his own selection from Shakespeare in 1996.
1993 Establishes Prince of Wales's Shakespeare School
1994 Sound Live, a residential music programme, is launched
1996 Becomes Patron of the Wordsworth Trust.
1999 Prince's Trust receives a Royal Charter

## Business, Community and Environment

1985 Becomes President of Business in the Community
1986 Becomes Chairman of Community Enterprise Awards
1990 Launches 'Seeing is Believing' days for senior business executives.
1990 Inaugurates Prince of Wales's International Business Leaders Forum (IBLF)
1992 IBLF takes over International Hotels Environment Initiative
1994 Establishment of Business and the Environment Programme at Cambridge
2002 IBLF sets up its Digital Partnership

# Resources

PRINCE OF WALES'S WEBSITE
www.princeofwales.gov.uk

PRINCE OF WALES'S FOUNDATION FOR
INTEGRATED HEALTH
12 Chillingworth Road,
London N7 8QJ.
T: 020 76196146
F: 020 77008434
E: enquiries@fihealth.org.uk
W: www.fihealth.org.uk

THE PRINCE OF WALES'S
INTERNATIONAL BUSINESS LEADERS
FORUM
15–16 Cornwall Terrace
Regent's Park
London NW1 4QP
T: 020 74673600
F: 020 74673610
E: info@iblf.org
W: www.iblf.org

DUCHY OF CORNWALL
10 Buckingham Gate
London SWIE 6LA
T: 020 78347346
F: 020 79319541

THE PRINCE'S FOUNDATION
19–22 Charlotte Road
London EC2A 3SG
T: 020 76138500
F: 020 76138599
E: rsuzuki@princes-foundation.org
W: www.princes-foundation.org

BUSINESS IN THE COMMUNITY
Web: www.bitc.org.uk

THE PRINCE'S TRUST
18 Park Square East
London NW1 4LH
T: 020 75431234
F: 020 754331200
M: 020 75431374
W: www.princes-trust.org

BUSINESS & THE ENVIRONMENT
PROGRAMME
Cambridge Programme for
Industry
1 Trumpington Street
Cambridge Cb2 1QA
T: 01223 332772
F: 01223 301122
E: bep@cpi.cam.ac.uk
W: cpi.cam/ac/uk/bep

SOIL ASSOCATION
Bristol House
40-56 Victoria Street
Bristol BS1 6BY
T: 0117 9290661
F: 0117 9252504
E: info@soilassociation.org
W: www.soilassociation.org

THE SCIENTIFIC AND MEDICAL
NETWORK
PO Box 11
Moreton-in-Marsh
Glos.GL56 OZF
T: 01608 652000
F: 01608 652001
E: info@scimednet.org
W: www.scimednet.org
    www.davidlorimer.net

# Bibliography

Aeschliman, Michael D., *The Restitution of Man*, Wm Eerdmans, Cambridge, 1998.

Alexander, Denis, *Rebuilding the Matrix*, Lion, London, 2001.

Allitt, John S., *et al., Monarchy*, Temenos, London, 2002.

Anderson, William, *The Rise of the Gothic*, Hutchinson, London, 1985.

—, *The Face of Glory*, Bloomsbury, London, 1996.

Ashman, Keith M., and Baringer, Philip S. (eds), *Science Wars*, Routledge, London, 2001.

Balfour, E.B., *The Living Soil*, Faber, London, 1975.

Bamford, Christopher (ed), *Rediscovering Sacred Science*, Floris Books, Edinburgh, 1994.

Barbour, Ian G., *Religion and Science*, SCM, London, 1998.

—, *When Science Meets Religion*, SPCK, London, 2000.

Beloff, John, *The Existence of Mind*, McKibben & Kee, London, 1962.

—, *The Relentless Question*, McFarland, New York, 1990.

—, *Parapsychology, A Concise History*, Athlone, London, 1993.

Berman, Morris, *The Re-Enchantment of the World*, Bantam, London, 1984.

Berry, Wendell, *What are People For?* Rider, London, 1990.

—, *Standing on Earth*, Golgonooza Press, Cambridge, 1991.

—, *Life is a Miracle*, Counterpoint, Washington, 2001.

Beveridge, W. I. B., *The Art of Scientific Investigation*, Scientific Book Club, London, 1955.

Bloom, Allan, *The Closing of the American Mind*, Penguin, London, 1987.

Bortoft, Henri, *Goethe's Way of Science*, Floris Books, Edinburgh, 1996.

Bradley, Ian, *God Save the Queen*, Darton, Longman and Todd, London, 2002.

Braudel, Fernand, *A History of Civilisations*, Penguin, London, 1994.

Bremner, Moyra, *GE and You*, HarperCollins, London, 1999.

British Medical Association, *Complementary Medicine*, Oxford, 1995.

Broughton, Richard, *Parapsychology, The Controversial Science*, Rider, London, 1991.

Brown, James Robert, *Who Rules in Science*, Harvard, 2001.

Brown, Lester, *Eco-Economy*, Norton, New York, 2001.

—, *The Earth Policy Reader*, Norton, New York, 2002.

Brown, Warren S., Murphy, Nancey and Malony, H. Newton, *Whatever Happened to the Soul*, Fortress Press, Minneapolis, 1998.

Buhler, William *et al., Science, Agriculture and Research: A Compromised Participation?* Earthscan, London, 2002.

Bulloch, John, and Darwish, Adel, *Water Wars*, Gollancz, London, 1993.

Burckhardt, Titus, *Mirror of the Intellect*, Quinta Essentia, Cambridge, 1987.
—, *Chartres and the Birth of a Cathedral*, Golgonooza, Ipswich, 1995.
Burnett, David, *A Royal Duchy*, Dovecote Press, Dorset, 1996.
Burrt, E.A., *The Metaphysical Foundations of Modern Physical Science*, Routledge and Kegan Paul, New York, 1924.
Bynum, W.F. and Porter, Roy, *Companion Encyclopedia of the History of Medicine*, 2 vols, Routledge, London, 1993.
Cadman, David (ed), *A Sacred Trust*, Temenos and the Prince's Foundation, London, 2002.
Capra, Fritjof, *The Web of Life*, HarperCollins, London, 1997.
—, *The Hidden Connections*, HarperCollins, London, 2002.
Churton, Tobias, *The Gnostics*, Weidenfeld & Nicolson, London, 1987.
Clunies-Ross, Tracey and Hildyard, Nicholas, *The Politics of Industrial Agriculture*, Earthscan, London, 1992.
Collins, Cecil, *The Vision of the Fool and Other Writings*, Golgoonooza, Ipswich, 2002.
Colquhoun, Alan, *Modernity and the Classical Tradition*, MIT, Boston, 1999.
Commission on Global Governance, *Our Global Neighbourhood*, Oxford University Press, 1995.
Conford, Philip, *The Organic Tradition*, Green Books, Devon, 1988.
—, *The Origins of the Organic Movement*, Floris Books, Edinburgh, 2001.
Coomaraswamy, Ananda K., *What is Civilisation?* Golgonooza, Ipswich, 1989.
Cornwell, John (ed), *Nature's Imagination*, Oxford, 1995.
Cousins, Norman, *Anatomy of an Illness*, Norton, New York, 2001.
Devall, Bill and Sessions, George, *Deep Ecology*, Gibbs & Smith, Utah, 1985.
Dimbleby, Jonathan, *The Prince of Wales*, Little Brown, London, 1994.
Dossey, Larry, *Space, Time and Medicine*, Shambhala, Boston, 1982.
—, *Beyond Illness*, Shambhala, Boston, 1984.
—, *Recovering the Soul*, Bantam, New York, 1989.
—, *Meaning and Medicine*, Bantam, New York, 1991.
—, *Healing Words*, Harper San Francisco, 1993.
—, *Be Careful What you Pray for*, Harper San Francisco, 1997
—, *Reinventing Medicine*, Harper San Francisco, 1999.
—, *Healing Beyond the Body*, Shambhala, Boston, 2001.
Downie, R.S. (ed), *The Healing Arts*, Oxford, 1994.
Dubos, René, *Mirage of Health*, Allen & Unwin, London, 1960.
Dupré, Louis, *Passage to Modernity*, Yale University Press, 1993.
Eccles, Sir John C., *How the Self Controls its Brain*, Springer, Berlin, 1994.
—, and Popper, Sir Karl R., *The Self and its Brain*, Routledge, London, 1977.
Edinburgh, HRH The Duke of, *A Question of Balance*, Michael Russell, Salisbury, 1982.
Ehrlich, Paul and Ehrlich, Anne, *The Population Explosion*, Hutchinson, London, 1990.
Fernando, Ranjit (ed), *The Unanimous Tradition*, Sri Lanka Institute of Traditional Studies, Colombo, 1991.
Filoramo, Giovanni, *A History of Gnosticism*, Blackwell, Oxford, 1990.
Foss, Laurence and Rothenberg, Kenneth, *The Second Medical Revolution*, Shambhala, Boston, 1988.

Foss, Laurence, *The End of Modern Medicine*, SUNY Press, New York, 2001.

Frankl, Viktor, *Man's Search for Meaning*, Hodder & Stoughton, London, 1959.

Fraser, Romy, and Hill, Sandra, *Roots of Health*, Green Books, Devon, 2002.

Gerber, Richard, *Vibrational Medicine*, Bear, Santa Fe, 1988, 1996.

Glyn-Jones, Ann, *Holding up a Mirror*, Imprint Academic, Devon, 2002.

Glynn, Ian, *An Anatomy of Thought*, Weidenfeld and Nicolson, London, 1999.

Goodwin, Brian, *How the Leopard Changed its Spots*, Weidenfeld and Nicolson, London, 1994.

Gore, Al, *Earth in the Balance*, Earthscan, London, 1992.

Goswami, Amit, *The Self-Aware Universe*, Simon & Schuster, London, 1993.

—, *The Visionary Window*, Quest Books, Illinois, 2000.

Graham, Gordon, *Universities: the Recovery of an Idea*, Imprint Academic, Exeter, 2002.

Graham-Smith, Sir Francis (ed), *Population: the Complex Reality*, Royal Society, London, 1994

Griffiths, Bede, *Return to the Centre*, Collins, London, 1976.

—, *The Marriage of East and West*, Collins, London, 1982.

Guénon, René, *Crisis of the Modern World*, Luzac, London, 1975.

—, *Fundamental Symbols*, Quinta Essentia, Cambridge, 1995.

Guiton, Jacques, (ed) *The Ideas of Le Corbusier on Architecture and Urban Planning*, George Braziller, NY 1981.

Hagger, Nicholas, *The Fire and the Stones*, Element, Shaftesbury, 1991.

Harremoes Paul et al (eds), *The Precautionary Principle in the 20th Century*, Earthscan, London, 2002.

Harman, Willis W. *A Re-examination of the Metaphysical Foundations of Modern Science*, Institute of Noetic Sciences, San Francisco, 1992.

—, and Clark, Jane, (eds), *New Metaphysical Foundations of Modern Science*, Institute of Noetic Sciences, San Francisco, 1994.

Harvey, Graham, *The Killing of the Countryside*, Vintage, London, 1997.

Henry, John, *Knowledge is Power*, Icon Books, London, 2002.

Hoey, Brian, *Majesty*, Harper Collins, London, 2001.

Holgate, Sir Martin, *From Care to Action*, Earthscan, London, 1996.

—, *The Green Web*, Earthscan, London, 1999.

Holton, Gerald, *Science and Anti-Science*, Harvard, 1993.

Huxley, Aldous, *Ends and Means*, Chatto and Windus, London, 1941.

—, *The Perennial Philosophy*, Chatto & Windus, London, 1946.

Inge, W. R., *The Philosophy of Plotinus*, Longmans Green, London, 1929.

Jahn, Robert G., and Dunne, Brenda J., *Margins of Reality*, Harcourt, Brace, Jovanovich, New York, 1987.

Jencks, Charles, *Modern Movements in Architecture*, Penguin 1971

King, Alexander and Schneider, Bertrand, *The First Global Revolution*, Simon & Schuster, London, 1991.

Kuhn, Thomas S., *The Structure of Scientific Revolutions*, University of Chicago Press, (2nd edition), 1970.

Laszlo, Ervin, *Macroshift*, Berret Koehler, San Francisco, 2001.

Lawlor, Robert, *Sacred Geometry*, Thames and Hudson, London, 1982.

LeShan, Lawrence, *Holistic Health*, Turnstone, Northampton, 1982.

Lewis, C.S., *The Abolition of Man*, Harper Collins, 1978.

Logan, Alastair H.B., *Gnostic Truth and Christian Heresy*, T & T Clark, Edinburgh, 1996.

Lomborg, Bjorn, *The Skeptical Environmentalist*, Cambridge University Press, 2001.

Lorimer, David, *Survival? Body, Mind and Death in the Light of Psychic Experience*, Routledge and Kegan Paul, London, 1984.

—, *Whole in One - The Near-Death Experience and the Ethic of Interconnectedness*, Arkana, London, 1990.

—, (ed), *Prophet for Our Times, the Life and Teaching of Peter Deunov*, Element, Shaftesbury, 1991.

—, (ed), *The Spirit of Science*, Floris Books, Edinburgh, 1998.

—, (ed), *Thinking Beyond the Brain*, Floris Books, Edinburgh, 2001.

Lovelock, James, *Gaia: A New Look at Life on Earth*, Oxford University Press, 1979.

—, *The Ages of Gaia*, Oxford University Press, 1988.

—, *Gaia: The Practical Science of Planetary Medicine*, Gaia Books, London, 1991.

—, *Homage to Gaia*, Oxford University Press, 2000.

Loye, David, *The Evolutionary Outrider*, Adamantine, London, 1998.

Margenau, Henry, *The Miracle of Existence*, Shambhala, London, 1987.

Margulis, Lynn, *The Symbiotic Planet*, Weidenfeld and Nicolson, London, 1998.

Maskell, Duke and Robinson, Ian, *The New Idea of a University*, Imprint Academic, Exeter, 2002.

Merchant, Carolyn, *The Death of Nature*, Harper and Rowe, San Francisco, 1980.

Midgley, Mary, *Science and Poetry*, Routledge, London, 2001.

Morton, James, *Prince Charles - Breaking the Cycle*, Ebury Press, London, 1998.

Mumford, Lewis, *The Highway and the City*, Secker and Warburg, New York, 1953.

Myers, Norman, *Ultimate Security*, Norton, New York, 1995.

—, *Managing the Planet*, Earthscan, London, 2000.

Nasr, Seyyed Hossein, *Man and Nature*, Allen and Unwin, London, 1967.

—, (ed), *The Essential Writings of Frithjof Schuon*, Amity House, New York, 1986.

—, *Knowledge and the Sacred*, SUNY Press, New York, 1989.

—, *The Need for a Sacred Science*, SUNY Press, New York, 1993.

—, *Religion and the Order of Nature*, Oxford University Press, New York, 1996.

—, *The Spiritual and Religious Dimensions of the Environmental Crisis*, Temenos Academy, London, 1999.

Naydler, Jeremy (ed), *Goethe on Science*, Floris Books, Edinburgh, 1996.

Needleman, Jacob, *The Sword of Gnosis*, Arkana, London, 1986.

—, *The Way of the Physician*, Arkana, London, 1992.

Nuttgens, Patrick, *Understanding Modern Architecture*, London, Unwin 1988.

Odent, Michel, *The Farmer and the Obstetrician*, Free Association Books, London, 2002.

Oldmeadow, Kenneth, *Traditionalism*, Sri Lanka Institute of Traditional Studies, Colombo, 2000.

O'Neill, Onora, *A Question of Trust*, Cambridge University Press, 2002.

Palumbi, Stephen R., *The Evolution Explosion*, Norton, New York, 2001.

Pelletier, Kenneth, *Sound Mind, Sound Body*, Simon & Schuster, New York, 1994.

Pert, Candace B., *Molecules of Emotion*, Simon & Schuster, New York, 1997.

Perry, Whitall N., *A Treasury of Traditional Wisdom*, Allen and Unwin, London, 1971.

—, *The Widening Breach*, Quinta Essentia, Cambridge, 1995.

Pfeiffer, E., *Soil Fertility*, Lanthorn Press, Sussex, 1983.

—, *The Earth's Face*, Lanthorn Press, Sussex, 1988.

Pietroni, Patrick, *Holistic Living*, J.M. Dent, London, 1986.

Porritt, Jonathon, *Playing Safe: Science and the Environment*, Thames and Hudson, London, 2000.

Porter, Roy, *The Greatest Benefit to Mankind - A Medical History of Humanity from Antiquity to the Present*, Fontana Press, London, 1999.

Pretty, Jules, *The Living Land*, Earthscan, London, 1998.

—, 'Can sustainable agriculture feed Africa? New evidence on progress, processes and impacts,' in *Environment, Development and Sustainability*, 1: 253–74, 1999.

—, and Hine, Rachel, 'The promising spread of sustainable agriculture,' in *Asia, Natural Resources Forum* 24 (2000) 107–21.

—, *et al.*, 'An assessment of the total external costs of UK agriculture,' *Agricultural Systems* 65 (2000), 113–136.

—, *Agri-Culture*, Earthscan, London, 2002.

Prickett, Stephen and Erskine-Hill, Patricia, *Education! Education! Education!*, Imprint Academic, Exeter, 2002.

Prochaska, Frank, *Royal Bounty*, Yale University Press, London, 1995.

Radhakrishnan, Sir Sarvepalli, *Eastern Religions and Western Thought*, Oxford, 1939.

—, *Religion and Society*, Allen and Unwin, London, 1947.

—, *Fellowship of the Spirit*, Harvard University Press, 1961.

—, *Religion in a Changing World*, Allen and Unwin, London, 1967.

Ravindra, Ravi, *Science and the Sacred*, Theosophical Society, Adyar, 2000.

Ray, Paul H., and Anderson, Sherry Ruth, *The Cultural Creatives*, Harmony Books, New York, 2000. Crisis in Higher Education.

Reeves, Marjorie, *The Crisis in Higher Education*, Open University Press, Milton Keynes, 1988.

Remen, Rachel Naomi, *Kitchen Table Wisdom*, Pan, London, 1996.

—, *My Grandfather's Blessings*, Riverhead, New York, 2000.

Prins, Gwyn (ed), *Threats without Enemies*, Earthscan, London, 1993.

Rose, Steven, *Lifelines*, Allen Lane, London, 1997.

Rudolf, Kurt, *Gnosis*, T & T Clark, Edinburgh, 1993.

Russell, Bertrand, *On Education*, Unwin, London, 1926.

—, *Education and the Social Order*, Unwin, London, 1932.

Sahtouris, Elisabet and Harman, Willis, *Biology Revisioned*, North Atlantic Books, Berkeley, 1998.

Schumacher, Fritz, *Small is Beautiful*, Jonathan Cape, London, 1973

—, *Guide for the Perplexed*, Jonathan Cape, London, 1977.

—, *Good Work*, Jonathan Cape, London, 1979.

Schweitzer, Albert, *My Childhood and Youth*, Unwin, London, 1924.

—, *The Teaching of Reverence for Life*, Peter Owen, London, 1965.

Seamon, David and Zajonc, Arthur (eds), *Goethe's Way of Science*, SUNY Press, New York, 1998.

Sharma, Ursula, *Complementary Medicine Today*, Routledge, London, 1992.

Shealy, C. Norman, *Miracles Do Happen*, Element, Shaftesbury, 1995.

Sheldrake, Rupert, *The Rebirth of Nature*, Century, London, 1990.

Sherrard, Philip, *The Rape of Man and Nature*, Golgonooza, Ipswich, 1987.

—, *The Sacred in Life and Art*, Golgoonooza, Ispwich, 1990.

—, *Human Image, World Image*, Golgonooza, Ipswich, 1992.

Skolimowski, Henryk, *Eco-Philosophy*, Marion Boyars, London, 1981.

—, *Living Philosophy*, Arkana, London, 1992,

—, *The Participatory Mind*, Arkana, London, 1994.

Smith, Huston, *Forgotten Truth*, Harper, New York, 1976.

—, *Why Religion Matters*, Harper, San Francisco, 2001.

Sorokin, Pitirim, *The Crisis of Our Age*, OneWorld, Oxford, 1992.

Spengler, Oswald, *The Decline of the West*, Allen & Unwin, London, 1934.

Sperry, Roger, *Science and Moral Priority*, Blackwell, Oxford, 1983.

Sterling, Stephen, *Sustainable Education*, Green Books, Dartington, 2002.

Stevens Curl, James, *The Oxford Dictionary of Architecture*, Oxford, 1999.

Tarnas, Richard, *The Passion of the Western Mind*, Ballantine, New York, 1991.

*Temenos Academy Review* 5, Autumn 2002.

Thomas, Sir Keith, *Religion and the Decline of Magic*, Weidenfeld & Nicolson, London, 1971.

—, *Man and the Natural World*, Penguin, London, 1983.

Tompkins, Peter and Bird, Christopher, *Secrets of the Soil*, Arkana, London, 1989.

Toynbee, Arnold, *A Study of History*, Oxford University Press, 1934–61.

—, *Civilisation on Trial*, Oxford University Press, 1948.

—, *An Historian's Approach to Religion*, Oxford University Press, 1956.

—, *Experiences*, Oxford University Press, 1969.

—, and Urban, G.R., *Toynbee on Toynbee*, Oxford University Press, 1974.

—, *Mankind and Mother Earth*, Oxford University Press, 1976.

—, and Ikeda, Daisaku, *Choose Life*, Oxford University Press, 1976.

Trapnell, Judson B., *Bede Griffiths, A Life in Dialogue*, SUNY Press, New York, 2001.

UNEP, *Global Environmental Outlook 3*, Earthscan, London, 2002.

Uphoff, Norman, *Agroecological Innovations*, Earthscan, London, 2002.

Velmans, Max (ed), *The Science of Consciousness*, Routledge, 1999.

—, *Understanding Consciousness*, Routledge, 2000.

Wales, HRH The Prince of, and Clover, Charles, *Highgrove: Portrait of an Estate*, Weidenfeld and Nicolson, London 1993.

—, *The Prince's Choice*, Hodder & Stoughton, London, 1995.

—, and Lycett-Green, Candida, *The Garden at Highrove*, Weidenfeld and Nicolson, London, 2000.

Wallace, B. Alan, *The Taboo of Subjectivity*, Oxford, New York, 2000.

Walton, John, Barondess, Jeremiah A., Lock, Stephen, *The Oxford Medical Companion*, Oxford University Press, 1994.

Watt, Sir James (ed), *Talking Health*, Royal Society of Medicine, London, 1988.

Watson, James B., *A Passion for DNA*, Oxford University Press, 2000.

Welburn, Andrew, *The Beginnings of Christianity*, Floris Books, Edinburgh, 1991.

—, *Gnosis, The Mysteries and Christianity*, Floris Books, Edinburgh, 1994.

Wentworth Thompson, Sir D'Arcy, *On Growth and Form*, Cambridge University Press, 1917.

Westlake, Aubrey T., *The Pattern of Health*, Element Books, Shaftesbury, 1985.

Whitehead, Alfred North, *Process and Reality*, Macmillan, London, 1978 (1929).

—, *The Aims of Education*, Ernest Benn, London, 1962 (1949).

Wilber, Ken, *Eye to Eye*, Shambhala, Boston, 1990.

—, *The Marriage of Sense and Soul*, Gill & Macmillan, Dublin, 1998.

—, *The Eye of Spirit*, Shambhala, Boston, 1997.

—, *Boomeritis*, Shambhala, Boston, 2002.

Williamson, G. Scott and Pearse, Innes, *Science, Synthesis and Sanity*, Scottish Academic Press, Edinburgh, 1980.

Wilson, E.O., *Consilience*, Little Brown, London, 1998.

Woodham, Anne and Peters, Dr David, *Encyclopedia of Complementary Medicine*, Dorling Kindersley, London, 1997.

Woodhead, Chris, *Class War*, Little Brown, London, 2002.

Woodhouse, Mark, *Paradigm Wars*, Frog, Berkeley, 1996.

Worldwatch Institute, *State of the World 2002*, Earthscan, London, 2002 (also previous years by the same publisher).

# Index